Ramones

An American

Band

ONES

An American Band

Jim Bessman
in association with the Ramones

ones

St. Martin's Press
New York

Design by Richard Oriolo
Title page photo by Godlis

Library of Congress Cataloging-in-Publication
Data
Bessman, Jim.
    Ramones : an American band / Jim
Bessman.
        p.   cm.
    ISBN 0-312-09369-1 (pbk.)
    1. Ramones (Musical group)   2. Rock
musicians—United States—
Biography.   I. Title.
ML421.R32B5   1993
782.42166'092—dc20
    [B]   93-16437
                                                  CIP
                                                  MN

First Edition: June 1993

10   9   8   7   6   5   4   3

For all the State of Wisconsin Ramones, but
especially Robin Gates, Sheila Ryan, Tom Herman,
Dennis Bowling, and Don Smock.

Contents

RAMONES get noticed...

First Album

New Album — Released Jan. 10, '77 "Ramones Leave Home"

"Just perfect. A" — Robert Christgau, Village Voice & Cream

"Ramones is a classic." — Rutgers Daily Targum

"Moronic and brilliant." — Nick Kent, New Musical Express

"This dangerous record must be withdrawn by the company and banned by shops." — Editorial, Scotland Evening Times

"The most amazing new band I've heard yet." — Lisa Robinson, Hit Parader

"My favorite album of the month." — Flo & Eddie, Blind Date, Phonograph Record Magazine

"My favorite group of the moment." — Juke Box Jury, Phonograph Record Magazine

"Great. Fantastic. Stupendous." — Lincoln Park (N.J.) Herald

"El Stinko garbage of the worst kind" — Dayton Journal Herald

"May or may not be the best album so far this year." — Paul Nelson, Circus

"My nomination for the best band in the land." — J. Poet, Rocky Mountain Musical Express

"The best young rock and roll band in the known universe" — Wayne Robbins, Newsday

"The most attractive example yet of this genre of rock." — LA Free Press

"The Ramones are the best new band to come into the public eye this year." — Craig Zeller, Aquarian

"They're great." — Charles Shaar Murray, New Musical Express

"Rotten. No musical promise or any cultural advances or redeeming social values. They deserve to be ignored." — Jim Girard, Cleveland Scene

"The Ramones stink. They have no socially redeeming value. I can't take it." — Mike Diana, Richmond, Va. Daily Press

"Ramones sounds more like a greatest hits than a debut album." — Richard Mortifoglio, Village Voice

"Incredible" — Cousin Bruce Morrow, Syndicated Column

"The last time I was insulted by something as bad as the Ramones was when Mary Hartman shot her husband in the crotch with a bow and arrow" — The Drummer, Philadelphia

"The next big trash band" — Walter Dawson, Memphis Commercial Appeal

"Irresistible" — Susan Shapiro, Sounds

"The starkest, first-take quality rock you've ever heard" — Pizza Platters Monthly, L.A.

"Worthless" — John Swenson, Crawdaddy

"The most radical album of the past six years." — Gene Sculatti, Creem

"This is it, America." — Dave Barton, Rock N Roll News, SF

"Degenerate no talents." — Steve Morrisey, Melody Maker

"Tough rock and roll at its raunchiest" — Chris Carson, Binghamton News

"Truly awful" — James Johnson, London Evening Standard

"For connoisseurs of bone-crunching rock only. All others beware." — Don Shewey, Pop Top, Boston

"America's worst rock band" — Kaye Bueno, Pittsburgh Music Magazine

"An amyl nitrite high" — Mark Jacobson, New York Magazine

"Indeed awesome" — Performance Magazine

"Crap. These boys will never make it." — Thom Gardner, Back Door Man

"Anyone who hates this record is an asshole." — Phast Phreddie, Back Door Man

"Truly overpowering" — Ian Ziodiac, LA Free Press

"A sizzling great...debut of the year" — Blast Magazine

"They're perfect, couldn't be better. Great musicians. Excellent musicians." — Jack Badger, Rock N Roll News, SF

"Recapturing the essence of rock" — Hollywood Daily Variety

"Merde. Je deteste ce disque." — Phillipe Garnier, Rock & Folk, France

"Perhaps the smartest band in America" — Lester Bangs, Creem

"The most hilarious album produced in years." — Melody Maker

"Walls of sound that narcotize all feeling" — Jan Hodenfield, New York Post

"The baddest sound around" — Denver Magazine

"Humorless poor taste performed by the missing links of rock and roll" — Ken Wilson, Hollywood Press

"Perfect. Phenomenal. Colossal." — Howard Klein, Record Rag, SF

"Avant-garde...neo-supremacist, beyond futurist. Total Trance" — Bruce Malamud, Music Gig

"None of your friends will like this record — it'll confuse the hell out of you." — Ralph Alphonso, Cheap Thrills

"Uniquely repulsive. Not a scrap of taste. The stuff of which bad myths are made" — Paul McGrath, Toronto Globe & Mail

"Burns holes in the mind" — Wilder Penfield III, Toronto Sun

"The Ramones have done it better than anybody else" — Steven Brailman, (publication untraceable)

"My God, is this really happening?" — Paul Budra, U. of Toronto Varsity

"Undoubtedly the best album of 1976" — Stennie Gunn, Farleigh Dickinson U. Gauntlet

"The Ramones win" — Peter Cowan, Oakland Tribune

"Oh no! This is grossly irresponsible" — Spokesperson for the Royal Society for Prevention of Accidents

"They don't waste their time — they waste you." — Stephen Ford, Detroit News

"The worst of New York punk bands." — Washington Post

"One hell of a rush." — Bob Sennet, Columbia Spectator

"Shocking material. I'm horrified." — James Dempsey, Member of Parliament, U.K.

"Destined to become a classic because it breaks away from all current standards. The REAL kings of heavy metal" — Marvin Jamerson, Collegiate Times

"You may never hear anything like this again. Rate it F-plus." — George Gesner, (publication untraceable)

"I give it an A" — Tom D'Antoni, Maryland Public Broadcasting

"There hasn't been an album in five years as strong or invigorating as this. It's as if a hydrogen bomb hit Herman's Hermits" — Howard Wuerfing, Washington Times

"Oldies are selling and these guys are in synch." — DeFleur, Head Magazine

"The most explosive of the new wave." — Paul Dabelia, Observation Post, City College of N.Y.

"Music to sniff glue by" — Marty Packin, Asbury Park Press

"The power of 70's heavy metal behind the melodic invention of AM radio mid-60's pop" — Wesley Strick, Blast

"Phew, what a scorcher!" — Kris Needs, Zig Zag

SIRE
Sire Records, Marketed by ABC.

Acknowledgments

First, of course, thanks to the Ramones, without whom there'd be no book, not to mention much, if not most, of the music we all love.

Special thanks also go to Josh Grier, who wrote the book proposal (since I had no idea how); Bill Carter, a book in his own right; and Jim Fitzgerald, an editor who "got it"—with the help of his daughters Zoe and Farrar.

I'm deeply indebted to Danny Fields, as is any rock fan, but I owe him above and beyond. Janis Schacht and Ida Langsam were also invaluable. So was Lauren Blanchard. And Liz Rosenberg, Bob Merlis, Karen Moss, and all at Warner Bros. Records publicity.

Thanks as well to the Ramones management team, especially Gary Kurfirst, Andrea Starr, Michele Esposito, and Ira Herzog.

In random order, I thank: Seymour Stein, Tim McGrath, Howie Klein, Linda Stein, Andy Shernoff, Daniel Rey, Roger Risko, Nancy Morgan, Andy Paley, Allan Arkush, Maureen Bell, Tony Bongiovi, Art Fein, Roberta Bayley, Lars Ulrich, Chris Frantz, Craig Leon, Vera Colvin, Bob Guccione, Jr., Marian Bell, Kevin Patrick, Joan Jett, Kenny Laguna, Chrissie Hynde, Allan Pepper, Donna Diken, Mark Volman, Howard Kaylan, Ed Stasium, Arturo Vega, Monte Melnick, Rodney Bingenheimer, Dennis McNamara, Linda Daniele, Carol Kaye, Dave and Langdon Schulps, Ira Robbins, John Holmstrom, Lisa Robinson, Roman Kozak, Lemmy Kilmister, Hilly Kristal, Marty Thau, Rick Johnson, Jane Friedman, Joan Tarshis, Suzanne Fritz, Kathryn Woods, Molly Reeve-Morrison, Rena Cohen, and Chuck Pulin, Alex Kuczynski, and Marion Flynn.

Editors over the years who let me write about the Ramones: Gary Sohmers, Frank Meyer, Ken Terry, Fred Goodman, and everyone at *Billboard*, as do others who have been too helpful to be overlooked: Steve Tatarsky, Andy Frances, Brian Chin, Chris and Alicia Capece, Tom Carson, Leslie Berman, Michael and Sharon Doucet, Steve Popovich, Mark and Ann Savoy, Bert Padell, Jake Fine, Walter Antoine, Janice Ginsburg, Davin Seay, Rachel Felder, Barbara Schneid, Mikele Stillman, Bob Oermann, Mary Bufwack, Chuck Juntikka, Rachelle Friedman, Chaya Schultz, Ray Rashid, Bahman Maghsoudlou, Phil Spector, Will Botwin, Lisa Clapes, Chuck Toler, Tim Onosko, Paula Sartorius, Shirley Divers, and Casey Fuetsch.

This is a short list.

"I love New York,
but we think of ourselves
as being more of
an American Band."

—Joey Ramone, August 1980.

"One-two-three-four!"

Like a drill sergeant, Dee Dee Ramone barked these numbers over Johnny Ramone's blasting buzz-saw guitar drone, and at Ramones concerts around the world, they were received as marching orders by an entire new wave of rock 'n' roll fans and musicians. By harking back to Ringo Starr's somewhat gentler count of the same 4/4 beat of "I Saw Her Standing There," the Ramones were now following in the Beatles heroic footsteps, calling forth the next generation to action.

But wait! Before we get too carried away by euphoric Ramonesmania, we hereby agree that it's silly—in fact down-right sacrilegious—to compare

"Hey, Ho!

Let's Go!"

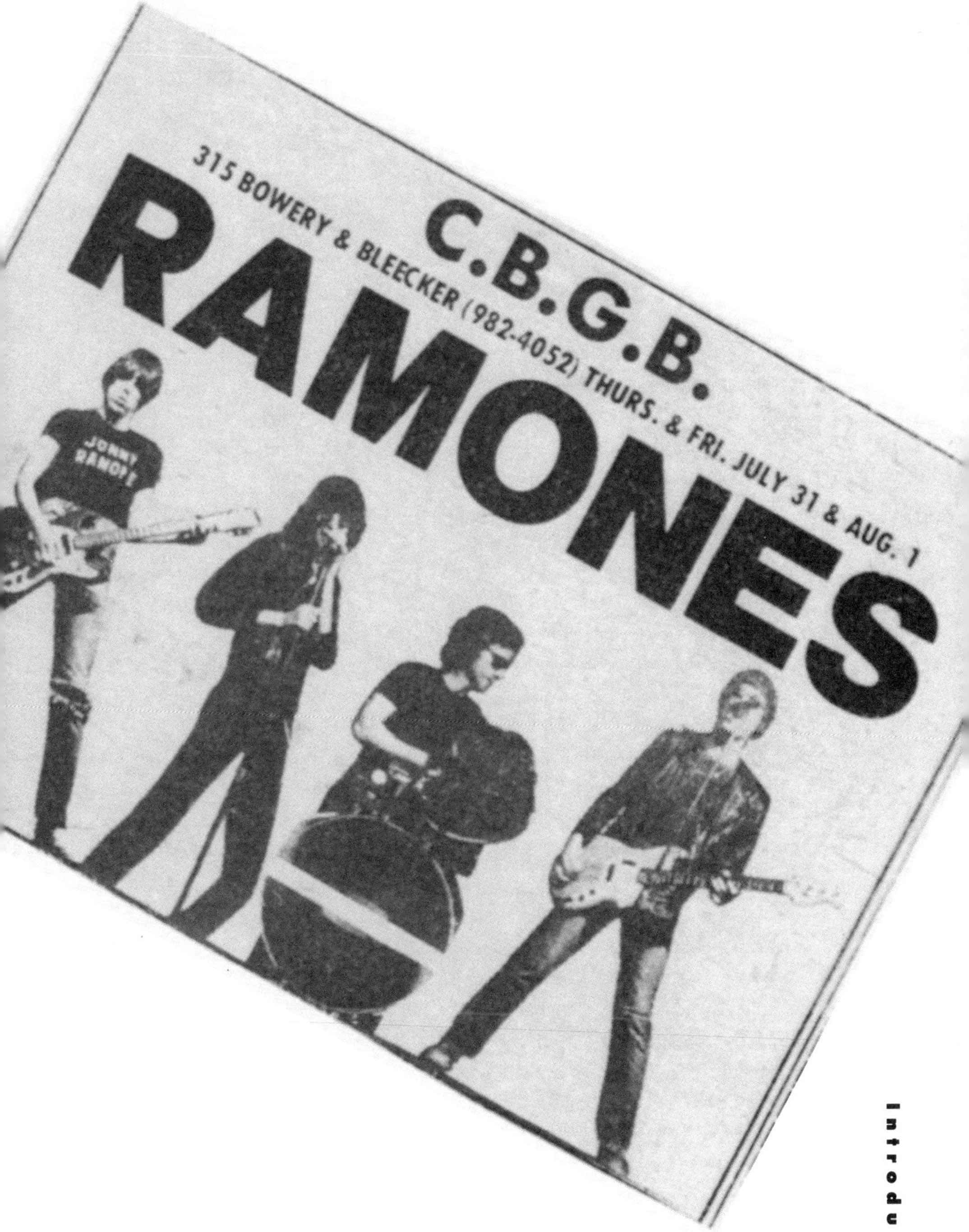
C.B.G.B.
315 BOWERY & BLEECKER (982-4052) THURS. & FRI. JULY 31 & AUG. 1
RAMONES

anything to the Beatles! It just ain't done! After all, the Beatles not only changed rock 'n' roll, they changed the whole world along with it. Never before and never again has one musical group had such universal and lasting impact. Besides, the Beatles had hit records galore, and the Ramones were never even one-hit wonders!

Yes, but at the same time, rock 'n' roll history shows that the Ramones actually *did* bring about such tremendous changes in music and style that comparisons with the Beatles were both instantaneous and common. Also, the Ramones kind of *looked* like the Beatles, at least in that they were four young guys, similarly dressed, with pseudo-Beatles moptops. The simple guitars-and-drums rock combo format was basically the same, too, as were the simple melodies and sentiments. After all, "I wanna be your boyfriend" is the next step after "I wanna hold your hand," and the power chording for which the Ramones music was notorious was really little more than an extension of the guitar crunch which opened "I Want to Hold Your Hand"—itself as revolutionary a sound in 1964 as anything punk rock would muster in its time.

And you didn't have to *think* about it, either. Like the Beatles, as soon as you heard the Ramones battle cry, "Hey, ho! Let's go!," you knew *who* it was, you knew *what* it was, you knew it was *for* you and *about* you. "We play for our generation—for *us*," Tommy Ramone once said. "If other people like it, that's great." And other people *did* like it, especially music critics everywhere, who hailed the band for ushering in a whole new era in rock 'n' roll, much as the Beatles had done slightly more than a decade earlier.

Of course, if you're already a Ramones fan, you already know all this. Otherwise, you're still laughing out loud at what would seem to be preposterous comparisons with the Beatles; that is, if you know who the Ramones are to begin with! Because even though the Ramones have lasted close to three times as long as the universally acknowledged greatest band of all time, they have yet to receive one iota of the Beatles mainstream success.

Now we can immediately dismiss any suggestion that the Ramones, simple as they were ("three chords, four leather jackets," observed one record company exec), simply weren't any *good*. Then why didn't they sell a billion records? Basically because at a time when disco and corporate/arena rock dominated radio playlists and record-company promotional budgets, the Ramones, as pioneers of a new musical trend, were *scary*, to put it mildly. They weren't cuddly-cute like the Beatles; in fact, they were almost a negative image of the Beatles. Where the Beatles smiled and joked, the Ramones stared blankly and sulked. Where the early Ramones were able now and then to come up with a romantic statement comparable to "I Want to Hold Your Hand," the early Beatles would never in a million years consider a song called "Beat on the Brat" (though

John Lennon would soon sing "I'd rather see you dead little girl," and, unlike most of the Ramones lyrics, it would be *no joke*).

But with the Ramones, such intense feelings of anger, anxiety, and the key word *frustration* were up front and center from the start. The Ramones, like all sixties children, had grown up on the Beatles, but by the early seventies, they'd grown up, period. Real life, sad to say, was no longer a three-minute love song. All the happy-days promises of TV sitcoms and commercials, parents and teachers, had turned into lies. The optimism and excitement of the Beatles in America the Beautiful of 1964 had been forever ruined by Vietnam, race riots, political assassinations, Watergate, and a seemingly unbridgeable generation gap. Besides, the Beatles had broken up in 1970!

An American band, where else but the White House, January '77. (Danny Fields)

So what was a poor boy to do except to sing for a rock 'n' roll band? Lucky for us as rock fans—and, no doubt, for society at large!—the disillusioned sixties kids who became the Ramones followed the path pointed out by the Rolling Stones in "Street Fighting Man" (which they would cover in 1985 for the B-side of a British twelve-inch single of "Howling at the Moon"). So these four guys from Queens who weren't related, who had little in common besides a love of rock 'n' roll and nowhere else to go, came together in 1974 as brothers, choosing to merge whatever individual identities they may have had into the Ramones for the good of the cause. Like the Three Musketeers—who, like the Ramones, started out as three and then became four—they would be one for all, all for one, the "one" being not only the group, but rock 'n' roll itself, and by extension, life. Because in the Ramones World of 1974, rock 'n' roll *was* life, just as it is in the Wayne's World of today.

At the same time, of course, rock 'n' roll in the pre-punk rock seventies was more *dead* than alive. Besides disco and the surviving dinosaur rock bands of the sixties, the commercial radio waves were dulled by the softer rock likes of the Eagles, Fleetwood Mac, the Doobie Brothers, Journey, Styx, America, Kansas, Foreigner, Genesis, Yes, ELP, Boston, Toto, Steely Dan, Queen, Elton John, Rod Stewart—you know, the kind of acts you expect to see now on VH-1. The psychedelic-era bands and performers of the late sixties had for the most part either faded away without a whimper, or, as in the cases of Jimi Hendrix, Janis Joplin, and Jim Morrison, just plain died.

On the other side of the spectrum were the theatrical glam, glitter, and shock-rock acts like David Bowie, T. Rex, and Alice Cooper, and the emerging heavy-metal rock bands, Led Zeppelin being the pace setter. But musicians like Zep guitarist Jimmy Page and drummer John Bonham were dazzling virtuosos who indulged in lengthy solos, while bassist John Paul Jones was a production/session master who had worked with virtually every major British pop star of the sixties. In other words, the rock music of the seventies—and it was now just called "rock"—was far removed from the abilities and interests of the kids who'd grown up on the rock 'n' roll radio of the sixties, who were now maybe just out of high school and finding out that the good old days of their youth were gone forever.

Much closer to these kids were the mid- to late-sixties garage bands like the Seeds, the Standels, the Shadows of Night, the Leaves, Count Five, and Syndicate of Sound, which seventies rock journalist and Patti Smith Group guitarist Lenny Kaye immortalized in his 1972 "Nuggets" compilation of sixties "punk." To borrow the Dead Boys' classic debut-album title, these bands were young, loud, and snotty, and while they were lucky to have had one hit—songs such as Count Five's "Psychotic Reaction" and Syndicate of Sound's "Little Girl," which the Dead Boys

SNIFFIN' GLUE...
AND OTHER ROCK'N'ROLL HABITS FOR...WHO ~~YOU~~ CARES!

28th Sept '76.

THIS ISSUE IS RARE.....RIP IT UP AND IT'LL BE RARER! Price: EMPTY YER WALLET, YOU BASTARD!

3½

PUNK special

100! CLUB
100 OXFORD ST.
W.1
7.30 till late.
Membership not required

"IT'S BACK TO JAZZ FROM NOW ON, WE CAN'T PLAY HERE AGAIN .... NOT AFTER TONIGHT"

SEX PISTOLS
CLASH
SUB WAY SECT
SUZIE AND THE BANSHEES
AND FROM FRANCE
STINKY TOYS

AND THE WONDERFULL
VIBRATORS
OPEN 7.30 pm. 60p in

the Damned

+ BUZZCOCKS.

PLUS STAR

WE'RE THE ONLY MAG, WHO KNOWS WHAT'S HAPPENING

later covered—they were cornerstones in the musical development of the disgruntled youth culture which eventually spawned the Ramones.

Now, there was one other noteworthy genre of seventies rock, though it could hardly be called part of a trend. This included the harder-edged, underground "pre-punk" bands: Detroit's MC5 and Stooges, and New York's Velvet Underground and New York Dolls. These groups sold few records, but they became a missing link between the once flourishing sixties rock scene and the punk rock, "new wave" movement that the Ramones kicked off in the mid-seventies—a time in rock history held by many to be as musically vapid as that between the first wave of classic rock 'n' rollers (Elvis Presley, Chuck Berry, Little Richard) and the British Invasion launched by the Beatles.

Basically, then, there was a real vacuum in terms of basic, straight ahead, rebellious rock 'n' roll. *Rebellion*, it should be noted, has long been considered by critics as a key ingredient of real rock 'n' roll. And the Ramones, as I have hinted, had plenty to rebel against, though all we need say for now is that they were very much the social outcasts they portrayed in their songs, guys who could sing so authoritatively about "going mental" only because they in fact had *gone* mental. "Adolescence was sure tough," they'd say, "especially when you don't grow out of it!"

These here were dead-end kids—who weren't even kids any more! But in that they were hardly alone. All across America, post–high school postadolescents were facing the cold hard fact of life: *this* is all there is. The American Dream, whatever it is, is "*No Fun*," for lack of a better way to put it than the Stooges classic song title, if not as bleak, perhaps, as the "*no future*" the Sex Pistols sang about. Celebrating the 1988 release of the thirty-song *Ramones Mania* compilation, Legs McNeil, who'd been chronicling the group since the beginning of punk rock, marveled in *Spin* magazine over the miracle that the Ramones had stayed together fifteen years and produced such a body of classic work. "But in reality," he wondered, "what else were they going to do?"

What else, indeed? While Johnny Ramone would have been satisfied with just one album, what the Ramones actually and amazingly did was to open the floodgates holding back the pent-up frustration and latent ambition of what would become thousands of bands of all kinds. Punk rock, new wave, new romantic, new music, techno-synth, hardcore/speed/ thrash metal, alternative, modern rock, postmodern—"There's a real straight line from the Ramones to Nirvana, for anyone who'd care to trace it," said *Spin* in its seventh anniversary issue, placing the Ramones alongside the Beatles, the Rolling Stones, Jimi Hendrix, Led Zeppelin, the Sex Pistols, and Public Enemy in pronouncing the seven greatest bands of all time. "No group in the last eighteen years has been more important or influential."

Need proof? Look at the T-shirts! The Ramones logo has adorned the chests of various members of groups including Guns N' Roses, Def Leppard, Metallica, the Cult, Skid Row, Poison, Anthrax, L.A. Guns, Megadeth, Bang Tango, Georgia Satellites, Wrathchild, Mr. Big, Kix, and the Damned; also seen sporting Ramoneswear have been John Lydon, Chrissie Hynde, Deborah Harry, Iggy Pop, and Alice Cooper. Meanwhile, Ramones songs have been performed by the varied likes of Skid Row, Sonic Youth, the BoDeans, the Godfathers, and Seductive Luck, not to mention Mojo Nixon, Pygmy Love Circus, Buglamp, the Creamers, Jeff Dahl, L7, the Flower Leopards, Bad Religion, and the Flesh Eaters—all of whom grace the Ramones tribute album, "Gabba Gabba Hey."

Most recently, the French group Casse Pieds covered "Beat on the Brat," while the German rock band Die Toten Hosen, in its punk rock tribute "Learning English, Lesson One," enlisted Joey Ramone to sing on their version of "Blitzkrieg Bop," cut to honor the Ramones ever-inspiring "staying power and uncompromising musical commitment." And not only did the groundbreaking synth-pop band Human League mention the Ramones in a song ("The Things That Dreams Are Made Of"), but Motorhead actually wrote a one-minute, twenty-five-second tribute to them. Excerpted from "Ramones": "Bad boy rock, bad boy roll/Gabba gabba, see them go . . . Bad boys then, bad boys now/Good buddies, mau, mau, mau."

Even in 1992, *eighteen years* after the Ramones emerged, came a new wave of "Ramones Clones," including Germany's Richies (their album title was the Ramones-derived "Out of the Basement"), Australia's Ratcat, and a band called the Exploding White Mice, whose name comes from *Rock 'n' Roll High School*, the legendary rock/teen flick which starred the Ramones. Ramones music, meanwhile, had also been featured in the soundtracks of the films *Times Square, That Summer, National Lampoon's Vacation, Get Crazy, Over the Edge, Roadkill, Car 54, Highway 61*, and, of course, Stephen King's *Pet Sematary*—not to mention a Budweiser beer commercial!

You know, when word got out that a Ramones book was (finally) in the works, the joke was that since their songs were so short, the book should only be four pages long! Well, we could fill those pages up and more with salutes and honors and accolades from fans and friends. I mean, none other than Tom Petty suggested that the Ramones should be an exhibition at the American Museum of Modern Art, with tour guides

THE RAMONES TUESDAY NIGHTS Call 263-8908 for info.

Introduction

WEEKLY SOHO NEWS

MATISSE AND THE RAMONES

WE HAVE IT ALL

every hour pressing a button causing Dee Dee Ramone to count out "One-chew-tree-faw," as the British journalists used to write it, and "Da Brudders" (again, the Brits!) doing their customary twenty songs in six minutes (Petty's slight exaggeration!) before the group moves on to the Robert Mapplethorpe photos! It was Bono who said that at U2's first TV audition, they played three Ramones songs—and got the gig!

Amy Carter wanted to meet the Ramones, and once brought along a phalanx of her father's presidential Secret Service agents to a Ramones soundcheck! Carly Simon said she was a Ramones fan when Joey and Marky performed at a Jerry Brown campaign rally! Everyone in the known universe loves the Ramones today. Indeed, they're the *Grateful Dead* of punk rock!

As we shall see, though, it wasn't always that way for a band that started out setting comic book–like lyrics to bubblegum music and wound up virtually reinventing rock 'n' roll, only to be misunderstood as violent and drug-crazed. Adopting the look of leather-jacketed street hoods (actually, it was just the way they always dressed!), they became musicians to fight back against teenage boredom and all that comes with it: no education, no jobs, no money, no cars, no girls. They had to learn their music as they made it because they couldn't do anything else, because there was nothing else they wanted to do.

And as we all know, the one tragedy about the Ramones is that they never got their just rewards for all they did for rock 'n' roll music and all of us who love it and live for it. They never had hit records, like Blondie and the Clash and the Knack and all the other bands that came and went in their wake, but they never made any sacrifices to fashion and always stayed true to who they were and still are.

And who *are* the Ramones?

Okay, so they aren't really *brudders*, er, brothers. In fact, they haven't even always been *friends*, as is obvious from the less-than-amicable departures of Richie and Dee Dee. Then again, obviously, neither were the Beatles, or the members of probably any other group that comes to mind. But through it all, "happy family" or not (to steal from their classic "We're a Happy Family"), commercial success or not, the Ramones maintained their integrity and total dedication to what brought them together in the first place: music. Rock 'n' roll music. "Something to Believe In," to quote their 1986 single. Just a few guys from Queens who didn't want to grow up, yet were "Too Tough to Die," to quote their 1984 album title.

In a word, then, theirs is a story of *survival*, and rock history has shown that in the Ramones case, it was a most unlikely and remarkable survival of the fittest.

he "Age of Aquarius" was long gone. The hippie generation was dead, but the "Blank Generation," as poet/punk-rock legend Richard Hell had labeled the withered remains of the sixties flower children, had grown up all over America, and they felt more like weeds.

Not that they who became the Ramones were flower children.

They who became the Ramones grew up in the middle-class suburb of Queens called Forest Hills, where the U.S. Open tennis tournament was held before it was moved to a bigger facility across from Shea Stadium. They also lived near Flushing Meadow Park, site of the 1964 World's Fair, where they

The Blank

Generation

would go hear rock concerts when they weren't out playing stickball or enjoying petty vandalism or cheap highs—before they figured out how to take out their frustrations through music.

From Manhattan, you take the E or F train to the Continental Avenue/Forest Hills stop, then take the 108th Street bus to 67th Street or so. It's a good half hour, maybe, but get out to Queens and you're in another world.

"Apart from a certain exaggeration in scale and proximity to New York [it] looks and feels like nine-tenths of the population territory of the modern U.S.A.," was how Hell described Forest Hills an early Ramones feature story he wrote for *Hit Parader*. "Giant hatchery brown-brick apartment houses along wide hot boulevards, with the spaces in between occupied by blacktop playgrounds, two-story drugstores with storage space or dentist's offices upstairs, ice cream parlors, fast food and supermarkets."

They hung out, he continued, at Jahn's ice cream shop in the summer, in floor stairwells in the winter. For kicks they'd go to Alexander's department store to watch people buy things. "Ain't it boring?" Hell wrote. "It's so fucking boring it's driving me crazy just writing about it."

Since he's the Ramones' frontman, we'll start with Joey.

He was born Jeff Hyman on May 19, 1951—though for many years he said it was 1952. His birthday is the same as that of Pete Townshend of the Who, one of his favorite bands; in fact, watching the Who during their first tour was one of the greatest things he ever saw.

Like most of his generation, Joey remembers listening to rock 'n' roll radio in the early sixties, to legendary New York jocks like Murray the K and the WMCA Good Guys.

"Rock 'n' roll was a savior. It gave you the sense of being an individual. It was something *you* had—nobody else but you. I remember my father getting me a radio that you hooked on the window sill and then listened to with an earphone. I used to listen to it under the covers and get caught!"

Though Joey, also like every sixties kid, credits the Beatles for their paramount musical influence on him, he was into music much earlier. When he was a kid, his grandmother, who played piano and sang at parties as part of a job at Macy's, and his father, gave him an accordion—which, in true Ramones fashion, he squeezed till there was nothing left of it. Then King Korn entered the picture.

"My mom used to go to the supermarket, where they gave out King Korn trading stamps—but she didn't collect them. So I looked at the catalog and saw they had a snare drum. I wanted to play the drums, so I *snared* her stamps and got a snare drum. Then I got a high-hat and started playing along to Beatles records and Gary Lewis and the Playboys and the Who."

When Joey was thirteen, granny kicked in a full drum set, which Joey eventually replaced with a "dream" kit modeled after Keith Moon's. Other drumming influences included Ringo Starr and Cream's Ginger Baker. His general musical influences, though, included all the pre-Beatles classic rock 'n' rollers, the British Invasion legends who followed, and really, just about everybody.

"The Beatles and Marc Bolan and T. Rex, the Stones and Jagger, Elvis Presley, Little Richard, Buddy Holly, Gene Vincent, Phil Spector, Ronnie Spector, Noddy Holder and Slade, the Who, early blues people, doo-wop, Herman's Hermits, the Stooges, MC5, Dave Clark Five, Beach Boys, Kinks, Gary Glitter, the Sweet, Del Shannon, Dusty Springfield, Dylan—there were just so many different styles that influenced me and conjured up the vast pool of my makeup! And John Lennon really played a major role, because of his character and antics, wit—his whole personality."

When Joey began to sing, though, Alice Cooper was a main role model. "Not just his singing, but the way he was living out a fantasy. I liked the whole theatrical glitter thing he was doing, and that he was very primal, like Iggy and the Stooges, which brought out the beast in me—the kind of insanity that was going on. In the beginning I really believed Alice, until I found out he wasn't really a necrophiliac and I got very pissed! Then I found out he was playing golf with George Burns, which kind of turned me off."

But Joey was also turned off by Forest Hills, where his parents divorced when he was eight. "It wasn't that bad of a childhood, but it was the broken home syndrome—I had three different fathers. But I never related to Forest Hills." Or Forest Hills High, for that matter.

Indeed, as he explained to the school's paper The Beacon in 1991, Joey was always his own person. "I never fit in there. There were people there who were eighteen, but they might as well have been sixty." His fondest memories, he said, were eating ice cream in the dean's office and getting a knife stuck in his back in the stairwell! But he also recalled playing drums in the basement of his mother's art gallery ("Mama Ramone" Charlotte, who like any good Jewish mother wanted her son to go to college, was an accomplished artist and collector) next door to the Trylon Cinema on Queens Boulevard, where he lived after she kicked him out of her apartment in Birchwood Towers, for his own good.

Which isn't to say he doesn't get along with his mom—he even appeared with her on TV on "Geraldo"! He even taught her how to smoke pot!

Joey gets along well with his dad now, too, though back then he and Noel Hyman, who owns a Manhattan trucking company, hardly saw eye to eye. In fact, it was his more open-minded Uncle Sy who was most supportive of the youngster's musical aspirations.

In his late teens now, Joey was going through an experimentation phase, journeying out to Manhattan and discovering himself.

"I always kind of liked having my life to myself, and never liked being told what to do. So I started venturing to the city and hung out in the West Village. It was winter, and I used to hand out fliers for massage parlors, and was always paranoid because store owners would call the cops and they'd be circling around you. But at age seventeen I was getting fifty dollars a week, getting paid by the hour. I used to go take a lot of fliers and dump them down the sewer and hang out somewhere and get a cup of coffee or read or go to the park and have a couple of beers. Then go back and get some more fliers."

But it wasn't a happy period. Joey didn't fit in well at home, at school, or in the neighborhood. Youthful experimentation with hallucinogenic drugs even landed him in a psych ward, planting the seeds, no doubt, for numerous future Ramones songs.

"We all were kind of loners and outcasts—and that's our audience," he would say years later, when he could look back and laugh. "We also shared this dark, black sense of humor that only a few people understood."

Johnny Ramone remembers those early years in a similar fashion. "The late teens are a very big period for kids, when you don't know what to do with yourself, when there's pressure to go to college and get a job. It's a crisis time, especially if you don't really enjoy school and aren't good at it. For me, those years were basically delinquent. Then all of a sudden one day, I was walking down the block and it hit me like a voice from above: What am I going to do with my life? Is this what I'm here for—to be delinquent? So I stopped doing everything that was wrong—no more drinking, drugs, or anything bad, which I'd been doing all day long, every minute of the day. Self-control can handle everything!"

John Cummings was born on October 8, 1951, the only son of a construction worker. All he ever wanted as a kid was to be a baseball player, and his love of the game—and the Yankees—continues to this day. "I've wanted to be a baseball player since I was five, but to be on the high school team you had to get a haircut, and even then I couldn't take any sort of discipline. Then I went to military school for two years in two places, and looking back, I did learn discipline. I think they should make it mandatory for everyone to go to boot camp for two months when they're eighteen."

The defining moment for the Ramones generation was the night of February 9, 1964, when the Beatles made their first appearance on the Ed Sullivan Show. Johnny had first become interested in music after Elvis Presley's famous performance on the legendary Sunday-evening variety show in 1957. He also liked such Presley-era contemporaries as Buddy Holly, Gene Pitney, Bobby Darin, Chuck Berry, Chubby Checker, and Dion, then when the Beatles and the other British bands hit, he—like millions of other teen dreamers—bought a guitar.

"I saw the Beatles and the Stones, then Led Zeppelin and Jeff Beck. I liked guitar bands like Hendrix and Cream, but I couldn't figure out how to play like any of them, so I just gave up."

Later, when Johnny saw bands like the New York Dolls, he would realize that you didn't *have* to play like a guitar god, and that most guitar gods cared more about self-indulgent guitar solos than songs! But first came several years of odd jobs, unemployment, and following his father, construction work. The goal at the time, simply, was to "try to be normal," which might have been achieved had Johnny not gotten a construction job in 1974 at a fifty-story building at 50th Street and Broadway in Manhattan, the same building, as fate would have it, where Dee Dee, his friend from across the street, also worked. "We used to sit outside for lunch every day and look at girls, and talk about starting a band."

Dee Dee, a one-time hairdresser and now a mail clerk, was born Douglas Colvin on September 18, 1952, and grew up mostly in Berlin. A mischievous army brat whose father was a career officer, he went to an army school in Munich and retreated into fantasy to escape his quarrelsome parents (they divorced when he was fifteen). Growing up in the streets, he would wander about World War II battlefields, collecting vintage helmets, gas masks, bayonets, and machine gun bullets. He and a buddy once took an old mortar shell found in Berlin and aggravated the elderly by setting off smoke bombs in it.

Less fun, though, was the beginning of his severe drug problems (including a fourteen-year heroin addiction), which would plague Dee Dee Ramone off and on throughout his adulthood. In a no-holds-barred tell-all he wrote for *Spin* after leaving the band, he recalled trading soldiers old war daggers for morphine, then turning on to pot, barbiturates, and glue when he moved to Queens, spending hours calling up certain phone numbers just to hear weird beeping sounds.

Musically, though, Dee Dee picked up guitar at age twelve. Since his mother preferred the Beatles and Ricky Nelson, he embraced the Stones and Jimi Hendrix. But he later liked Paul McCartney and Wings, and even had an autographed bio of the Scottish bubblegum sensation the Bay City Rollers. The first time he saw a rock group, he knew that that's what he wanted to do, and at high school dances, instead of dancing with the girls, he would stand at the front of the stage and just stare at the band in amazement.

Dee Dee's high school experience was otherwise as uneventful and unpleasant as that of the rest of the guys. In those days, he said, girls wouldn't even look at you unless you had a Corvette. Needless to say, he didn't have a 'vette, and for a long time, he didn't have a girlfriend, and when he finally did get one, she was so ugly he didn't like her much anyway. He didn't like school much, either, and mainly hung out with the other guys around the flagpole outside. He was finally asked to leave, he said, when he couldn't figure out the list of credits. They wanted him to take academic stuff, anyway, when all he wanted was to take shop.

Finding American kids couldn't compete with his sense of style, Dee Dee began frequenting the discotheques—nightclubs like the Sanctuary, Tamerlane, and Superstar. Here he discovered the Dolls, and was blown away when he first saw Iggy and the Stooges, what with Iggy painted gold and throwing up during a thirty-minute, three-chord set, and guitarist Scott Ashton with a Nazi swastika emblazoned on the back of his motorcycle jacket.

Dee Dee remembered meeting Johnny on the sidewalk and talking with him about the Stooges. They all lived pretty much next door to each other then, in an apartment complex in Forest Hills. Dee Dee, Johnny, and Joey—they were the three future first Ramones, and the fourth was Tommy Erdelyi.

Tommy was born in Budapest, Hungary, on January 29, 1952, and came to the U.S. with his family when he was four.

"I first met Johnny in the cafeteria at Forest Hills High School. We talked about music and stuff, and we put a group together—Tangerine Puppets. It was sort of like a young garage band [they played songs by the Shadows of Knight, Bo Diddley, the Stones, and Count Five], really wild and energetic. Johnny would have his guitar slung really high and dive around wildly, using it like a machine gun. One day we played at the high school and we were hopping around, and Johnny ran into a girl with his guitar and we got banned from school. After high school we went our separate ways for a while, but we stayed in touch. I'd ask what he was doing and recommend getting a band together, because I thought he was a great performer and very talented."

After high school, Tommy, who played guitar, found work as a recording engineer at the fabled Record Plant in Manhattan, where he worked on Jimi Hendrix's Band of Gypsies sessions (he would often convince a doubting Hendrix that the guitar tracks laid down the night before weren't awful but great), jazz guitarist John McLaughlin's "Devotion" album, and "Mountain Climbing," from the band fronted by gargantuan guitarist Leslie West—another Forest Hills emigre.

Meanwhile, back on Broadway, Johnny and Dee Dee decided to go to Manny's Guitar Center on 48th Street and buy guitars. On January 23, 1974, Johnny (who keeps records of all the important Ramones dates) bought a blue Mosrite guitar for fifty dollars—because that was all the money he had. But Mosrite, which can be tinny like a Fender but has the rich sound of a Gibson, was also a make used by few players besides the Ventures—which suited Johnny's rugged individualist streak perfectly. But it was no big deal; as he once noted, all guitars sound the same if you play them loud enough! Later on he bought a sunburst Mosrite (a renowned spendthrift, Johnny paid two hundred dollars for it since he was buying amps at the same time and the salesman knew he had money!) to have on hand at gigs, since at least one string would break per set. (He also has a white Fender stratocaster, which he used on "I Wanna Be Your Boyfriend" to get the desired tinnier sound.)

Dee Dee picked up a fifty-dollar DanElectro bass, which he later smashed before stepping on a Gibson Firebird, still later buying his first Fender Precision from Fred Smith of Television (who told him never to sell it—but he did). Four days later they had their first rehearsal, and when Tommy found out that his friends now had guitars, he sort of became their manager. By this time he had also discovered the Stooges and the Dolls, as well as "Nuggets"—Lenny Kaye's prized album compilation of sixties garage-band punk rock. But most important, Tommy was now running his own little rehearsal place on East 20th Street at Park Avenue South in Manhattan with yet another Forest Hills High School chum, Monte Melnick—truly, the *fifth* Ramone.

A stocky, soft-spoken guy with an interest in architecture and the requisite fortitude of Job, Monte has been with the Ramones since they caught on enough to need a soundman. Now tour manager, Monte is responsible for everything from coordinating the eight-man crew to making sure Joey gets on the plane! As he says, he's everything from babysitter to psychiatrist, booking agent to travel agent, paymaster to van driver. But before all this, he was bass guitarist in a local glitter-era band with Tommy, called Butch. After that he was in a country-rock band called Thirty Days Out, which recorded two albums in the early seventies for Reprise (Tommy received engineering credit) and opened shows for the Beach Boys, Tom Rush, and Captain Beefheart.

When the group split up, Monte did a little session work, then joined Tommy in designing Performance Studio. The group that became the Ramones was Tommy's pet project, and when they began rehearsing there in March 1974, they were Johnny on guitar, Dee Dee on rhythm and vocals, and their friend Joey on drums, though brief mention is made here that at the very beginning there was another Ramone, Richie, who played bass while Dee Dee played guitar. But Richie couldn't keep up, and after only two days of rehearsals he became a mere historical footnote.

A year or so earlier, Joey was singer in a band called Sniper—sort of "a glitter band with a lot of attitude," Joey said, specializing in lyrics about violence and perversion. For Joey, who'd been in other bands and once auditioned as a drummer for one-hit pop singer Keith ("98.6" was No. 7 in 1967; Joey played Ginger Baker's "Toad"), Sniper was the first band he put together in which he was the singer. Aye, at six-foot-three, every inch a singer.

To make ends meet, though, Joey did a lot of odd jobs, the last as a street vendor of fad items like plastic flowers in Greenwich Village. "They were acrylic flowers, like stained glass. I was the first person to bring them into Queens, and I did so well I hired someone. I mean, one day I made three hundred dollars. Then one time in the city near Macy's, I opened shop at the wrong time. A cop said I had to move because he was getting complaints, so I picked up my box and started working around the corner. Then a police car with the door open pulled up and a guy says, 'Get in,' and I'm sitting there with the chestnut man and the pretzel vendor and in front was the girl selling hot dogs. I got one phone call, so I called the company I worked for, but they fuckin' ignored me, which really pissed me off. So I had to spend the whole day in jail. I'd never tasted a chestnut 'til that point—and they were really good!

"Then the paddy wagon came at seven P.M., and they put me in with all the hookers and handcuffed me to a coke dealer. I was a nervous wreck! They put me in a cell in the Tombs on Center Street with all these derelict degenerates. There were like thirty people in there until ten P.M., when I went before the judge. I was charged with peddling without a license, and a civil-liberties lawyer said to plead guilty or spend three more days in jail, with a two dollar fine or something. I'd taken all this fuckin' abuse, so the next day I took as many flowers as I could and never came back. I wanted to kill somebody and burn the whole place down!"

Luckily, Joey was getting noticed at the Coventry, the early seventies glitter joint on Queens Boulevard where Kiss used to play and the Dictators were the reigning house band. The Dictators, it should be stated, were the punk rock band that really slipped through the cracks. They were the kings of the hill before there *was* a hill.

Let us digress. The Dictators were the last link in the pre-punk rock chain connecting the early rock 'n' roll punks like Elvis Presley and Eddie Cochran and Gene Vincent, the early Beatles and Stones and the rougher-edged British Invasion groups like the Animals and the Who, the post–British Invasion American garage bands of the "Nuggets" set, and the early seventies punk-rock lead-ins—the Stooges, MC5, Velvet Underground, New York Dolls, and finally, the Dictators.

"Basically, we were a bunch of Jewish wise-ass guys from the Bronx with a New York wise-ass sense of humor," says Handsome Dick Manitoba (real name Richard Blum), the Dictators lead singer, and one of rock 'n' roll's unsung heroes. To illustrate, this snippet from the 'Tators "Master Race Rock": "We're the members of the Master Race/Got no style and we got no grace/First you put your sneakers on/Goin' outside to have some fun/C'mon Guys! Let' Go!"

No, it wasn't pretty. But it was *early*. A year ahead of the Ramones, the Dictators spoke for their generation in like fashion: "My favorite part of growin' up/Is gettin' sick and throwin' up/It's the price you've got to pay/For eatin' burgers every day."

Sadly, the Dictators weren't for everyone, and disbanded after a few poorly received albums—but not before leaving their mark. Joey would catch them at the Coventry when he wasn't playing there himself. This was back in 1973–74.

"It was the only place for bands to play original music," recalls Andy Shernoff, who spelled his name *Adny* when he was the Dictators bass guitarist. "At that time, Max's Kansas City only had bands that were on tour, like Marley and Springsteen. The Mercer Arts Center in Manhattan had original bands, but mainly the Dolls and a few other groups. Most bands had to do the bar circuit, which meant playing cover songs.

"Joey used to sing for a band called Sniper." Manitoba vividly remembers "this tall, skinny, hunched-over guy" who stood out in a room full of weird glitter-rock types. Recalls Joey: "I was into dressing up in my own style. I had a black satin-like jumpsuit made of stretch material with a bullet chain hanging around the groin with the zipper open, and elbow-length black leather gloves and a chain. I had pink-lavender boots with six-inch platform heels, a leather jacket, black sunglasses, long hair. It was pretty androgynous, but in those days you could let go. Still, a lot of people wanted to kill me!"

Joey remembers meeting Dee Dee when he came to see Sniper, then meeting him again at a Dolls show at Kenny's Castaways. "I knew John from seeing him around and hanging out after high school. He and Tommy were friends, and he was in a band with my brother Mitch. Then I got to be friends with Dee Dee, and he and John were friends, too. He mentioned me to John, and John called and asked me to be in a band.

"I thought John and Dee Dee looked really cool. John had the same kind of haircut as now, and his presentation was the same as when he plays—a very intense demeanor. We didn't have the superficial image of bands today. Maybe we were more dressy in the glitter days, but the later look became jeans, sneakers, leather jackets—what we wore when we walked around the street. We are like we seem."

But back to the Performance Studio. Again, it was Dee Dee, bass and lead vocals, Johnny on guitar, and Joey on drums.

"They brought their stuff down and plugged in, and they were awful," recalls Tommy. Monte remembers laughing when he saw them—which was the reaction most people had at first. "These guys came in and banged out basic stuff, which at that time was pretty scary!" But Tommy, at least, heard *something*.

"They were terrible, but they were *great*. I could tell right away that they were exciting, interesting, and funny. They kept coming back every week and rehearsing and got better and better. Dee Dee sang most of the time, but every now and then Joey sang, and he had a pretty good voice. But Dee Dee would get hoarse after a few songs."

On March 30, the Ramones played their first gig, a showcase at the studio. Monte recalls that the guys sent out their

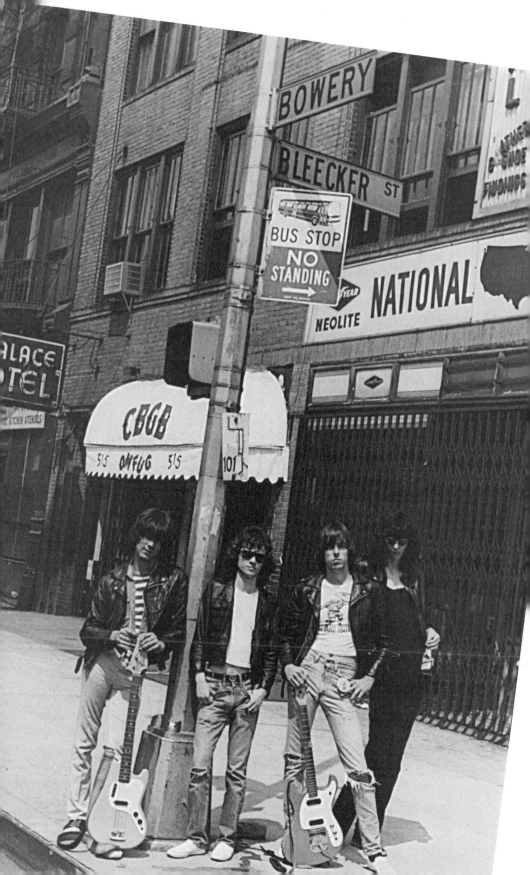

own fliers, and that admission was two dollars. About thirty people showed up, and Dee Dee was so nervous that he stepped on his bass and broke it!

"We invited all our friends down to see us and they all hated it and didn't want to be our friends anymore," says Johnny. "We weren't ready to play before anyone!"

Tommy would later tell *Punk* that Joey was a very good drummer, who played with such power that he was known to beat through the hardware! As for Joey's cymbal technique, Tommy said that he created so much sound you couldn't hear the rest of the group! Then in July, Tommy, who had up till now been the manager/motivator, saw that the band, which had been pretty much a hobby, was getting so good that it was becoming both avant-garde and potentially commercial.

"Things started happening. Joey was working on what later became 'Judy Is a Punk,' and I noticed there was something here that went beyond what it was initially, that was unique and artistically valid, that could lead to a breakthrough.

"Joey really wasn't the best drummer, and by this time they were playing faster and faster—which is one thing they could do. So we started auditioning drummers, and we'd get guys coming in with shag haircuts, straight out of Led Zeppelin. You got to understand, this was the mid-seventies! So I'd sit down and show them what I had in mind, though I never played drums in my life! But they couldn't get it, so the guys said, 'Why don't you play the drums?' I thought about it and figured it might be fun, so I got a one hundred dollar drum set to go along with their cheap guitars.

"I was always a guitar player, and was frustrated by the drums. I just wanted a simple backbeat, a nice four-four like the drumming on the Stax records, or Charlie Watts, but those guys threw me off. So I just started playing what *my* guys were playing, and it turned out kind of neat. Technically I played all wrong but it gave me a nice style. I had no idea how to play—just what I heard in my head, I suppose."

Which fit in well with the rest of the guys. Once again, Johnny—with the others—tried to figure out how to play other groups' songs, and once again failed. This time, though, no one gave up. As Dee Dee told then-journalist Howie Klein after admitting he didn't know the notes on his bass, "You have to realize, I have no talent. So how could I play? What I *can* do is just all I could ever do—just thump away on one string." Anything else, of course, would have been too much.

And even though the Ramones could technically play only what they knew—which was basically what they had just *learned*—and never really departed from what would be called the *minimalist* style which they both invented and perfected, the day would come when they would be recognized as true musicians. Indeed, in 1987, Dee Dee would be asked to explain his technique to *Guitar*: "I don't play a melodic style, I don't play fourths or fifths, scales or anything like that in bass progression. The bass line I play is the same line as the guitar plays. I just play the note of the chord and I stay on that. It's sort of a box pattern and I just hammer it out."

Simple, yet historic. He added that he liked the bass because it was strong: "I played in a violent style. It's a violent explosion of my feelings." For the record, he was then playing a custom-made ESP Surveyor, with both Jazz and Precision pickups to get more power. He'd have preferred a Precision body, but felt they were too heavy.

For his part, Johnny developed his style out of a "limp wrist action" that isn't so much limp as it is straightforward and relentless. "Other people try to play like the Ramones and don't sound the same," he says, "because they play with their arms. But I didn't play guitar until I learned with the Ramones, basically counting a downstrum, 'one-two-three-four.' All downstroke and barre chords. I just learned to play by the numbers!"

Says Ed Stasium, who came on board later to produce the Ramones and play the more complicated guitar parts, "Johnny makes it sound simple, but I can't do it, and I bet Eddie Van Halen can't. Not for an hour! No one else can do what Johnny Ramone does."

Now, in all fairness, when Johnny was featured in *Guitar Player*, the mag was flooded with complaints! But as he explained to Joan Tarshis in 1991 in *Guitar for the Practicing Musician*, "I'm an entertainer. The only time I ever say I'm a musician is when you have to fill out forms, when they ask you what your job is. I write down musician, but I'm never comfortable with it."

Turns out Johnny doesn't even keep a guitar at home. He hasn't improved since he started playing—and doesn't want to! "I've always felt that the people who changed, changed for the worse," he said, singling out Jimmy Page and Keith Richards as bad examples. "Only the Beatles changed successfully from album to album. If Elvis would have stayed the same . . . he would have been fine."

He went on to explain that basically, he'd been laid off his construction job, and got together with a couple friends and decided to form a band and have fun. Maybe they'd get to do an album. Otherwise, all he wanted to do was feel that the Ramones were the best punk band around, which is all they intended to be in the first place. "I'm totally satisfied with that," he concluded. "I've been very fortunate to be the best I can be."

And the fastest.

he following text was mailed out in a mid-1974 flier under the underscored heading, "THE RAMONES":

The Ramones are not an oldies group, they are not a glitter group, they don't play boogie music and they don't play the blues. The Ramones are an original rock and roll group of 1974, and their songs are brief, to the point, and every one a potential hit single.

The quartet consists of Johnny, Joey, Dee Dee, and Tommy Ramone. Johnny, the guitarist, plays with such force that his sound has been compared to a hundred howitzers going off. Joey, the lead singer, is an arch villain whose lanky frame stands threatening center

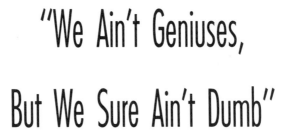

"We Ain't Geniuses, But We Sure Ain't Dumb"

—Tommy Ramone

A very early Ramones performance.
(Bob Gruen)

stage. Dee Dee is bass guitar and the acknowledged handsome one of the group, and Tommy is the drummer whose pulsating playing launches the throbbing sound of the band.

The Ramones all originate from Forest Hills, and kids who grew up there either became musicians, degenerates, or dentists. The Ramones are a little of each. Their sound is not unlike a fast drill on a rear molar. Contact Tom Erdelyi, Loudmouth Productions, Forest Hills, N.Y.

The Ramones legend—and myth—had begun.

Even their name was steeped in legend. Back when the Beatles were known as the Silver Beatles, Paul McCartney called himself Paul Ramone. That was the name the Ramones chose from a list of fifty or so possibilities (one that luckily missed the cut was "Spice"!), because according to Joey, it had a certain ring to it, like "Eli Wallach"; while according to Dee Dee, they liked the producer Phil Ramone (Billy Joel, Simon and Garfunkel) and "Ramones" sounded like an outlaw gang name. And, according to Johnny, they figured nobody else would name themselves that.

The group also figured that no one would care about their *real* last names, so they decided to simplify everything by going with their first names and tacking on the chosen surname. It was as if they were brothers—but they weren't.

In the beginning, though, the idea was to do everything together. The group identity—via same last name, same style of dress (their leftover glitter look quickly gave way to their everyday motorcycle jackets, jeans, and sneakers garb), and a presentation of overall solidarity—was strictly adhered to. That's why the songwriting credits on the first albums go to the Ramones as a group—no individual recognition.

Many of the early songs actually were written with the guys at least somewhat together, though. A major influence then was the late sixties bubblegum rock of groups like the Ohio Express and the 1910 Fruitgum Company, whose No. 5 hit "Indian Giver" would be a Ramones British B-side more than a decade later. Scotland's Bay City Rollers, who also dressed alike (in plaids) and sent teenyboppers into Beatles-type hysteria, provided another formative role model. Says Johnny: "For the first year we looked at them as competition, even though they were big and famous and we were just kids from the neighborhood. But they were the only other bubblegum group at the time. Looking back, I guess, we were kind of crazy!"

The Rollers had a No. 1 U.S. hit in 1976 with "Saturday Night," the high point of which was the chant spelling out the title. The Ramones admittedly borrowed the concept in opening their "Blitzkrieg Bop" with what became the universal "Hey, ho! Let's go!" chant. But attempts to cover Rollers songs or tunes by any other groups proved futile.

"We tried to figure out other people's songs at the first rehearsals, but we couldn't because we had just started to play," Johnny continues.

"So we decided to write our own songs, from the first or second rehearsal. We wrote 'I Don't Wanna Walk Around With You' the first day."

Actually, Joey had already written songs—and self-described "decadent and perverse" poetry—prior to joining the Ramones. In fact, both "I Don't Care" and "Here Today, Gone Tomorrow" were proud earlier efforts. Another obviously important influence on the band's writing, and Joey's in particular, was the Stooges' Iggy Pop, who had already plumbed the depths of post-adolescent frustration and boredom with gut-wrenching intensity. One Stooges song, "Search and Destroy," from the 1973 album *Raw Power*, is legitimately hailed as a harbinger of the forthcoming punk-rock explosion—and its chief sensibility: "I'm the world's forgotten boy/The one who's searchin' to destroy."

Hearing the Stooges was like letting the beast out, Joey said. Ex-Velvet Undergrounder Lou Reed, whose raw delving into society's underside also broke open the so-called new wave, provided additional inspiration, as did Jonathan Richman, the cultish leader of the Modern Lovers (and the first person to ever *dance* to the Ramones!), whose romantic idealism masked a dark sense of humor that Joey could relate to, together with his tendency to write out of his own experiences.

Of course, the Ramones experiences, as evidenced by their early songs—"Beat on the Brat" and "Now I Wanna Sniff Some Glue" are easy examples—were very much different from the experiences and songs of anyone else! These guys were hardly model citizens. In leather jackets, they looked like hoodlums and in fact were "general nogoodniks," as Johnny admitted to one interviewer. They wrote songs about sniffing glue only because they had, in fact. One of them even tried robbing a drug store on Queens Boulevard once, but instead broke into a laundromat by mistake. So the comedy of errors that had become their trivial lives were naturally reflected in their lyrics. Again, part of it had to do with the fact that they had just started playing, and therefore had to write simple songs about the simple but crazy things that seemed normal to guys who were into comics and cartoons, war relics and movies, mental illness and rock 'n' roll. Dark stuff, but funny stuff.

And no *politics*. The Vietnam War was over, and the Ramones had no tolerance for the likes of sixties protest/hippie types like Dylan, Joan Baez, or Country Joe and the Fish. While Joey remembers getting tear-gassed while protesting the war, Dee Dee once recalled heckling antiwar demonstrators. Of course, both Johnny and Dee Dee were patriotic products of military schools and politically conservative, if not thoroughly *disinterested*. Remember, this was the "Me Decade" of the seventies—no one really cared much about politics anyway. And while the Ramones may have been part of the Woodstock generation, none had had any desire to go to Woodstock.

"We were fans of the Stooges, and Slade was still around," says Johnny.

RAMONES

Blitzkrieg Bop····Beat On The Brat····I Wanna Be Your Boyfriend····Havana Affair····Judy Is A Punk····I Dont Wanna Go Down To The Basement····I'm A Nazi Baby····53rd & 3rd····Now I Wanna Sniff Some Glue

MAX'S KANSAS CITY
FRIDAY & SATURDAY
AUGUST 6 AUGUST 7
WITH HARRY WITH THE
TOLEDO SCREWS

"When we came out we were a cross between bubblegum groups and the Stooges."

England's working-class, hard-rocking Slade is noteworthy for two reasons. Joey learned breath control from the vocal coach who taught Slade's Noddy Holder (and Bette Midler!), and John has said that both Slade and the New York Dolls convinced the Ramones that you didn't have to be instrumental virtuosos in order to have great songs and be exciting performers.

Ah, the New York Dolls. Let us digress again.

Whenever they talk about the New York Dolls, they always say, "Too much, too soon." It was the title of their second and last album (released in 1974), and it became the epitaph for one of the most important and least appreciated bands in rock 'n' roll history. Fronted by the brilliant David Johansen, who would achieve some stardom years later as cocktail lounge-lizard Buster Poindexter, the Dolls were a glam band in that they dressed in transvestite chic and wore lipstick, but they were punk in that they were musically untrained and raucous. Their sound derived from Stones-style hard rock rooted in R & B, their lyrics reflected the mixed-up mores of the early seventies (Johansen would carry signature song "Personality Crisis" into his solo performances), and their image was outrageous enough to turn off nearly everyone outside New York City limits. Their commercial failure was taken as proof positive that New

York's incipient underground rock scene didn't stand a chance above the surface.

In New York, though, the Dolls ruled, and their roost, in 1972–73, was a decaying theater complex in Soho called the Mercer Arts Center. An air-conditioner mogul with an interest in theater owned the place, but there weren't enough good shows available to fill the eight small rooms, so he allowed rock bands to perform there on off nights. Besides the Dolls, the heavy hitters there were Wayne County, the campy transsexual punk rocker who became Jayne County after her operation, Ruby and the Rednecks, and Eric Emerson and the Magic Tramps. Emerson was an Andy Warhol "superstar" and a seminal figure of the budding New York underground rock scene, but alas, he was one of many who would die before it took off.

And alas, so would Mercer. Emerson and the Tramps were rehearsing one day, when the wall behind them collapsed, and the whole place had to be torn down, but not before the house bands, especially the Dolls, had left their mark on a generation of musically inclined New York street kids who wanted it before they knew how to get it.

"That's why the Dolls were such an influence," Johnny continues. "We saw them, and realized that they were a great band and that they really didn't play well at all. So maybe we didn't need to play guitar twenty years to play rock 'n' roll—which was never what rock 'n' roll was about!"

Nope. As the Ramones already knew, rock 'n' roll was about seizing the moment. But for the Ramones, in the beginning, the moment was entirely negative. After "I Don't Wanna Get Involved With You," the second song the Ramones wrote was "I Don't Wanna Walk Around With You," which was more or less the same song:

> I don't wanna get involved with you
> That's not what I wanna do
> Come knocking on my door
> I'm gonna knock you on the floor
> I don't wanna get involved with you
> That's not what I wanna do.

Then came "I Don't Wanna Be Learned, I Don't Wanna Be Tamed" (the title was also the entire lyric, with Joey anglicizing "tamed" into "timed"!), then "I Don't Wanna Go Down to the Basement." They didn't write a "positive" song until "Now I Wanna Sniff Some Glue."

The songs, since the Ramones were new at writing, were brief—nothing over three minutes until their fourth album. And by the time of their first gig, despite their initial trouble at learning cover songs, they

A Ramones publicity shot that ended up being used on their first album Ramones. (Roberta Bayley)

had down the Bobby Fuller Four's "I Fought the Law" and Tommy Rowe's "Sheila." The set list for that disastrous first gig, by the way, was "I Don't Wanna Go Down to the Basement," "I Don't Wanna Walk Around With You," and "Now I Wanna Sniff Some Glue," plus the now-extinct "I Don't Wanna Be Learned, I Don't Wanna Be Tamed," "I Don't Wanna Get Involved with You," "I Don't Like Nobody that Don't Like Me," and a tune penned by Joey called "Sucubus," which was dropped because no one liked the title.

By the time Tommy took over as drummer (after six months of auditioning for drummers by the band), "It's a Long Way Back to Germany," "Babysitter," and "Blitzkrieg Bop" had been added to the repertoire.

"Our early songs came out of our real feelings of alienation, isolation, frustration—the feelings everybody feels between seventeen and seventy-five," says Joey. "They directly resulted from fascination with a lot of different things. Like Dee Dee was heavily into comic books, and we were all into B films and horror films and sci-fi, you know, 'I Don't Wanna Go Down to the Basement.'

" 'I Don't Care'—people thought that was nihilistic but it really sort of evolved out of being in a heavy depression, some sort of insanity—mental illness. I wrote 'Beat on the Brat' at the time I was living in the Birchwood Towers in Forest Hills with my mom and brother. It was a middle-class neighborhood, with a lot of rich, snooty women who had horrible spoiled brat kids. There was a playground with women sitting around and a kid screaming, a spoiled, horrible kid just running rampant with no discipline whatsoever. The kind of kid you just want to kill. You know, 'beat on the brat with a baseball bat' just came out. I just wanted to kill him.

"A funny thing, when the song came out on the first album, the intro was a bubblegummy sort of thing, right out of the Ohio Express or the 1910 Fruitgum Company—our influences. But a lot of people said we were really stupid. 'Beat on the brat.' They didn't get it. Then you'd explain it and they'd say, 'That's not stupid.' An album review in England even said it was an anti-child-abuse song, which I guess it really is indirectly!"

Essentially, then, what the Ramones had done was blow apart and recreate the music they

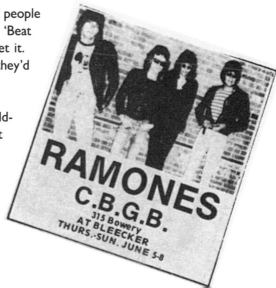

RAMONES
C.B.G.B.
315 Bowery
AT BLEECKER
THURS.-SUN. JUNE 5-8

loved out of bits and pieces of the pop culture that had hacked them up and spit them out.

"The one thing we had in common was that we all felt like square pegs that couldn't fit in," says Tommy. "But out of that came our creativity. We all liked bubblegum music that other people despised, one-hit wonder records, Phil Spector, the English rock scene, and the Top Forty radio of the era. We were called a minimalist band, and in a lot of ways that's true. I used a ¼ beat with minimalist hitting and syncopation, opening and closing the high-hat to add texture at the appropriate moments. I hit cymbal crashes sparingly, but always in places where they meant something. In working with a song, I'd hear a sonic wave: I'd try to get the feel like I was riding a surfboard and rising with the wave and hitting the shore like a tsunami."

Dee Dee exploded the rhythm with his voice and bass, Johnny's hyperspeed double-strum power-chording invented a new guitar style, and Joey's uniquely weird British-accented Queens English had surprised them all. As Joey reflects, "Pop music that was exciting, spirited, and fun, and *three minutes*, wasn't being recorded anymore. Each song or album had a half-hour drum or guitar or keyboard solo. So we simplified it and made it pure. We put the emotion and guts and attitude back in."

Speaking with interviewer Joan Tarshis, Johnny summed it up this way: "Basically, I got laid off from my job as a construction worker, and got Dee Dee and a couple friends and decided to do a band and have fun." Maybe they'd do an album and that's as far as they would get before going back to the real world, this time for good. Except then they started coming out with songs that were undeniably *different*. "We decided to basically write some crazy bubblegum music." Maybe *too* crazy, but catchy to the max—and with a little hard work and determination, it became obvious to them, at least, that the Ramones could offer the world an alternative.

All they needed now was a place to play.

arly in 1976, legendary rock scene maker Danny Fields reported in *Music Gig* that Lou Reed was an avid fan of a new New York band called the Ramones. The band, he said, was making their own cassette tape of a recent performance at CBGB, a biker bar on the Bowery that was "the mecca" for all the New York underground bands. "It's still difficult to get record executives down there, but for visiting musicians and journalists, especially those from the West Coast and England, the club is the number-one musical must on any visit to the Big Apple."

Number 315 Bowery, at the dead end of Bleecker Street and in the heart of hell, is a world-famous

Other Music

For Uplifting

Gourmandizers

Hilly Kristal, owner and operator in front of his club, CBGB-OMFUG in the mid 70s. (Photo by Godlis)

address. There still stands CBGB, a boxcar-shaped bar where someone once observed that if you put anything down you could consider it stolen within five minutes.

Perhaps that's too harsh, but the eternally grungy 167- by 25-foot room remains situated in a Skid Row area of flophouses, soup kitchens, gas stations, restaurant supply stores, and precious little else besides those who have no way out. Greenwich Village is nearby, so is the less beckoning East Village, Chinatown, and Lower East Side, but it's the Bowery—maybe once the home of the colorful Bowery Boys of the thirties movie lore, but lately the home of hopelessly downtrodden Bowery bums.

In December 1973, Hilly Kristal, a beefy ex-Marine and veteran nightclub operator whose praises will be sung as long as there are new bands looking for a place to play, opened a new club, CBGB–OMFUG, which would forever be known as CBGB's—CB's, for short. The initials stood for "Country, Bluegrass, and Blues," but it was the overlooked

OMFUG—"Other Music For Uplifting Gourmandizers"—that was about to change the world.

At this time, New York's live music scene was mainly made up of the touring superstar rock concert acts of the early seventies. Little of note was left from the underground outside of "Berlin"-era Lou Reed, the declining Dolls, and Wayne County.

One of the biggest problems was that there was practically nowhere to play. After Mercer Art Center's walls came crumbling down there were basically the Coventry in Queens and a few Manhattan clubs including the 82 Club, Mother's, Kenny's Castaways, and Max's Kansas City. Then one day in the spring of 1974, two young guitarists named Tom Verlaine and Richard Lloyd happened to walk past 315 Bowery just as Hilly Kristal was outside putting up his new club's awning. They stretched it in telling Hilly that their band Television could play country, bluegrass, and blues, as well as *originals*. TV's originals, of course, were about as far away from the designated CBGB's music as every band that followed in their footsteps—but none more so than the Ramones.

"I think we saw a little tiny ad in the *Village Voice* for Television, who started out there a month before us," says Johnny. "So we said, 'Let's try and go play there.' "

Hilly had opened CB's with country music and poetry readings until he decided to let Television play Sundays. "Then this group from Queens, the Ramones, were pushed on me," Hilly recalls. "They played and got into their famous seventeen minute set: seventeen minutes of twenty songs, very loud and high energy, from one to another to another. Nobody had ever done that before. It was like hitting people over the head, but by the time you were saying, 'I can't take it any more!' they were finished."

The joke at the time was that seeing a Ramones set was like entering a small Oklahoma town: Blink and you'll miss it. They played eternally at 78 rpm., one critic said, as if they had only fifteen minutes to live. The main purpose behind each song seemed to be to finish it as quickly as humanly possible, and if there were complaints afterward that the set was too short (and there *were* complaints!), well, the Ramones said, you got what you paid for—just without the stupid stage patter in between songs!

It was said, too, that the sets were seventeen minutes long (some said fifteen minutes) because the Ramones didn't know enough songs for a more standard set length, though it was also noted that few Ramones songs clocked in at even two minutes *tops*. Equally noteworthy, of course, was the headbanging sound akin to chainsaws cutting through a forest, and lyrics worthy of an institutionalized psychopath. Just your normal, everyday stuff from middle-class suburban kids with no hopes of ever getting out.

They did the whole set over and over and over again, then over again some more. Sometimes they'd stop and argue with each other, sometimes

MEET THE RAMONES

New York's Phenomenal Pop Combo

AT C.B.G.B. 315 Bowery

TuesDAYS — 10 + MiDNite

Getting the word out themselves!
Homemade handbills that the band posted
up around CBGB's and elsewhere.

Dee Dee would count his "One-two-three-four!" and each guy would start a different song. Sometimes something went wrong and one or more would storm offstage. But eventually they got it right. "Nobody is going to like you guys, but I'll have you back." Thus spoketh Hilly to Joey. Let there be light.

The Ramones first CBGB's gigs took place August 16 and 17, 1974. Playing there every week, they would have seventy-four performances under their collective belt by the end of the year.

Tommy, who had started on drums only two weeks before the first CB's show, described the scene as straight out of film director John Waters's outrageously tasteless masterpiece, *Pink Flamingos*. The first audience was basically the club's bartender and his dog. Then came the Andy Warhol crowd, then the intellectuals, then the kids. Admission was two dollars, with the band getting a percentage of the door.

"We were trying to create a club scene," says Johnny. "Clubs were only for Top Forty cover bands, otherwise there were only rock concerts. And people wouldn't go to the Bowery because it was a slummy neighborhood with bums—but it wasn't that dangerous. At the beginning at CB's, they had two or three people playing in a theater group, who were all a bunch of nerds to me. I'd go to rock concerts and back to Queens, but I'd never see people like this!"

No doubt Johnny hadn't seen anyone like the Cockettes, either. They were the notorious transvestite group from San Francisco, which was also stationed at CB's early on. One of them, Tomata du Plenty, later became lead singer of the Screamers. Then there was Arturo Vega, a young actor/painter from Chihuahua, Mexico, who lived in a loft around the corner from the club, who later became (after Monte Melnick became the fifth) the sixth Ramone.

THEY DON'T WANT TO
BUT THEY WILL
— HELD OVER AGAIN —
THE
RAMONES
C.B.G.B.
THURS. – SUN. 315
BOWERY

"I met Dee Dee because he used to see a girl named Sweet Pam who lived upstairs. She was also with the Cockettes, and the Ramones opened for them at least once. I was also at CB's, in an off-off-off-off-Broadway drag show called 'Savage Voodoo Nuns.' I played Connie, a girl who wanted to join a convent to become a famous virgin! We opened for the Ramones once. I'd been a rock 'n' roll fan all my life, but in the early seventies nothing was happening. So I was waiting and hoping for a change, and then I saw the Ramones and thought they were good, but too funny to be true or important. Then I realized they were for *real*. They were so original and powerful!"

Arturo became the first person to work for them, at first carrying and setting up equipment, later running the lights as well. Arturo also started creating the band's ads and posters, as well as the fliers which they diligently sent out to attract journalists and other music business types. But most important, Arturo devised the merchandise which, along with constant touring, virtually kept the Ramones alive.

Monte, meanwhile, soon became the band's sound man, monitor man, roadie, "and everything else." The Performance Studio had served a purpose, but the place had never been properly insulated, and after a while the neighbors complained about too much noise. Besides, Tommy had joined the band.

"Because I was a musician at the time, I didn't like them when I started working for them," says Monte. "Musicians couldn't like the Ramones, because musicians are technical, and the Ramones aren't technical."

No, the Ramones weren't technical. Just what they *were*, though, immediately became an argument.

"The Ramones were unbelievable," says rock journalist Ira Robbins, founder of the now defunct *Trouser Press* magazine and editor of its legacy, the authoritative Trouser Press *Guide to New Wave Records.* Robbins had attended a Ramones Performance Studio gig, which had also featured the local club bands Tuff Darts (then with soon-to-be rockabilly revivalist Robert Gordon) and The Fast.

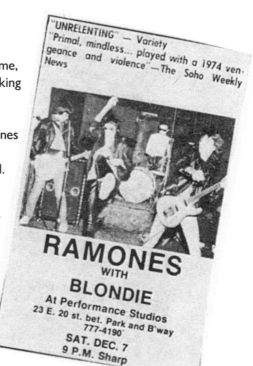

"They were Jan and Dean played really fast, and I though they were pathetic and very bizarre. Joey looked like an amphibian in the early days, like he'd been dragged out of a swamp. I mean, he was ten feet tall and wrapped around the mike stand like a tree limb, with shades and hair in his eyes. He looked like a creature from Mars who'd never seen the sun!

"CB's hadn't started yet, and Max's booked showcase bands instead of underground acts seven nights a week. If you weren't in with the Max's crowd you never played there. There were fifty to one hundred people there, and I was sitting on the floor near the stage. Johnny had a blue Mosrite, and I remember watching him play and not really liking them, then I noticed Johnny had this really cool trick: The pick guard of his guitar was turning from white to bright crimson red. Then I realized that he'd split his finger on his hand from endless up and down strumming, and he was spraying the entire scratch plate with a fine, aerosol mist of blood."

Robbins saw them again, several times, at CB's. "I was with Binky Phillips of the Planets, a Who-inspired band around the time of the Dolls, the Dictators, and The Fast. We stood in the back making fun of Dee Dee counting off the songs—every single song!—twenty-two songs in twenty minutes. So we counted each song, too, and collapsed with laughter. I just couldn't take them seriously because they were such a jokey kind of band. Then I got into a knock-down, drag-out argument with my friend Scott Isler [another *Trouser Press* staffer] over whether they were totally worthless or the greatest band that ever lived and the greatest

**Joey on the cover
of *Punk* magazine as
illustrated by John Holmstrom.**

art statement of the twentieth century. I confess that I really misunderstood them at first. This was long before they made a record, and they just blasted out their three-chord songs and when they got to 'California Sun,' which had four chords, they left one chord out! Even with a four-chord song they were a three-chord band! I was so shocked by their minimalism that I thought there was nothing there, but in hindsight, of course, I realized Scott was absolutely right."

John Holmstrom is another journalist and Ramones contemporary who didn't know what to make of the band at first, but would later make plenty out of them. The future founder/editor of *Punk* magazine (he currently publishes *High Times*) also came from a middle-class suburb (Cheshire, Connecticut), but was politically radical and artistically inclined. Enrolled at Manhattan's School of Visual Arts, he had studied with *Mad* magazine founder Harvey Kurtzman and comic book legend Will Eisner (*The Spirit*), and had immersed himself in the early seventies downtown Manhattan arts scene.

Like everyone else, Holmstrom had grown up in the sixties on rock 'n' roll; his favorite musicians were the same as the Ramones, and he felt equally disenfranchised by the lifeless music that was masquerading for rock in the seventies.

"I picked up the Dictators first record and went nuts over their humor, and I liked the Ramones because they sounded like a heavy-metal bubblegum group. The Dictators were crude and loud and dumb, but I always thought the Ramones had a special class and intelligence, a simplicity that took sophistication to appreciate.

"I went to see them one Sunday night at CB's when there were only forty people in the audience, and I was blown away! They did their twenty-minute sets in those days, but this one lasted a half hour, and they didn't say a word, which I liked. It was the perfect rock show, perfectly timed, not boring—bim, bam, boom! It was very radical and threatening but very artistic, and so well executed that I had a hard time figuring out if they were really punks in leather jackets who would kill you for looking the wrong way or if they were just posing. There was always that edge, and I couldn't figure it out: Was this a put-on? Were they really from the streets or just rich kids pretending to be punks? They were stripping rock

'n' roll down to the bare essentials and hitting the perfect chords over and over again, but they were also making a musical artistic statement, so they couldn't be just punks—or idiot savants. Once I met them I realized that they fell somewhere in between!"

Chris Frantz, however, never had any doubt. The Rhode Island School of Design grad and drummer for the fledgling Talking Heads had moved to a loft three blocks from CB's. The first time he went to the club was in September 1974. "I walked in and the Ramones were playing, and I realized, 'This is it!' " says Frantz. "They were extremely *arch* in a musical way, and had a whole fashion statement: pretty serious jeans and black leather jackets. In the days of glitter rock 'n' roll they were pretty rough and extreme—the volume was real loud, the songs were short. In those days they'd stop in the middle of songs and argue, and then 'One-two-three-four!' and they'd start again. Maybe someone would get the chord change or tempo or lyrics wrong, and they'd stop periodically and yell at each other and start again. But they really appealed to me. I liked black music, as well as the Stooges and the Velvet Underground—fairly extreme white rock 'n' roll, and the Ramones were *extremely* extreme. They were really like *art rock*, not like Yes or ELP, definitely not into it just to sell records or get girls, but they *cared* about making an artistic statement. To me, that was the essence of the Ramones."

As a neat side benefit, Frantz had also discovered a place for his band to play, and soon the Talking Heads, along with Television, the Ramones, the streetwise poet-turned-punk-priestess Patti Smith, and the sixties girl-group-derived Blondie had put CBGB's to the fore of a suddenly rejuvenated New York rock underground.

But neither Holmstrom nor Frantz had just stumbled on CB's and the Ramones, for the media had been there already. Since they were revolutionary in their image and musical approach, the Ramones quickly became media darlings—whether they were loved or as often as not, hated. "It was quite startling, but after a few months everyone was talking about them," Hilly recalls. "I'll never forget one night Linda Ronstadt pulled up in a limo and came in. I think she lasted four minutes. She smiled when she walked out, but I think it was too much for her!"

What she had seen, as Richard Hell described it, was a singer who hid his eyes with oval shades, who was built like a praying mantis with the coloring of Snow White. Not to mention that guitarist whose face seemed frozen in a permanent grimace, nearly scowling, perhaps to overcome the pain in his bleeding hands.

Other writers also had a field day with the Ramones. Johnny, with his Moe Howard haircut, was likened to a Three Stooges stand-in, and cited as the first guitarist to engage himself in a full-fledged glaring match with his guitar (it was a draw!). Dee Dee, the Ramones designated heartthrob, was otherwise noted for his ability to stare blankly at an equally blank

wall. Tommy's most complimentary comparison was with a wind-up toy. Joey was a young broomstick of a lead singer who could only have come from another planet —were he not from Forest Hills. In June 1975, Albert Goldman, the controversial biographer of Elvis Presley and John Lennon who was then *Life's* rock critic, remarked that the Ramones sounded like they escaped from under somebody's garage.

Most critics, though, were ecstatic. "Brevity is the soul of wit and it's right at the heart of the Ramones music," wrote the *Aquarian's* Craig Zeller, capturing an early CB's gig with appropriate spirit. "This is one group that will never be accused of dragging out a number. The word's 'solos' and 'slow' are not in their vocabulary and they would be at a loss trying to define words like 'subtlety' or 'nuance.' These guys are speedin' punk maniacs and they know it and various combinations of shades, T-shirts (one of which has 'Captain America' emblazoned across the front), black leather jackets, and dungarees ripped wide open at the knees (that's lead guitarist Johnny again). The main purpose in doing a song seems to be finishing it as fast as is humanly possible while they play at the speed of light and at a pace roughly that of a buffalo stampede, what with lead singer Joey slur-snarling out the vocals while Johnny and Dee Dee (that's right, Dee Dee) lay their guitars like runamok threshing machines with the drums all smashing cymbals and slam bang pounding the background. This is the big beat at its crudest, noisiest and most simplistic. It's also rock, at its most direct, exciting and igniting ... and just like the Beach Boys it's fun, fun, fun. In between songs there's a pause of about four seconds before they rev up into the next one ... as the set progressed audience members started yelling out the countdown (accompanying Dee Dee's one-two-three-four), prompting Dee Dee to switch over to German. . . . Lead singer Joey, nicknamed Snake, long and slithery with hair falling around his neck in thick curly ringlets undulating all around the mike. Seldom makes any moves on stage except to occasionally kick his right leg out and back hard and jerk his head down to the side if the other guys come down particularly hard on a note; same with Johnny, who chords ferociously and at such a relentless pace that his hands really are a blur. I'm sure he gets a finger transplant every other week so he can continue to play like there's no tomorrow."

Alan Betrock, in a May 1975 issue of *Soho Weekly News*, compared the Ramones sound to a streamlined, yet still "vehemently compact" mix of early Velvet Underground, Shadows of Knight, and the Stooges. "It's rock 'n' roll the way it was meant to be played, not with boogie or pretense, but just straight freshness and intense energy. Sort of out of the garages and onto the stages again."

But press acclaim was hardly restricted to New York. In November 1975 Charles Shaar Murray, in an overview of New York's CBGB's/punk scene for England's *New Musical Express* (NME), said that the Ramones were a band that London's rock scene could really use. "They're simultaneously so funny, such a cartoon vision of rock 'n' roll and so genuinely tight and powerful that they're just bound to enchant anyone who fell in love with rock 'n' roll for the right reasons. . . .

"They aren't worried about being genuinely creative, and if you told them that they provided a unique insight into anything they'd probably piss on your shoes, and you'd deserve it, too. They ain't glitter queens. They ain't a blues band. What they do is fire off ridiculously compressed bursts of power chords . . . and nuthin' but hit singles or what would be hit singles, if there was any justice in this crummy world."

He went on to discuss the other New York rock bands that had erupted forth out of the Ramones volcano, and concluded that while British bands played better, they lacked the New Yorkers' "abnormally high energy level [and] the desire to combine traditionalism with experiment by cutting rock right down to the basic ingredient that made 'em like it in the first place and then rebuilding from there."

In the final analysis, Murray concluded, "what all of these bands have in common is that they're representing the fifties and sixties in a way that could only be the seventies."

CBGB's, by default, had become the Fillmore East of the seventies. Despite what *Rolling Stone* depicted as an "ambience of piss and disinfectant," even the highbrow *New Yorker* recognized the club's "coherent social and musical aesthetic," as represented by scores of odd-named bands whose most common characteristics were that they were new, unsigned, and unknown beyond their home base. Besides the handful of previously mentioned forerunners and the equally important Dictators, Mink De Ville, and the Heartbreakers (starring ex-Dolls Johnny Thunders and Jerry Nolan and ex-Television bassist Richard Hell), these now included such scene stalwarts as Tuff Darts, The Fast, the Miamis, and the Shirts.

"There are other talented and promising bands around," *Phonograph Record*'s Vince Aletti acknowledged, "but none seem so strong as the Ramones, a group which has lots of folks really excited. Their tunes, all teenage rockers, sound the same, but they're so great and energetic that no one seems to notice or care."

One journalist, though, stood out from the pack.

Lisa Robinson, then as now, was one of the most important and visible rock journalists on the scene. Not only did she edit *Hit Parader*, but, along with her husband and Richard Robinson (who would produce David Johansen's magnificent solo albums) and pre-Patti Smith guitarist Lenny Kaye, she also ran *Rock Scene*, a teen-oriented picture magazine which relied heavily on backstage pix taken by the big-time rock photographer Bob Gruen. While she closely covered superstar rock acts like the Stones and Led Zeppelin, she also had her ears to the underground, where the buzz from the Ramones was deafening.

The legend goes that one night she and another journalist flipped a coin to see who would go to see the Ramones, who'd been bugging both of them to attend a gig. Robinson either won or lost the coin flip, but either way she's the one who went.

"I really loved Led Zeppelin," says Lisa, "but after spending several tours with them and watching lengthy guitar and drum solos, I saw the Ramones—with all their songs under three minutes!—and thought it was such a refreshing change. I thought they were really charming, and that for the time, their energy was a much-needed shot in the arm. So I'd just go see them all the time. Nobody was doing anything like that! I wrote about them, and Bob did several photo spreads of the Ramones for *Rock Scene*, which we put out just for fun, though it later turned out to be much more influential than we ever thought it would be."

Robinson's specialty was lively gossip, which, in addition to publishing in *Rock Scene*, she syndicated to the *Chicago Sun-Times* and *The New York Post*. She was also American editor for *NME*, which was interested in Led Zeppelin and the Stones, but more interested in Patti Smith, Television, and the whole CBGB's scene. "They [NME] had this big love affair with U.S. punk and rock 'n' roll music, but they covered it in a very intellectuallized way, and I was just gossip and features and frivolity," explains Lisa.

But what Robinson wrote went a long way, as would the written words and similar stature of another major New York rock scene maker whom the Ramones were desperately trying to attract.

anny Fields was the other journalist who won or lost the fabled coin flip with Lisa Robinson.

"We sent him fliers all the time because we'd seen his name on MC5 and Stooges albums," says Johnny. "We didn't know who he was or what he did, but we figured that if he liked *them*, maybe he'd like us."

What Danny Fields had done could fill another book. The co-editor of *16 Magazine* and a weekly columnist for *Soho Weekly News*, Fields was a Warhol-era rock 'n' roll Renaissance man who enjoyed opera and compared hard rock music to a Bach fugue. In the late sixties he was a publicist at Elektra Records, where he was considered

"I Call It

'Rock Rock'"

THE HEARTBREAKERS

THE RAMONES

Wayne County DJ

New Year's Eve Champagne Party

refreshments provided $7.50 (includes everything) at THE SEA OF CLOUDS club 5 E. 16th St. 5th fl. continuous music doors open at 11 PM call 255-59

the "resident hippie." But he also had a&r input (meaning he was a talent scout) and signed and managed the radically political MC5 (the Detroit hard rockers' name stood for Motor City Five) and the Stooges, another Motor City pre-punk band which substituted moral outrage with decay. Elektra also was the Doors label, though Fields didn't get along very well with Jim Morrison. But he was eventually fired for defending MC5's right to have the word "fuck" on its album jackets and print ads, and was later fired from a publicity stint at Atlantic for openly detesting Emerson, Lake and Palmer.

Fields then worked for prominent club operator Steve Paul's management company (whose clients then included Johnny and Edgar Winter) prior to hosting an FM radio show and becoming a major editor/columnist covering the likes of Television and Patti Smith. Now one of the most experienced and astute forces in New York's music scene, Fields likened the music business of the mid-seventies to a "big government in crisis," a far, far cry from the glory years of 1965–67, when groups like Jefferson Airplane, the Byrds, Yardbirds, and Doors made their debuts alongside the Beatles ("Sergeant Pepper's Lonely Hearts Club Band"), the Stones ("Their Satanic Majesties Request"), the Beach Boys ("Pet Sounds"), and Bob Dylan ("Blonde on Blonde").

Rather, the music of the day was dominated by the California sounds of the Eagles, the Doobies, Linda Ronstadt, and America, "pathetic Xeroxes of Xeroxes," Fields said. Rock bands were never hard enough for him, or else they had too much blues influence. But he refused at first to see the Ramones, who were bombarding him with invites and phone calls, because from the sound of their name, he thought they were a cha-cha band that played salsa music! Then came the fateful coin toss.

"They [the Ramones] weren't the only act that was bugging us both, so we tossed a coin one night, and I went to see one act, she [Lisa] went to see the Ramones. I figured we'd got them both out of our hair, then next day she called and said they were great and just perfect for me: Their songs were short, they looked adorable, had great energy, no guitar solos—they were just fabulous! She knew my attention span wasn't very long, and I guess she liked the idea that they had a gimmick—a great name, they all wore jeans and white T-shirts and black leather jackets, and sneered. It sounded very good to me, so I went to see them at CB's."

Robinson was right. Fields loved the Ramones.

"They were what the world needed at that time. They were so cute, and I thought they had hit tunes. 'Beat on the Brat' and 'Blitzkrieg Bop' were so catchy—'Blitzkrieg Bop' became a beer commercial eighteen years later, so *someone* thought it was catchy enough." While journalists had taken to calling the Ramones music punk rock, Fields preferred "rock rock."

By now, even Johnny knew that the Ramones had something special. "We were still naive toward the whole situation. All I wanted to do was one album and go back to my job as a construction worker; I didn't know how hard it was being a musician. But early in 1975 CB's started to happen. Patti got signed, Lou Reed came down, Warhol. Alan Vega of Suicide said, 'This is what I've been waiting for!' I can't believe that some people liked us, but I felt we were good and would become big."

So did Fields, who realized that the Ramones represented both his past accomplishments and future objectives, and decided to take them on. "I think it was late 1974 when I borrowed money from my mother to buy them equipment. That was their condition of management: They needed a manager and money. 'Manager' means 'grownup,' and 'grownup' means 'money.' " A little of which would have to go a long way.

Johnny remembered one gig in the city where the Ramones and the Heartbreakers had to split fifty dollars. When the band began, they were making fifty dollars a week; even by the time of their fourth album, that salary had only tripled.

Still, at the end of 1974, they kicked in one thousand dollars, and in eight hours, cut a fifteen-song demo. It was just basic tracks and vocals and mixes of most of the songs that made up their first album, but Johnny felt the demo was actually *better* than the first album. Recalls Tommy,

"We put a promo package together, sent it out and got rejected everywhere."

Joey and Dee Dee, who had lived together in Joey's mother's gallery on Queens Boulevard when the Ramones started (they barricaded themselves behind paintings and paint cans to rehearse and to ditch the beat cops), were now living in Arturo Vega's loft. Here Vega, who supported himself by painting supermarket produce signs (example: "PEAS—67 CENTS A POUND"), was creating the Ramones main income source: T-shirts.

Most of the Ramones T-shirt designs were derived from the black-and-white photograph of an American bald eagle belt buckle pictured on the back of the Ramones self-titled first album (that photo, by the way, was clipped from a self-portrait Vega had taken in a dime-store photo booth).

"I saw them as the ultimate all-American band," says Vega. "To me, they reflected the American character in general—an almost childish, innocent aggression. Then the first time I went to Washington, D.C., I was impressed by the official atmosphere of the buildings and agencies and all the flags everywhere. I thought, 'The Great Seal of the President of the United States' would be perfect for the Ramones, with the eagle holding arrows—to symbolize strength and the aggression that would be used against whomever dares to attack us—and an olive branch, offered to those who want to be friendly. But we decided to change it a little bit. Instead of the olive branch, we had an apple tree branch, since the Ramones were American as apple pie. And since Johnny was such a baseball fanatic, we had the eagle hold a baseball bat instead of the [Great Seal's] arrows."

The scroll in the eagle's beak originally read "Look out below," but was later changed to "Hey, ho! Let's go!" The arrowheads on the eagle's shield came from a design on a polyester shirt Vega had bought on 14th Street, while the letters of the band's name, spelled out in block capitals, were little more than plastic stick-ons. Sales of these T-shirts would not only keep the Ramones going for many years, but would finance Vega's first trips with the band to California and Europe. But those were still a ways down the road.

Meanwhile, the CB's scene was nearing the boiling point. "We were friendly but competitive toward the other bands," says Johnny, "even though they were nothing at all like what we were doing. Our only real competition that I thought was good was Johnny Thunders and the Heartbreakers. Talking Heads was a little different, and Blondie was a girl group. We were a total different thing." But with all the media gravitating toward the Bowery, and Patti Smith signed to Arista Records, it was only a matter of time before the record business, in its time-honored fashion, jumped on the bandwagon until the bandwagon collapsed. But could the Ramones, so contrary to record-business norms in music, lyrics, and image, possibly be next?

On June 23, according to Johnny's records, the Ramones auditioned for the small independent label Sire Records, which offered them a singles deal for "You're Gonna Kill That Girl," but the band declined, opting to hold out for an album deal. The next day they auditioned for Steve Paul's Blue Sky label, and the next, for Arista.

Paul was at least interested enough in the band to have them play an unannounced concert set at a July 11 date at the Palace Theater in Waterbury, Connecticut, in between headliner Johnny Winter and the New York band the Stories, who had a No. 1 pop hit in 1973 with "Brother Louie." This gig, as it turned out, became the first of numerous nightmare bookings which continued until the band finally got an agent who understood how to place them.

"The crowd cheered, and I thought, 'Great! They know the Ramones!'" recalls Johnny, who realized his mistake when it started raining bottles three songs later. As Dee Dee wrote in *Spin*: "The lights went on, and everyone was standing up cheering, because they thought we were Johnny Winter ... but as soon as we started playing, that crowd turned ugly. I've never got so many bottles or firecrackers or so many people giving me the finger. The people were just so upset with us, and after that we didn't want to play anymore. We said 'Forget it. This is no fun.' But we were too involved to turn back." And as Tommy said shortly afterwards, "It goes with our music. We're giving out World War III, and they're giving it right back."

In mid-July, CB's ran a nightly series of dates featuring the many unsigned bands that had placed the club so prominently on New York's cultural map. Headlining the "CBGB Summer '75 Rock Festival Showcase Auditions" were the Ramones, who also benefitted the most from the heavy U.S. and U.K. press turnout. As Johnny recalls, "*Rolling Stone* had a one-page article and we were three-fourths of it."

Then, on September 19, the Ramones visited 914 Studios in Blauvelt, New York, where they cut demos of "Judy Is a Punk" and "I Wanna Be Your Boyfriend" for former New York Dolls manager Marty Thau. "Johnny Thunders used to tell me about them and said I should get in touch," says Thau, who in 1991 released these two comparatively crudely recorded and mixed tracks in "The Groups of Wrath," a compilation of songs by the other New York groups he had been involved with, including the Dolls, Blondie, Suicide, and Richard Hell and the Voidoids.

Thau had been approached to manage the Ramones but was hoping to become a record producer. The Ramones tracks were his first efforts, and having heard that Sire had once looked at the group, he contacted Craig Leon, the label's a&r assistant. "He was surprised I had Ramones recordings. When I went there and played the tapes for him, his eyes lit up and he played them for Seymour Stein, and related back to me that they had dispelled any doubts they had that the Ramones were recordable."

In the audience at CBGB's: Brian Ferry (drinking),
Patti Smith, and above her, Janis Schacht.
(Danny Fields)

Seymour Stein, a legendary "great record man" who delights in demonstrating his boundless enthusiasm for all things musical, had founded Sire in 1966 with writer-producer Richard Gottehrer, who had co-written the Angels 1963 girl-group revenge classic "My Boyfriend's Back" and in 1965 had had his own smash hit, "I Want Candy," with the Strangeloves. The label's early output consisted primarily of European acts licensed to Sire in America. These acts included Fleetwood Mac and Chicken Shack, then on England's Blue Horizon label (of which Sire was half owner); the Dutch group Focus, which had had the 1973 pop hit "Hocus Pocus"; and England's Climax Blues Band.

Craig Leon, meanwhile, worked at a small studio in Florida where Climax had rehearsed, before Gottehrer convinced him to move to New York in 1973. The goal at Sire now was to sign its own bands, and Leon was out there every night looking. "Patti Smith was my A-number-one choice, but unfortunately she got signed to Arista. But I liked all the New York bands: the Ramones, Television, Talking Heads—those three were all together. Most people at the time felt that the Ramones couldn't make a record or tour—especially after what happened with Johnny Winter. But I felt they could make a real revolutionary record."

Admittedly, Leon was "low guy at a very small record company." But his confidence in the band was borne out by Linda Stein, Seymour's equally colorful ex-wife, who came down to see the band during its three-night stint during the first week of October at Mother's, a club on 23rd Street.

"It was a gay bar for elderly gays," recalls Linda Stein, who had been a schoolteacher prior to assisting her ex-husband at Sire. Now Manhattan's "realtor to the stars" and manager of Danish rapper Lucas, Mrs. Stein had come down to Mother's at Fields's request, subbing for her flu-stricken husband.

"It was really a cold, winter, snowy night," she says. "Of course, they did 'Blitzkrieg Bop' and all the standards. I was fascinated by the simplicity of the lyrics and beat, and Dee Dee, who was always so sexy and cute! I came home and told Seymour, 'You gotta sign them!' Two or three days later they auditioned for Seymour at some rehearsal space and he was very taken by them and signed them. Soon after we went to Midem [the annual international music industry convention in Cannes] and I remember him walking down the Croisette [Cannes' main drag] and saying, 'Are you sure they won't laugh at me in England?' "

Thau's demos and the fact that the Ramones had a legitimate manager whom he'd known for years were the key factors in Seymour Stein's decision to take a chance with the Ramones. "I'd become aware of the Ramones and the other CBGB bands as part of the Bowery phenomenon, and after Linda came back with such glowing reports, I saw them within a week. Quite literally, they blew me away. Apparently, people were taken aback by them, or saw all their songs as one continuous drone, but their melodies were very catchy and stayed with me, dancing around in my head, and it was absolutely clear that for better or worse, underneath it all was a pop-band mentality."

There was, however, one major sticking point. "I don't know if I should admit it, because I got over it very quickly, but I wasn't very pleased with the Nazi references in the songs. You can't throw away twenty years of Jewish upbringing in Brooklyn, nor do I want to. So I spoke to them about it, but decided that Sire wasn't the kind of record company, and I wasn't the kind of music person, to restrict anything, and I went along with it. But admittedly, I was a bit uneasy about it."

The Ramones legend is that they were signed by Sire for the paltry sum of six thousand dollars—the advance for production of their first album. "Apparently they'd been to a lot of other companies, and most of them wouldn't even listen," Stein continues. "Those that did rejected them instantly, so they were quite desperate to make a deal."

But unbeknownst to the Ramones, Stein himself was quite desperate, too. As an independent label, Sire was dependent on other companies to distribute its records to stores, and had gone through a series of distributors, ending up at Paramount Records. Paramount was then sold to ABC Records, where Steely Dan and Jimmy Buffett ruled the roost. Stein entered into a new deal with ABC, and things were going very well until the ABC executive who negotiated the deal got axed, and the new guy declared himself not at all happy with the existing Sire contract.

"They did everything possible to force us into changing the deal, so now I didn't have any money, and it was hard enough just to pay salaries each week. So I told the Ramones that the only way I could make a deal, because what I loved was their *songs*, was if I could do their publishing deal as well. So we made a song demo, and I called Roland Rennie, one of the forgotten souls of the music business, who in his heyday was the first managing director and president of Polydor Records in England, but was now involved in song publishing there for Chapel Music. I took the receiver and said, 'Listen to something revolutionary!' and let it rip for six minutes before realizing what the call was costing me! So I took down the phone and asked him what he thought. He said, 'Seymour! I've been screaming at you! I can't make it out!' So I was about to say, 'Roland, trust me!' but I didn't have to. He said, 'Seymour, if you feel that passionately, I'll take the subpublishing!' Now the money I got for the subpublishing deal was quite high, and I used it not only to make the publishing deal with the Ramones, but also to make the record deal and pay them their first advance, which was six thousand dollars. To this day, I'm grateful to Roland."

Fields also remembers getting as much as twenty thousand dollars from Sire to buy equipment and feed the band, then regularly using Stein as a "bank," taking out small amounts of money whenever they were broke, though they all knew how to live cheaply; Dee Dee actually lived in Danny's apartment for a while, and Joey stayed there as well.

The year 1975 saw the dawn of the era of huge signings and advances from the major labels, but Sire was basically a small fish. "We weren't contenders at all in any way, shape, or form," Stein continues. "So we had to jump on the trends before there was even a whiff of them being trends to begin with."

Remember, this *was* 1975. "Guys were flipping around in the air in million-dollar stage shows and playing as many notes as they could on records," says Leon, "but the Ramones were the exact opposite. They were a return to the pop ethic of sixties rock 'n' roll and Phil Spector, which had been lost."

On February 2, 1976, the Ramones began recording their first album for Sire. On February 19, they finished.

O

n April 7, 1976, Sire Records publicist Janis Schacht sent out the following press release:

SIRE SIGNS THE RAMONES

Seymour Stein, managing director of Sire Records, has announced the signing of the Ramones. The Ramones, who are easily one of the best-known and most-loved groups on the New York/CBGB's circuit, recently completed their first album for the label, *Ramones*, recorded at New York's Plaza Sound Studios and produced by Craig Leon.

It is rumored that the record will be marked "Play loud but not too loud," as the album registered on the mastering equipment at Sterling

"Shoot 'em
in the Back Now"

**Jayne County,
formerly Wayne County,
a familiar face on the
early punk scene.
(Danny Fields)**

Sound as one of the "hottest" records ever cut. In fact, several pieces of expensive equipment were irreparably damaged when the first reference copy of the album was cut.

The high-energy album contains fourteen tracks, such as: "Beat on the Brat," "Judy Is a Punk," "I Don't Wanna Go Down to the Basement," and "Blitzkrieg Bop" (the projected single). The album's running time is just under thirty minutes. The agreement with Sire was made by the group's manager, Danny Fields, who in the past was responsible for discovering and signing the MC5 and the Stooges.

Ramones is scheduled for an April 23 release and Sire Records is marketed by ABC Records.

*   *   *

The fourteen songs on *Ramones* clocked in at twenty-eight minutes, fifty-two seconds ("I Don't Wanna Go Down to the Basement" was an opera-length 2:35). The album cost $6,400 to produce, when average costs were well over $50,000, and recording superstar acts sometimes surpassed $500,000.

Schacht was absolutely right about the damage to the studio equipment.

"We really were trying to make the hottest record ever," says Craig Leon. "It was mastered at Sterling Sound by Greg Calbi, who's one of the best mastering engineers, but it was one of his first projects. When we first brought the master tapes in to actually cut the record, it was so loud that the cutter head cut right through the acetate disc and completely blew the cutter head!"

But the recording process itself was also memorable. "Ramones" was recorded at Plaza Sound in Radio City Music Hall, a gigantic art-deco facility where the great conductor Arturo Toscanini used to rehearse the NBC Symphony Orchestra and where Radio City's famed dancers the Rockettes practiced as well. The dimensions of the place were such that Tommy needed a metronome with a flashing light so everyone could see it from a distance (the pointer was set to the extreme right position, which was the fastest); Dee Dee was in one room, Johnny around the corner in the Rockettes' room.

By now the Ramones had so much material that they basically cut the first thirteen songs they had written, pretty much chronologically—an arrangement very similar to a typical CB's set. They usually did only two takes of each song, at one point cutting seven in a row without stopping. "If everyone was like them, record companies would have no worries," Seymour Stein recalled in the "Lifestyles of the Ramones" home video. The day they cut the seven tracks, he noted, they were *depressed* because they weren't able to do *more*.

The Beatles first album, *Meet the Beatles*, was one role model the Ramones followed for their first album, and they tried to approximate that record's split which emphasized the bass line on one side, guitar on the other. The guitar sound Leon wanted to get was similar to that on Hawkwind's British hit "Silver Machine." And nodding to his idol Phil Spector, he layered different instruments and sounds together to broaden the Ramones minimalist base.

It's necessary to note here that the Ramones played their own instruments, since a lot of people, even to this day, question whether they actually *can* play. Which isn't to say that they play *everything*, as the Ramones, like most recording groups, get a lot of studio help. So no, they didn't themselves perform on Radio City's huge Wurlitzer pipe organ on "Let's Dance," for instance, nor on the Byrds-like twelve-string guitars, tubular bells, and glockenspiel which Leon padded into "I Wanna Be Your Boyfriend."

As for the songwriting, while all songs were credited to the group, Joey was the force behind "Beat on the Brat," "Judy Is a Punk," and "Chain Saw," while Dee Dee wrote "53rd & 3rd," "I Don't Wanna Walk Around with You," and "Now I Wanna Sniff Some Glue." Tommy wrote "I Wanna Be Your Boyfriend" and the music for "Blitzkrieg Bop" to Dee Dee's lyrics. Dee Dee and Johnny collaborated on "I Don't Wanna Go Down to the Basement" and "Loudmouth." "Let's Dance" was a cover of the 1962 hit by Chris Montez.

Tommy also received associate producer credit (under the name T. Erdelyi), since some of his techniques from the demo production were used on the album.

"When we were done, they asked us if we wanted to listen to it, and we said forget it," Johnny told *Trouser Press*.

All they needed now was a cover photo. Sire had already commissioned a photographer, but the results were terrible. Meanwhile, Roberta Bayley, who worked the door at CB's and had begun taking pictures of the bands, had quickly knocked off three rolls of black-and-white film on the boys for a *Punk* magazine feature. When Sire saw her contact sheets, they offered her $125 for the cover shot and publicity stills as well.

"I'd taken them right off First Street, around the corner from CB's, in front of a wall by a vacant lot," recalls Bayley, who, in true punk fashion, had been taking pictures only a few weeks. "I had quite a few others from that session, but the one on the cover was a classic."

Sure enough, the "Ramones" cover portrait would be recognized in a 1992 issue of *Rolling Stone* as one of rock's one hundred best album covers, "on the same page as *Meet the Beatles*—but also the same page as a Toto album!" Bayley remembers that then, as now, the Ramones hated having their picture taken.

"Somehow I made them look the same height. There's a three-foot difference between Tommy and Joey, but Joey's slouching down, and Tommy's standing on something and looking up."

The pose, of course, was pure Ramones. In black leather jackets, sneakers (they wore Keds, since it was an American brand!), frayed jeans, cartoon T-shirts, dark sunglasses, just standing there against the wall looking back at you. Over the next few years the Stones, Queen, and even Billy Joel would steal their look.

"We just wanted to get it over with," recalls Johnny of the historic shoot. "Just a picture of us standing there, outside Arturo's apartment. I know covers are important—I bought a Stooges album because of the cover. But we were never comfortable taking pictures, and I still feel very foolish doing it. You want the band to look cool, because image is very important, and the photographer says, 'Do something!' But we don't do nothing. You don't want to put your arms around somebody, so you all just stand there, and then they make you feel more uncomfortable!"

Joey and Deborah Harry posing for the Mutant Monster Beach Party issue of *Punk* magazine in 1977. (Roberta Bayley)

Bayley, who went on to become staff photographer for *Punk* and recently researched a documentary film on the late Johnny Thunders, would never again "formally" shoot the Ramones. And despite her classic "Ramones" cover, Sire chose photographer Moshe Brakha to shoot the cover of the second album. "First they wasted their budget on some guy whose pictures they never used, then they wasted another three thousand dollars for a terrible album cover," Bayley marvels. "Doesn't the music business suck?"

In 1976, it was hard to answer no. All you had to do was look at the charts. As the Ramones were recording *Ramones*, the No. 1 Top 40 hit was Paul Simon's "50 Ways to Leave Your Lover." As the album was being released, Johnnie Taylor's "Disco Lady" was No. 1. "Disco Duck" (Rick Dees) was another chart-topper that year, as were "I Write the Songs" (Barry Manilow), "December, 1963 (Oh, What a Night)" (the Four Seasons), "Let Your Love Flow" (the Bellamy Brothers), "Welcome Back" (John Sebastian), "Silly Love Songs" (Wings), "Afternoon Delight" (Starland Vocal Band), "You Should Be Dancing" (Bee Gees), "(Shake, Shake, Shake) Shake Your Booty" (KC & the Sunshine Band), "Rock'n' Me" (Steve Miller), and "Tonight's the Night" (Rod Stewart).

Obviously, "Blitzkrieg Bop" never had a chance.

> They're formin' in a straight line
> They're goin' through a tight wind
> The kids are losing their minds
> The Blitzkrieg Bop
>
> They're pilin' in the back seat
> They're generatin' steam heat
> Pulsatin' to the back beat
> The Blitzkrieg Bop
>
> Hey, ho! Let's go!
> Shoot 'em in the back now!

Now, those of us who have waited so patiently—well over fifteen years—for the Ramones to become big *always* like to say things like, "Gee, the music business sucks." And it's true that in 1976, radio wasn't particularly geared to a line like "Shoot 'em in the back now!" In all fairness, neither is today's radio! But there were other Ramones songs radio *could* have chosen—on *Ramones*, for instance, it was "I Wanna Be Your Boyfriend," which Sire released as the album's follow-up single (backed with the live versions of "California Sun" and "I Don't Wanna Walk Around With You," which were later released on "All the Stuff (and More)—Volume I").

Hey little girl, I wanna be your boyfriend
Sweet little girl, I wanna be your boyfriend
Do you love me babe? What do you say?
Do you love me babe? What can I say?
Because I wanna be your boyfriend.

Indeed, what could any radio programmer with an eye on the teen/ young adult demographic say against lyrics like that? But there were plenty of other problems.

Being from New York never helps, but having to follow the commercial debacle of the New York Dolls, especially in such a "safe" musical climate, full of aging "dinosaur" rock acts and cavemen radio programmers, couldn't have hurt the Ramones more. Then again, look at the rest of the album!

Beat on the brat!
Beat on the brat!
Beat on the brat with a baseball bat, oh yeah!
What can you do?
What can you do?
With a brat like that always on your back
What can you lose?

Even if you knew Joey's story behind "Beat on the Brat," you might not sympathize. And how many grownups could relate to "Now I Wanna Sniff Some Glue":

Now I wanna sniff some glue
Now I wanna have something to do
All the kids wanna sniff some glue
All the kids want something to do.

And, God forbid, "Loudmouth":

Well you're a loudmouth baby
You better shut it up!
I'm gonna beat you up
Well you're a loudmouth, babe!

Or worse yet, "53rd & 3rd":

Then I took out my razor blade
Then I did what God forbade

Now the cops are after me
But I proved that I'm no sissy!

Or Seymour Stein's nightmare, "Today Your Love, Tomorrow the World":

Well I'm a shock trooper in a stupor, yes I am
Well I'm a Nazi schatzi, you know, I fight for the fatherland
Little German boy, being pushed around
Little German boy, in a German town

Of course, Stein wasn't alone in taking offense.

"I don't understand why people get upset and call us Nazis," Dee Dee complained in *New York*. "It's terrible. We wrote the songs because we watch a lot of war movies."

"Havana Affair," whose lyrics mixed CIA intrigue with a Cuban talent show, seemed to combine old war-movie plots with spy movies and even Elvis movies. "Chain Saw" was a more direct ode to the guys' fave flick, "Texas Chainsaw Massacre," while "I Don't Wanna Go Down to the Basement" showed the influence of watching too many sci-fi/horror movies.

"It's all one big war, ya know," Tommy said in *Interview*, in which the Ramones explained that "53rd & 3rd" dealt with a destitute 'Nam vet they'd met who'd been reduced to hustling sex, who was crying in his beer and saying how he'd murdered someone. Added Dee Dee, "All these places are a battlefield, y'know, from the stage to the streets."

And Forest Hills was never far from their thoughts. "It's the perfect place to grow up neurotic," Tommy said. "It was horrible," said Dee Dee. "I broke into the wrong store, and half of us got caught," said Johnny.

"We'd write about teenage problems," Johnny now says in retrospect, "songs about growing up, being nobody, having a hard time finding a girlfriend, teenage boredom, not knowing what to do with yourself. Songs we felt comfortable with, not like what other bands were singing. There was always a theme, mental illness—something *everyone* can relate to. Everybody around you has their own neuroses. I remember people from the neighborhood would disappear for awhile and they'd be in the looney bin. Too much LSD. Certain friends committed suicide. Stuff like that. We just brought out the humor. Of course, later on in life I wondered, what am I doing? I can't believe the things I would do back as a kid!"

But getting the lyrics was only half the battle. Anyone brain dead from the music of 1976, which meant virtually *everybody*, still had to deal with the Ramones sound and fury.

Now might be a good time for old fans to slap "Ramones" on the old turntable—if it still works. Otherwise, the "All the Stuff (And More)—Vol. I" CD will do just fine. Now picture yourself somewhere in the bowels of America's ultimate theater, Radio City Music Hall, in a room where Toscanini conducts the NBC Symphony Orchestra, where the Rockettes practice their high-kicking unison dance routines. Suddenly there's a jet engine roar of guitar noise, a bass line buzzing like a thousand angry bumblebees, drumming which could power a militia, and above it all, a distinctly Queens-by-way-of-Liverpool commander barking out warped teen-pop psycho-melodramas.

But as riveting and unprecedented as is the total *sound* of it all, you can't help but notice that it's all absolutely right and everything's in its place—less-is-more perfection. Like the best of sixties rock 'n' roll, these songs run on their own internal logic. Everything—chord changes, cymbal crashes, melodic turns—is anticipated from that which immediately precedes it, because that's the way it's supposed to be. *It can be no other way.* As Joey says after the first verse of "Judy Is a Punk," just as his idol Peter Noone did in the Herman's Hermits hits, "I'm Henry VIII, I Am": "Second verse, same as the first"—which really says it all.

That's one way of looking at it. The other, offered by one Pittsburgh critic, runs like this: "I suspect the kids on 'Romper Room' could come up with something better without much effort." The Ramones, he said, were trying so desperately to become America's worst rock band that it would be an oversight not to acknowledge such a moronic effort.

"We really like people who hate us," answered Tommy in an interview. "Good or bad, hate or love, we deliver entertainment and people on both sides never leave disappointed. Boz Scaggs was at one of our San Francisco shows and said he didn't like us at all—but he stayed for both sets!"

The May 22 issue of the record business tradepaper *Cash Box* carried this review of "Blitzkrieg Bop": "The Ramones is one of the first bands to break out of the New York rock scene that we've read so much about. Theirs is a hard-rock style, crudely fashioned yet infectious in its energy. The tune is powerful, and the band's street punk stance is all part of the music. From the album 'Ramones,' this should get played on all progressive FM outlets."

"Ramones" sold six-thousand copies its first week out. It entered the *Billboard* charts at No. 198, then went to No. 194, then No. 181 the third week, with a "bullet" indicating substantial sales activity. But except for a few daring radio stations, mainly in New York and California, the album got no radio play.

"They were too real, too authentic," says Denis McNamara, now a record company a&r man, but an early and longtime champion of the

Ramones during ten years at the Long Island progressive/modern rock station WLIR-FM.

"Radio was still in the progressive, underground era—before 'alternative.' The programming hierarchy felt the Ramones were too dangerous, or that their reputation was too dangerous, considering the kind of acts that were accepted by radio at the time."

Rodney Bingenheimer, however, was as far away from the traditional radio programming hierarchy as the Ramones were from traditional radio programming. Known as L.A.'s "Prince of Pop," Bingenheimer had been a major rock scenemaker since the sixties; in 1976, he launched his "Rodney on the ROQ" new wave/sixties show on KROQ-FM, and the Ramones were his first guests. Meanwhile, up at San Francisco's KSAN-FM, future Sire Records General Manager Howie Klein was starting up one of the country's first punk-rock radio shows because of his first Ramones sighting.

Klein had moved to the Coast from New York, where he'd gone to college in Long Island and knew Danny Fields from booking the Doors into Stony Brook. "I ran into him again in 1976, and he asked me to check out his band at CB's. I told him I really wasn't into rock anymore, thinking he had some kind of band like Journey or REO. But I ended up going anyway, and my whole life changed right then and there! I immediately went to San Francisco and started the radio show."

Vin Scelsa, one of New York's "old hippie deejays" was the guy who played the so-called "fringe bands" at WNEW-FM. The afternoon that the much-ballyhooed local band's debut album came into the station, Scelsa dropped everything and threw it on the air. He lasted through "Blitzkrieg Bop" and "Beat on the Brat," but halfway through "Judy Is a Punk" he'd heard enough.

"I turned on the mike and said, 'What is this crap? What is this noise?,' took the needle off and the album off the turntable and flung it across the room," Scelsa recalled in the home video *Lifestyles of the Ramones*. But the album was still intact, and after taking it home and listening to it some more, he brought it back a few days later and recanted. "I said, 'I was totally and completely wrong about the Ramones. This is a great new revolutionary rock band.' "

Ira Robbins also experienced a dramatic change of heart. The *Trouser Press* editor remembers attending Sire publicist Janis Schacht's "earsplitting" album-listening party at the label's West 74th Street brownstone, and being "completely knocked out" by *Ramones*.

"I hadn't had so much fun in ages. I'd seen so many of the New York underground groups live, but in the studio, they just didn't deliver. The adventure of their live shows would always be missing, the anything-can-happen weirdness. I mean, Television's appeal as a live band was watching

At the Bottom Line,
watching the Ramones, are Seymour Stein
(at left), Linda Stein (center). To her left
are Andy Warhol and theater and book critic Donald Lyons.
To her right is Warhol associate Vincent Fremont.
(Danny Fields)

them collapse! Richard Hell fell over in the middle of the set. Richard Lloyd broke five of his six guitar strings and kept playing because he didn't have another set. But the record was polished and well-played, but not *true*.

"But the Ramones were one group that got better for me on record. Their album made perfect sense, and was the first New York record that was significantly better than their live show. Live, everything was fragmented but blurred together, but the album had such great production that everything came through. When Tommy hit the cymbal on 'Blitzkrieg Bop,' it was a *life-changing experience*. It was the biggest cymbal ever recorded! It was like setting off a detonation—a torpedo hitting a ship."

In *Hit Parader*, John Holmstrom wrote, "Their music is very basic and you may not understand it at first listening. It may sound 'monotonous,' but if you listen a few times you'll find that it's simplicity is tasteful and effective. . . . Although they play rock 'n' roll, it's not the fifties sound at

"Ramones" (Sire). I love this record—love it—even though I know these boys flirt with images of brutality (Nazi especially) in much the same way "Midnight Rambler" flirts with rape. You couldn't say they condone any nasties, natch—they merely suggest that the power of their music has some fairly ominous sources and tap those sources even as they offer the suggestion. This makes me uneasy. But my theory has always been that good rock and roll should damn well make you uneasy, and the sheer pleasure of this stuff—which of course elicits howls of pain from the rock and roll musicianship crowd, e.g. Dr. Feelgood's aficianados at the Bottom Line—is undeniable. For me, it blows everything else off the radio; it's clean the way the Dolls never were, sprightly the way the Velvets never were, and just plain listenable the way Black Sabbath never was. None of which is to suggest that it's as important as any of these, Black Sabbath included. Just perfect, a minor classic. And I hear it cost $6400 to put on plastic. A.

—Village Voice,
June 14, 1976

(Reprinted by permission of Robert Christgau and the *Village Voice*)

all. It's hard rock but it isn't overbearingly obnoxious. They play songs like early Beatles and Rolling Stones but they're better than the Beatles or the Stones. I guess they sound like the Ramones."

Sire saw the glowing Ramones press notices, and exploited them from the outset. Promotional label copy noted, along with the "pulsating beat of their music which never falters" and the "power of an approaching artillery fire," on the fourteen album tracks, pointed to the "unorthodox amount of press [the Ramones received] for a previously unsigned band"—specifically, all the reviews in *Rolling Stone, Creem, Circus,* the *Village Voice,* and the English music weeklies *NME* and *Melody Maker.* "The critics who have heard the album are already heralding it as one of the most important releases of 1976. With careful concentration in key markets including New York, Boston, Cleveland, Detroit, and Memphis, the Ramones could equal or surpass the sales interest now garnered by Kiss, Aerosmith, and Black Sabbath."

A full-page *Billboard* ad for "Blitzkrieg Bop" borrowed a *Punk* magazine photo layout stringing together performance shots of the band with cartoon balloons of the song lyrics. An album ad announced, "The Ramones are so punky you're gonna have to react!" and included quotes excerpted from reviews in *Circus* ("The Ramones are out to relive the roots of rock by mauling them"); the *Village Voice* (Christgau: "The last time I caught them I walked home high"); *Hit Parader* (Holmstrom: "This album is pure TNT"); and *NME* (Charles Shaar Murray: "They're just bound to enchant anyone who fell in love with rock 'n' roll for the right reasons").

An ad in *Billboard* on June 19 ran quotes from *The Aquarian's* Craig Zeller ("The Ramones are gonna smash you to smithereens . . . and slam you up against the wall screaming for more"); *Newsday's* Wayne Robbins ("The Ramones are the best young rock 'n' roll band in the known universe"); *The New York Times'* John Rockwell ("An abstraction of rock so pure that other associations get left behind"); *Cash Box's* Phil DiMauro ("Occupying a musical slot somewhere in the dark netherworld between Herman's Hermits and ZZ Top, the Ramones are presently in the position to expose their brand of New York Bowery rock to a national audience"); *Walrus* ("Their album defines their style well, putting them at the front of the ravers. They will lead all our fifteen-year-olds into the sea"); *NME's* Nick Kent ("This record poses a direct threat to any vaguely sensitive woofer and/or tweeter lodged in your hi-fi"); the *Voice's* Christgau ("Hard, loud, fast and tuff, this is the most cleanly conceptualized New York rock show there is to see"); *Soho Weekly News's* Kenneth Tucker ("I played it constantly when I first got it and still slap it on for an instant energy rush"), *Circus's* Ernest Leogrande ("The Ramones are precise and relentless as a rushing pulse . . . it's all adrenaline chords at a terrific speed. The Ramones are out to relieve the roots of rock by mauling them"); and the Rutgers *Daily Targum's* Bob Sennett ("Punk with commercial potential . . . it's about time.") At the bottom of the ad Sire inserted the line, "Today New York . . . tomorrow the world."

But would it play in Peoria? A letter to the editor of *Circus* "congratulated" writer Paul Nelson for making some readers waste money on the Ramones. Nelson, wondering if the Ramones would get the mainstream acceptance that had evaded the Dolls, said that the band "represents a kind of idealized Top Forty music. Not the real thing, but what Top Forty music should sound like." In other words, like sixties bands such as the Beatles and the Beach Boys—though in the same issue, Georgia Christgau duly noted that Ramones songs weren't about holding hands or driving cars, but about *not* liking girls and getting into fights.

"The way [Nelson] raves about the Ramones, you'd think they were another Aerosmith or Zeppelin," the reader protested. "If he thinks that guitar-smashing the same chord for an hour, with lyrics that my baby sister could write, and a singer who sounds as if he woke up with some new disease of the vocal chords is rock 'n' roll, he should be banned from writing!"

No, not everyone got it.

eviewing *Ramones* in the May 21, 1976 issue of *The New York Times*, John Rockwell, noting that the Ramones were the second mid-seventies New York underground band to release a nationally distributed album (following Patti Smith), called it a "highly stylized extension of the [punk] idiom."

What the Ramones do, he continued in a scholarly tone, "is deliver a nonstop set of short, brisk, monochromatically intense songs" where "conventional considerations of pace and variety are thrown calculatedly to the winds." While the tunes sometimes sound like formula pop, he added, "the effect in the end amounts to an abstraction of rock so pure that

Birth of a

Nation

SNIFFIN' GLUE...
AND OTHER ROCK'N'ROLL HABITS,
FOR ~~PUNKS~~ GIRLS! (3) SEPTEMBER '76.
THE MAG THAT DOESN'T LIKE GIVING YOU 'UP TO DATE' NEWS ON THE MUSIC SCENE
WITH
THE DAMNED ☆ SEX PISTOLS ☆ IGGY POP ☆

other associations get left behind. It will be interesting to see if the Ramones can extend their range; if they can't, it will all seem in retrospect like an amusing gimmick. But even now you have to admire it as an assertion of style."

By now everyone was talking about "punk rock." What it meant, though, was open to question. As Johnny pointed out, the Dictators and the Heartbreakers were punk, but Television and Blondie?

As we've seen, in its loosest definition, "punk" encompassed everyone from Elvis Presley to the Beatles to the mid-sixties garage bands. In 1972, *Creem* declared Alice Cooper "Punk of the Year," and in January, 1976, the first issue of *Punk* featured Lou Reed on the cover. (This was actually the second *Punk* magazine; Billy Altman had also put one out three years earlier.)

Punk magazine was as much a reaction against commercial journalism as the Ramones were a reaction against commercial music. Writer and "resident punk" Legs McNeil came up with the name, apparently because Telly Savalas always said "You lousy punk!" to the villains in "Kojak." McNeil and cartoonist/journalist John Holmstrom founded the remarkably offbeat, hand-lettered publication, which featured interviews, features, photos, cartoons, and an alienated sensibility to match that of the Ramones. While it only published sixteen issues and lasted through 1979, it definitely made waves.

The April 1976 issue had a great Holmstrom cartoon on the cover of Joey Ramone standing against a brick wall with "RAMONES" graffittied in blood and contained, among other things, a Ramones "cover story," interviews with David Johansen, the Heartbreakers, and Richard Hell, not to mention one of Legs's "famous persons" interviews, this one with Boris and Natasha of "Bullwinkle" cartoon fame. The issue also featured a Holmstrom editorial playing dictionary, changing the meaning of "punk" from a description for "the boys [in prison] who give up their ass to the wolves," or "an insult to young would-be hoods from more experienced hoods," or even "a young ruffian" to something else again.

Rather, Holmstrom defined a "punk" as "a beginner and inexperienced hand." In this context, then, Holmstrom saw "punk rock" as a medium where "any kid can pick up a guitar and become a rock 'n' roll star, despite or because of his lack of ability, talent, intelligence, limitations and/or potential, and usually does so out of frustration, hostility, a lot of nerve, and a need for ego fulfillment." Rock 'n' roll is "a very primitive form of expression—like cave paintings or jungle sculpture," he continued. "It takes a lot of sophistication—or better, none at all—to appreciate punk rock at its best or worst (not much difference). Punk has become a catchword for a lot of critics to describe New York underground rock, most of which is not punk rock."

The late journalist Lester Bangs, whose band Birdland included Joey's brother Mickey Leigh, also offered a useful working definition of "punk" in *National Screw:* "Music made by teenage slobs who were proud of it [which was about] the perpetuation of adolescence and the cultivation of infantilism by (a) getting drunk and staying that way, and (b) living with your parents till you're forty."

Punk summed up the attitude bluntly: "We don't believe in love and any of that shit. We believe in making money and getting drunk." But Holmstrom had every reason to fear that record companies would jump on the punk bandwagon, as the mass media had already done, and dilute the term "punk" until it meant nothing, and no one liked it.

"We never called ourselves punk rock," Tommy told an interviewer. "We're young kids playing music—energetic, innocent, white, and middle class." They never called themselves punk rockers, maybe, but the Ramones sure epitomized the term. As Dee Dee once explained, punk was motivated by *hatred*—pure, adolescent hatred of parents, society, even music.

And for all anybody knew, maybe even of *music journalists*—perish the thought!

"I guess I thought they really *were* punks," says the hardly timid Lisa Robinson, who admits to feeling nervous around the Ramones early on. "Not that I thought they'd pull out a knife and cut you, but they had an aura of danger and violence around them that was probably contrived. They *were* loud and dark and angry. But their songs had melodies like the Beach Boys'—just with much more of an edge. In retrospect, they weren't at all threatening."

Sire publicist Janis Schacht, who helped close down CB's with Joey every night for four years and sewed the seat of his jeans together before gigs, remembers that at first, interviewers were terrified to be alone in the room with the Ramones. "It was the funniest thing. They thought they were in the room with axe murderers, when the Ramones were more frightened than *they* were! Nobody visualized them as these middle-class kids!"

Of course, there was that song about beating on the brat with a baseball bat, right?

One of the fun things about record-business hype is the promotional item, commonly known by the Yiddish word *tshatshka.* Seeing as though the Ramones were such baseball fans, and that they did have this song about baseball bats, well, Schacht came up with one of the all-time great *tshatshkas* in the form of miniature Louisville Sluggers. The fifteen-inch black bats, which cost fifty cents apiece to produce, were to be engraved with "Beat on the Brat," except that the manufacturer refused because of the implied use of the bat as a weapon. So U.S. versions of the bat bore the "Blitzkrieg Bop" song title, while the U.K.'s had "Ramones—

A Hit on Sire Records." Joey used to toss them out into the audience after singing "Beat on the Brat"—now you'd pay upwards of one hundred dollars to get one!

But it was Arturo Vega's hand-silkscreened T-shirts that kept the Ramones going. The only problem now was, going where? "Getting a manager and a record contract was easy," says Johnny. "Finding a booking agent was the hardest thing."

With their debut album out and generating a tremendous amount of press exposure, if not sales, it was time for the Ramones to move beyond their safe CBGB's haven.

On May 10 and 11, the Ramones played their first "prestige" gig, at the famous Bottom Line showcase club, opening for English pub-rock kings Dr. Feelgood. No more than a five-minute walk northwest of CB's, it was light years away in class.

It was also one of the first shows with new equipment, particularly new Marshall amps. The afternoon soundcheck was so loud that cars stopped in front of the club, and people got out to see what the deal was. Not that the date wasn't successful (Andy Warhol was among the celebs who showed for the Ramones whopping thirty-minute set), but the Ramones were hardly meant for the Bottom Line's intimate atmosphere. Joey wouldn't sing there again until he did a songwriters' showcase in 1991 for Vin Scelsa.

But if the Ramones were to happen on a scale beyond downtown Manhattan, they'd have to leave town and try to pick up where the Dolls left off. "I had to book clubs myself, and it was just hell," says Danny Fields. "The established places didn't want us, because they'd already heard about us, we were punk rock, or we weren't right for the crowd they drew. So we went from town to town, giving the clubs one dollar for every two we took at the door. We also diddled with six or seven small booking agencies, using our press."

Boston, Toronto, Washington, D.C., Chicago—these were early foreign outposts on the Ramones tours. Along the way, one indignant, ignorant Rhode Island club owner called the sheriff when the group left the stage, unaware that their sets were only twenty minutes long! And in Youngstown, Ohio, the band got directions to Cleveland from one Stiv Bators, the late, great singer for the Dead Boys. Stiv had the Ramones follow the car he was in, and when he climbed out the window to flash the Ramones a ninety-mph moon, Joey was so impressed that he got the Boys their first gig at CB's, where they became regulars and signed on as management clients of Hilly Kristal.

Then there was The Chance in Poughkeepsie, New York, where Roger Risko a representative Ramones superfan, first saw the band that same summer of 1976, and later married his wife, Nancy Morgan, in commemoration! "By the first pause for a quick guitar change by Johnny, a retrieved mike stand for Joey, and an adjustment for Dee Dee's amps, about half the audience made for the streets," recalls Roger. "Their rejection became my motivation to stay, to listen, to drop my preconceived, socially deceived attitudes and become reborn. I went home and shaved off my Cat Stevens beard and went off to my old faithful record store to find their just-released first album, *Ramones*—a name which not only sounded like a gang to join, but a new identity for the musically homeless, like me. Now I was no longer Roger, I became *Roger Ramone!*"

Well, if Roger Ramone's transformation sounds farfetched, still to come was July 4, 1976, the day that transformed an entire *nation*.

That's the date of the first Ramones show in England, where they opened for the Flamin' Groovies, San Francisco's fifties/sixties-influenced band which, like the Ramones, did little commercially but enjoyed much cult appeal among punk/new wave era groups. "On the two-hundredth anniversary of our liberation from England, we went back and gave 'em something in gratitude," Danny Fields told *The New York Times*.

Their first night was at the Roundhouse in London (sharing the bill with the Stranglers), playing to a sellout crowd of two thousand, as compared to the fifty or so that had showed up at CB's. The next night they did a club gig at Dingwalls. In two nights' time, members of probably every U.K. punk group destined to turn the music business upside down (many of them still unformed) saw the Ramones: the Sex Pistols, the Clash, Generation X, the Damned, and the Pretenders.

"I was trying to get a band together when I saw them at the Round-house," says Chrissie Hynde, who wrote for *NME* before forming the Pretenders. "The punk scene in London was very closely knit and anti-everything. The Ramones were the only 'outside' band that everyone looked up to. Sid Vicious learned to play guitar by shooting speed and staying up all night and playing Ramones records! They were his favorite band."

Joey remembers Hynde, Johnny Rotten, and Joe Strummer among the many English dignitaries who came backstage to express their debt of gratitude, for both the impact of the concerts, and the influence of "Ramones." It must have come as a big shock for the Ramones to be greeted as conquering heroes here, when back home they couldn't get arrested, but the U.K. has always been quicker both to embrace and to cast off new bands and trends, because it's a small country, less dependent on radio, with an aggressive national music press. So it made all the sense in the world for a young, hard, fast band like the Ramones to arouse the British populace, even as America slept.

It was also the "Summer of Hate" for the U.K. Led by the Sex Pistols and its sacrilegious anthem "God Save the Queen," England's punk scene differed markedly from that in the U.S. In England, punk was largely a

July 4, 1976
—America's bicentennial
gift to England. Joey
in front of the infamous London
music hall the Round House.
(**Danny Fields**)

working-class phenomenon, totally artless, and not at all broadly styled, as were the diversified CB's bands. Emerging from the early seventies pub-rock epitomized by basic, hard-driving bands like Dr. Feelgood, Brinsley Schwarz, and Ducks Deluxe, these musicians were angry, snotty, sneering, and disdainful types embodied by the Sex Pistols immortal lyric, "We're so pretty, oh, so pretty *vacant*—and we don't care!" Musically, they owed much to the Ramones and the Heartbreakers; stylistically, they followed the fashions set by Sex, the punk boutique run by Malcolm McLaren. Earlier, McLaren had informally managed the final New York Dolls lineup into oblivion, and had brought back to England Richard Hell's style of dress—dark glasses, disheveled short hair, leather jacket, and torn shirts. In England, the punks added safety pins to their look, worn as both clothing accessories and facial ones.

Out of Sex, of course, came the Sex Pistols, and it was the truly repulsive image portrayed by the Pistols and their compatriots (repulsive,

**Nancy Spungen
(center), flanked by
photographer Leee Black Childers
(at left), and Sid Vicious, awestruck
by his idol Dee Dee.
(Danny Fields)**

that is, to the media-establishment types who might have been willing to
give the comparatively innocent Ramones a chance) which gave punk rock
its horrendously unacceptable identity.

Sad for the Ramones, the very real and major differences among punk-
ers were overlooked. The British punks were generally younger and
politically minded, as they came out of socially deprived backgrounds with
little reason for optimism. Not that the Ramones outlooks were bright;
they were all on unemployment and living on the Bowery when they
started the band, and, as Johnny observed, the Bowery looks worse than
anything in England, where they complain about standing in line for the
dole when in the U.S. the Ramones couldn't even get food stamps.

But musically, the Ramones and the other New York punk bands were based largely on a classic rock 'n' roll foundation that had vanished from the airwaves, and couldn't be found in Brit-punk either. They also retained a sense of humor.

By the time the Ramones finally invaded the U.K., their album had been the No. 1 import, and the music press had touted them as far back as last year's "CBGB Summer '75 Rock Festival Showcase Auditions."

"Someone must have written a big article," says Johnny, "because when we got there, everyone was there to see *us*."

According to *NME*'s reviewer Max Bell, that first London gig was on the hottest, steamiest, and dirtiest night of the year, and Dee Dee's mike went dead before the Ramones even started. "The appeal is purely negative, based on their not being able to play a shit or give a shit. The thinking process involved in evaluating their performance is non-existent."

The Ramones material, Bell continued, strung together "a selection of imbecilic adolescent ditties whose sole variation lies in the shuffling of three chords into some semblance of order." Laughing at the show, he suggested that you take them in the intended spirit, or go home.

Then again, Sid Vicious followed Dee Dee Ramone all over the place, the Sex Pistols followed the Ramones, and so did everyone else. A week after the Roundhouse, the *Sniffin' Glue* fanzine started up. Soon, it was said, every song on "Ramones" had become the name of either a fanzine or a band. And in September, the Ramones also caused a *furor*.

Again, it had to do with sniffin' glue, namely, "Now I Wanna Sniff Some Glue"—the song.

"Glue Sniff Death Shocker," screamed the headline of the August 19 *Glasgow Evening Times*. "Ramones in Teenage Glue Death Outrage," answered the September 11 *NME*. The ruckus was about a perceived epidemic of glue-sniffing among Scottish youth, resulting in over twenty deaths and three hundred arrests.

"I'm horrified," said James Dempsey, a local parliamentarian. "How is it possible that a song like this can be on sale when twenty children have already died from the effects of gluesniffing?"

Dempsey had been alerted by a concerned parent, and sought to get the offending Ramones record removed from store shelves, as did other officials and newspaper editorialists. Of course, "Ramones" had come out long after the first glue-related death. Phonogram, the Ramones distributor in Scotland, denied any link between the song and the sniffing.

"The song was just a goof," said Joey at the time. "We really were just writing about teenage frustration." Added Danny Fields, "War films aren't banned on the grounds that they advocate violence." In years to come, similar arguments would be heard in defense against moves to ban heavy metal and rap records for allegedly promoting everything from satanism and suicide to violence against women and the police.

Meanwhile, *Ramones* was selling three hundred copies a day throughout Britain—considered fifteen times the normal rate expected for a group which never had a hit single. Sire snapped up fifty copies of the "Glue Sniff Shocker" article to send key U.S. press people.

In a May 1977 interview in *National Screw*, the Ramones admitted sniffing glue in the past, but stressed that it was very dangerous and "pure poison."

"It's a message song," they said, acknowledging its popularity at concerts, where kids often threw tubes of glue on stage. "They can relate to the trauma of adolescence."

Dee Dee and Jordan, the premier model from Vivienne Westwood's clothing shop, Sex. (Danny Fields)

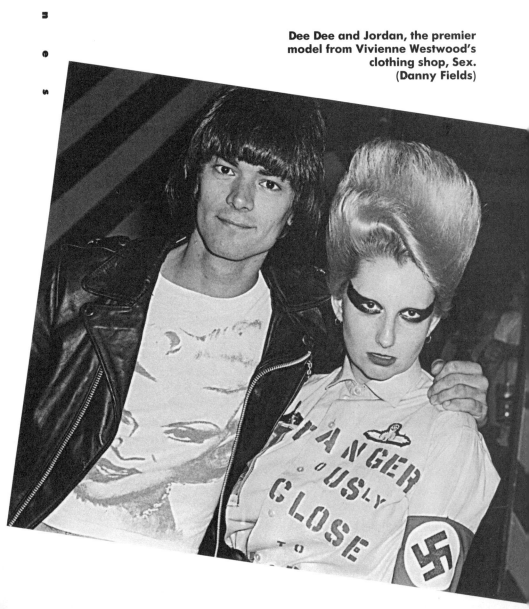

Shortly after returning from their historic English debut, the Ramones headed in the opposite direction.

On August 11 and 12, the Ramones played the Roxy in Los Angeles, again with the Flamin' Groovies. The local press was ready.

In a "thought" piece for the paper's August 1 "Calendar" section, the prominent *Los Angeles Times* critic Robert Hilburn, recalling the parental outrage which greeted such fifties rock 'n' roll pioneers as Bill Haley and Fats Domino, asked, "Can you imagine the reaction of a mother—already alarmed over her teenager's aggressive behavior toward a kid brother—after noticing the

Meanwhile,

Back in the States ...

teenager's fascination with this tale of sibling rivalry ['Beat on the Brat']?"

But after comparing the band members in the *Ramones* cover shot to the futuristic thugs portrayed in "A Clockwork Orange," Hilburn then suggested that the group was more of a joke than a threat. "Virtually every current commercial guideline in rock is broken somewhere in the Ramones debut album. The songs are too short ... the lyrics are dismal; the musicianship is rarely above that of the average garage band and the relentless tempo and tone show almost no variation. . . . Even supporters of the band acknowledge the group's crudeness."

In the *L.A. Free Press*, opening night at the Roxy was covered thusly: "Their lead guitarist dropped his pick in mid-song (we haven't seen that done in years) and shortly thereafter the lead whiner fell backwards, hooking his mike stand in the bass player's guitar strap, disrupting their intensity for a few short minutes that were the highlight of their set. One observer stated that he could've formed a better band off Selma Avenue—if you get his meaning."

Performance also saw fit to report Joey's fall, and had him "babbling such nonsequitur nonsense as 'This is for you Rasta fans.'" And a reviewer who was probably too stupid to behold the Ramones awesome *concentration* noted that while one of the Groovies broken guitar strings necessitated a five-minute break, Johnny broke a string and didn't even notice!

Then again, L.A. man-about-town Art Fein, also writing in the *L.A. Free Press*, played off the famous Bruce Springsteen rave review in declaring, "I have not seen the future of rock 'n' roll, but I have seen the Ramones and that may be even better.... They stood there pounding monotonously and mercilessly with their own cretinous originals and some other people's, with no regard for pronunciation or 'art,' blasting musical pretensions to dust, and encoring with Chris Montez's 'Let's Dance,' which for me, at least, beats the hell out of Bruce Springsteen doing the Ronettes."

Fein has since gained renown as host of the long-running L.A. cable show "Li'l Art's Poker Party" and author of *The L.A. Musical History Tour*. "They really woke me up out of the mid-seventies slumber," he recalls. "They did fifteen songs in thirty minutes and levitated me from my seat! Then the lights went on and I went over to the other rock critics, and they were all puzzled, because nothing had been written yet, and even though they knew they had a great time, they didn't know if it was *okay* to like them!"

Then it was off to San Francisco, where the *San Francisco Examiner* declared, "Just when we've found the answer to swine flu, along comes the Ramones." The wiseguy at the paper also had fun with Tommy's early flier: "The Ramones hail from Forest Hills, New York, where you either grow up to be a musician, a dentist, or a degenerate. . . . With the Ramones, it's a toss-up."

SNIFFIN' GLUE...
AND OTHER ROCK'N'ROLL HABITS,
FOR THE NEW-WAVE! ④ OCT'76.

What, this isn't a joke. If you want something funny buy MAD. Anyway, this issue is priceless.

THE CLASH

BUZZCOCKS ✱ SAINTS ✱ PATTI SMITH NEW LP.

Ramones and
their U.K. counterparts,
Chrissie Hynde (far left)
and members of the Damned.
(Danny Fields)

Luckily, Howie Klein was there, too. "Halfway through the set, I had a barely controllable urge to lift a chair over my head and break it," he wrote. At least *he* got it. But the Savoy had to close down after the Ramones gig there, after the cops demanded the club install a three thousand dollars soundproofing following complaints from neighbors about noise—and the club couldn't afford it.

Klein also observed the effect that the Ramones had on the local community: Everyone began starting their own punk bands.

"A lot has to do with honesty," Tommy told *The Music Gig*. "What happened was that all the really bored people bumped into each other and started hanging out in the same places. There was a feeling among those people about what was missing in the music they were listening to, and they changed it. The feelings were constant and stronger than they are in most areas, and that's why the music comes off with more conviction."

The November 20 issue of *Billboard*, in a front page analysis by the late Roman Kozak (who would later write the excellent account of the CBGB scene, *This Ain't No Disco*), recognized that the record business was now fully behind the punk rock underground, what with Atlantic releasing the "Live At CBGB's" double-album compilation, Sire signing Talking Heads, Elektra signing Television and the Dictators, and Private Stock signing Blondie. Leading the pack were the Ramones, who had begun recording their second album in late October at Sundragon Studio.

Johnny revealed that the album would break new lyrical ground in talking about "pinheads" and "geeks," "being good boys" and "headbanging." Tommy hinted that musically, it would be heavier and more melodic, with more bite as well as "more of a singalong quality."

This time the production was credited to Tony Bongiovi and T. Erdelyi, with Edward "Stasiun" engineering, though the correct spelling was *Stasium*. Another honorary Ramone, Stasium had cut his engineering and production teeth working with the likes of Gladys Knight & the Pips and Sha Na Na, as well as various disco projects. Bongiovi was a veteran producer and engineer, having worked at Motown and the Record Plant, where he brought in Tommy Erdelyi back in the Hendrix days. A friend of Stasium's father was building a studio with Bongiovi—completing the circle.

"I'd been working in Canada for ten months, and hadn't even heard of the Ramones," says Stasium. "Everything was so safe at that time: 'Rumours' was a big record, 'Hotel California' was just out, the first Boston record, for God's sake! Then I went with Tony to CB's, and it was *shocking*."

They recorded the album at a tiny studio on 21st Street off Fifth Avenue, spending maybe twice as much as on "Ramones," but cutting the basic tracks very quickly. "I thought it would be one of the biggest things ever done, or one of the biggest flops ever done," says Bongiovi. "It was a grinding wall of sound."

"Ramones Leave Home" was completed in time for an early January release. Its fourteen songs totalled just under thirty minutes, and included two certified Ramones classics.

"Pinhead" probably condenses the Ramones to their prime essence:

> Gabba Gabba
> We accept you
> We accept you
> One of us.
> I don't wanna be a pinhead no more
> I just met a nurse that I could go for.
> D-U-M-B
> Everyone's accusing me.

There it is. Anyone who's ever been to a Ramones show knows it, since it's the show's climax, when Bubbles, the Ramones longtime roadie,

The Ramones, the Steins, and cop-dressed Elton John backstage after a concert in 1976. (Danny Fields)

donned a pinhead mask and bobbed a sign with "GABBA GABBA, HEY!" painted on it, while Joey and Dee Dee pointed accusingly at each other while spelling out "D-U-M-B!"

Written by Dee Dee Ramone, "Pinhead" derives from the grotesque horror film *Freaks*, which was made in 1932 by *Dracula* director Todd Browning and starred actual sideshow freaks in a truly horrible revenge plot. The "Gabba gabba, we accept you" opening chant was a slight modification of actual movie dialogue (it was closer to "gooble-gobble") chorused by the freaks to the beautiful blonde who has married one of them for his money—a major mistake, it turns out. It's obvious why the Ramones—themselves considered freaks by much of the record industry, if not the record-buying public—could relate.

"I guess we could identify with him," Johnny said to a reporter. "*Mental health* . . . it's a subject you have to deal with every day. It's like therapy: Sing about it and you're all better."

If not, there's always "Gimme Gimme Shock Treatment," a group co-write, which offered the perfect panacea and remains a Ramones concert staple. Continuing the theme, "What's Your Game" had to do with an insane girl who just wanted to be like other girls, while "Suzy Is a

Headbanger" (whose "mother is a geek") was another fun-filled freak peek.

"Leave Home" also had another war movie outtake in "Commando," which offered the following "rules": The laws of Germany; Be nice to Mommy; Don't talk to commies; and Eat kosher salamis. "You Should Never Have Opened That Door" was akin to "I Don't Wanna Go Down to the Basement" in its horror-movie origins.

The self-explanatory "You're Gonna Kill That Girl" again showcased the Ramones classic rock 'n' roll roots, this time with a melodramatic intro straight out of Dion and the Belmonts smash hit, "Runaround Sue." "Oh Oh I Love Her So," besides its wonderful evocation of innocent teen romance ("I met her at the Burger King/We fell in love by the soda machine"), musically evoked Freddy Cannon's "Palisades Park." And "California Sun," of course, was a cover of the Rivieras' 1964 hit.

Then there was the catchy "Swallow My Pride," "Leave Home" 's first U.S. single. The vague lyrics ("Winter is here/And it's going on two years/ Swallow my pride") expressed displeasure over the commercial failure of "Ramones," some of which was directed at the record company. After all, when the president of ABC Records (Sire's distributor) came down to see the band at CB's, he reportedly wore a powder-blue leisure suit! If so, "Leave Home" 's lead track, "Glad to See You Go," which offered up Charles Manson as a role model, must have sent him into paroxysms.

> Gonna take a chance on her
> One bullet in the cylinder
> And in a moment of passion
> Get the glory like Charles Manson

This song was about Dee Dee's ex-girlfriend, Connie, now deceased. Connie, who had earlier been seeing New York Doll's bassist Arthur Kane, nearly cut his thumb off once, apparently because she was jealous of his going out on tour. She later chopped up Dee Dee's behind with a beer bottle; Dee Dee, according to Legs McNeil and John Holmstrom in *Spin*, freely admitted he'd probably be dead now had he not broken up with her.

One New York radio programmer, at the very least, refused to play "Leave Home," not surprisingly interpreting "Glad to See You Go" as a glorification of mass murder. But one other album cut, "Carbona Not Glue," was so hot to touch that it had to be taken out entirely.

Carbona was the name of a cleaning fluid that the Ramones turned on to when the hobby shop back home got hip to the fact that the guys had another use for glue other than building model airplanes. So after the "glue sniff shocker," it made sense, perhaps, that now they preferred Carbona:

I'm not sorry for the things I do
My brain is stuck from shooting glue
Carbona not glue.

It was another joke, of course. The rest of the lyrics blamed an overindulgence on TV, paint, and even roach spray for the sorry situation of sticking oneself in the closet. But the joke was on the Ramones, for unbeknownst to them, Carbona wasn't a generic name but a corporate *trademark*. To avert a potential lawsuit, then, the track was substituted, in the U.K., by "Babysitter," a lovely teen-pop confection about sharing the couch "with my special one" while she babysits (which was also the B side to the U.S. single "Do You Wanna Dance"). The U.S. replacement was "Sheena Is a Punk Rocker," which was cut at Sundragon the following April, after release of the first pressings of "Leave Home," which still included the offending track. Since "Carbona" has never been officially released since then, these first copies of "Leave Home" are worth as much as thirty dollars apiece today.

"Danny Fields asked us to listen to the album before it came out, and we told him that 'Carbona Not Glue' was the best song ever written," recalls John Holmstrom. "He said, 'I was afraid you'd say that. That's what everybody says, but we can't release it.' I guess it's all part of why the Ramones were never big."

The Beach Boys-like "Sheena," incidentally, featured Stasium's own guitar-playing as an adjunct to Johnny's. The single, which at least four CB's girls claimed to be the inspiration for, made it to No. 48 on the charts. Then *Ramones luck* struck again, when "60 Minutes" did a sensationalized story on the Sex Pistols and the British punk scene. The sight of spikey hairdos and safety pins through eyelids probably cemented the media impression of punk as angry, violent, and socially unacceptable, dooming "Sheena"—and anything referred to as "punk rock"—to death before birth.

"The English punk thing started and brought incredible notoriety, especially with Malcolm McLaren wanting to get the Sex Pistols on the front page, and 'God Save the Queen' taking on everything," says Fields. "The word 'punk' became an albatross. People thought if you had a punk record, the walls would crumble down! While the Ramones were the most unpolitical entity in the world, *culturally* they meant something scary. 'Punk' meant *criminal*, somebody who would beat you up. No one saw beyond the sense of irony in the Ramones lyrics, like 'Beat on the brat with a baseball bat,' which I thought was enchanting—not dangerous sentiments! But even if promoters and radio wouldn't touch them, they brought joy to the press. Finally there was something to write about!"

Before "punk" gave way to "new wave," then, *Ramones* placed eighth

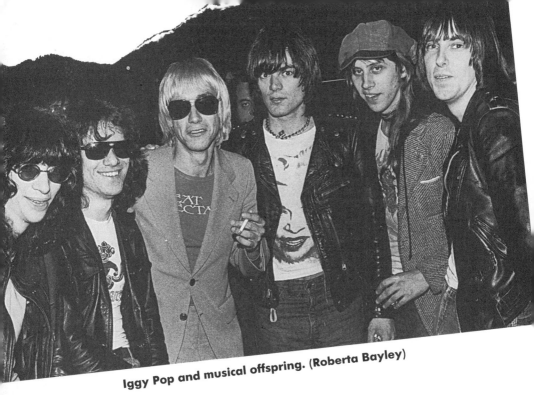

Iggy Pop and musical offspring. (Roberta Bayley)

in the 1976 *Village Voice* "Pazz & Jop Critics Poll," way ahead of Bob Dylan's *Desire*, in between Joni Mitchell's *Hejira* and Rod Stewart's *A Night on the Town*. For the record, Stevie Wonder's *Songs in the Key of Life* won, while Graham Parker and the Rumour, Patti Smith Group, and the Modern Lovers were the only other new wave artists in the top thirty, a list otherwise represented by the likes of Boz Skaggs, Thin Lizzy, David Bowie, Bob Seger, Bob Marley, Steely Dan, and Jackson Browne.

Creem's annual readers' poll, meanwhile, had the Ramones album at No. 16 (the top three spots were taken by Aerosmith, Peter Frampton, and Led Zeppelin). They were both the No. 10 best group (Aerosmith, Kiss, and Led Zep were at the top) and the No. 10 *worst* group (Bay City Rollers were No. 1), the No. 3 best *new* group (behind Boston and Heart), and the No. 5 "punk of the year" (following Steven Tyler, Lou Reed, Elton John, and Patti Smith). And *People*'s year end issue even singled the band out as "musical personalities to watch" along with Elvin Bishop and the Fifth Dimension's Marilyn McCoo and Billy Davis.

But a dream punk tour of the U.K. with the Sex Pistols never materialized when there wasn't enough time for advance promotion. And Joey missed a "Leave Home" listening party when he was hospitalized for an ankle operation, which also caused cancellation of Christmas weekend at CB's, and New Year's Eve in Los Angeles.

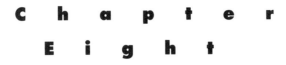

amones Leave Home," as one critic put it, was a slap in the face to anyone who thought the Ramones were musically limited to a single-album release. Of course, as *Interview* said, it was hard to picture the Ramones leaving home, "or maybe it's just hard to picture Mr. and Mrs. Ramone. Then again, they could be perfectly normal people. It could be radioactive fallout that did it."

My friend Rob speculated that it was such a big step for the Ramones to leave home that they had to name their album after it. "I think it was that we had just spent a week on the road," explains Johnny.

To herald the January 10 release,

"Ramones Gabba No Moss"

—review headline in English music paper *Sounds*

Joey in front of their first poster. (Danny Fields)

Danny Fields went through hundreds of press clippings and culled sixty-two choice quotes for a full-page *Village Voice* ad, which later became a promo poster. "I looked for superlatives, either love or hate," he said, "and they weren't hard to find!" Sure enough, the blurbs ranged from "Phew, what a scorcher!" (*Zig Zag*) to "They don't waste their time—they waste yours" (*Detroit News*).

Fields soon needed a second scrapbook.

"Leave Home" quickly earned an "A-minus" from Robert Christgau in the *Village Voice*: "People who consider this a one-joke act aren't going to change their minds now. People who love the joke for its power, wit, and economy will be happy to hear it twice." In *Rolling Stone*, Ken Tucker determined that if the album title implied "a certain broadening of experience, its main evidence on the new record is an occasional use of harmony and the boys' discovery of Carbona." But he suggested that while the band was as intense, direct, and witty as ever, their hard rock was so pure that they might still be taken for a "freak novelty."

Trouser Press staffer Scott Isler, the stalwart Ramones defender against Ira Robbins's initial attacks, wrote in *Crawdaddy* that even while a second Ramones album might be considered "a contradiction in terms," the band might in fact long outlive the "p—k" craze. He also acknowledged that as songwriters, the group was coming perilously close to "dare I say it?—poetry" in lines like "Now I wanna be sad alone" from "Now I Wanna Be a Good Boy."

In *NME*, Charles Shaar Murray credited them with learning a few new tricks like minor chords, Merseybeat changes, and "lyrics that are crass and nasty in a far more mature manner than the more straightforward viscious innocence of their debut album. . . . In other words, it's magnificent." Also in *NME*, Mick Farren praised the Ramones minimalism: "The world needs . . . a band who've distilled all moral, political, and social philosophy down to the phrase 'gabba gabba hey'—and needs it now."

John Rockwell, reporting on the New York underground for *The New York Times*, philosophized, "What the Ramones do is string a manic run of short songlets together in one cumulatively rising chain. On a first hearing all the songs sound the same, and dark suspicions arise that the group couldn't do anything else if it wanted to. But especially in performance, one realizes that a Ramones set or album has to be conceived of as a whole, with each songlet a piece of a larger mosaic. The Ramones are generally considered New York's archetypal punk rockers, the local inspiration for London groups like Eddie and the Hot Rods, the Sex Pistols, and the Damned. But actually the Ramones stance is so patently deliberate, so artfully assumed, that pure punk primitivism is left far behind."

In summary, Rockwell agreed that the Ramones were indeed "minimal" (as were Talking Heads), but only because they ultimately chose to say "something that was clear and simple." As far as Tommy was concerned, the songs were short and to the point because otherwise the guys lost interest. He suggested that TV commercials were at fault for their short attention span. Whatever the case, critic Gene Sculatti nailed it: "Don't talk to me about rock 'n' roll unless you've played 'Ramones Leave Home' several dozen times."

But it was now time for the Ramones to leave home again. A local February 2 gig at My Father's Place in Long Island was noteworthy, drawing an anti-punk group which implored followers to "confront the pagan punk populace with a style of heckling that will raise hackles." But then it was off to Los Angeles, and five sell-outs at the Whiskey (February 16–20), with Blondie opening, and dignitaries, including the Kinks Ray Davies along with Phil Spector, in attendance.

From April 23 through June 6 the Ramones returned to Europe, bringing along Sire and CB's mates Talking Heads.

"I remember Johnny's girlfriend at the time wore a black rubber dress with armpit hair sewn onto it!" Heads drummer Chris Frantz marvels admiringly. "But they always had this whole vibe of leather, loudness, and *extreme* girls, in high heels and usually some kind of bondage dress, with bleached blonde hair done up really big! I hung out with Dee Dee quite a bit. We used to get a pot buzz together and explore Amsterdam or Paris or London. It was their second time there, but my first trip to Europe, and it was the best tour I ever had. Every place we played was full—not that they were that big, but compared to CB's they were huge. Then we'd go out all night and travel to the next show and it was just a great time."

Frantz remembers Johnny as being a bit suspicious of the Heads, and he was right. "They were always a bunch of intellectuals," says Johnny. "They just sat there reading. You couldn't ask Jerry [keyboard player Jerry Harrison] a question, he'd go on reading for an hour! And Tina [bass player Tina Weymouth] complained that we had roadies to handle our equipment instead of doing it ourselves, like they did. Kids don't want to see you carry your own equipment! But we were friends."

Just totally opposites. As Harrison recalled in the video "Lifestyles of the Ramones," while the Heads looked forward to Paris and its continental cuisine, the Ramones couldn't wait to get there because it had a McDonald's! In Marseilles, meanwhile, the Ramones used so much power that they blew out France's entire second-largest city!

Linda Stein also has vivid recollections of the tour. "It was like 'Spinal Tap.' We rented a little red minivan and went to see the Sex Pistols, and Johnny insisted that everybody have the same seats going as coming, and there was a major fight on the way back because Tina insisted on changing her seat!"

As for the Sex Pistols, Johnny, for one, wasn't impressed. "After seeing

THE BLITZKRIEG BOP!!

PHOTOS-DANNY FIELDS   WORDS-©THE RAMONES   CONCEPT-J. HOLMSTROM

them I realized they couldn't compete with us," he says. "We were aware from the start that if our playing was limited, we still had to compete with the Aerosmiths of the world. So we needed certain things, like lights, a drum platform, good P.A. system. They were a good group, but they had tiny little amps when they were supposed to be loud and powerful. Maybe they were supposed to be unprofessional, but it was a total amateur show."

The key word here was *professional*. Through the years, Johnny has always come under fire for being a tough authoritarian. Maybe it was his military schooling, but for Johnny, there was one right way to go about things, which happened to be *his* way. They didn't call him "the Führer" for nothing. Then again, he was an avowed animal lover, whose pet cat had no name—since animals don't have names in nature!

"I try to maintain a punk-type attitude, but be nice to people who are nice people," Johnny concedes. "I never liked the part of the music business where they expect you to be jolly and cheerful about everything, you know, like to get you on this show or that show. I don't want to be on that show! I hate that show! I don't care! I'm no ass-kisser."

"It was like school, and Johnny was the principal," continues Stein. "When we toured England, anybody five minutes late would get fined twenty-five dollars. No dilly-dallying. He used to scare me in the beginning, but after Danny told me to stand up to him he became very sweet. It really was the most efficiently run trip, not what you might expect with the Ramones."

Recalls Fields, "Johnny was extremely bright and dedicated, with a great sense of justice and honor—a real *mensch*, with a strong focus on

(Danny Fields)

what had to be done. He didn't tolerate foolishness or mistakes or sloppiness, so he could be hard on you—but not without reason. He kept a record of every gig in a little notebook, so he always knew where we'd been and how many came. He was very shrewd."

Vera Colvin, who married Dee Dee in 1977 and has been separated from him since a month before he quit the band in 1989, remembers with some bitterness that Johnny's tight rule over the band, and especially its image, prevented Dee Dee from publicizing his marriage. You know, the group identity thing, which at this point was still intact and zealously guarded. But she does give Johnny credit for his strong stance against getting high before shows—which only happened once, at that first Performance Studio gig, when they got drunk to settle their nerves, then played so badly they embarrassed themselves in front of their friends.

"Dee Dee fucked up only when he was off the road," says Vera, who still goes by Vera Ramone. "The band had strict rules about drugs on the road, and for Dee Dee, they had to."

So there existed this dichotomy within the Ramones. "They were the most well-behaved people, *period*," says Stein. "I always thought it was funny how people were so scared of them, and asked me how I could go on the road with them. But everybody went to bed early because they had to be up early. They didn't like the Talking Heads because it was art music—and the Ramones couldn't be more repulsed! They liked Blondie, but they *really* hated everyone, including me, and especially each other! But that's what's so adorable about them: To know them is to understand them."

Adds Fields, "They were sort of within themselves. I remember a long car ride, and occasionally someone would say something, but mostly they'd look out the window."

They spent a lot of time together in cars and vans. No wonder they got on each other's nerves. "They'd be together twenty-four hours a day or *more*, with no privacy," says Vera. "After three months of hating each other they'd go back on the road and everything was okay."

Back from Europe, they played their first Madison, Wisconsin, gig on June 23 at a club called El Tejon. "We were getting four hundred and fifty dollars, but the guy docked us for not playing long enough," says Johnny. I myself was at that gig, but I don't remember the set length. Johnny remembers that the band was now playing five jobs a week, doing a forty-minute set in thirty minutes.

The next important date was August 16, but not because it was a Ramones gig. That was the day that Elvis Presley died, and the reason it sticks out here is that it was also the day that Fields and Stein met with Premier Talent, the booking agency behind such superstar rock acts as Led Zeppelin and the Who.

"Critics were going *nuts*," Johnny says, "but we still had a hard time breaking into concerts—where Aerosmith and Kiss were the rule."

Besides their ill-fated Johnny Winter warm-up, the Ramones had un-pleasant experiences opening for the likes of the Kinks, Peter Frampton, and even Toto! One night they opened for Blue Oyster Cult before twenty thousand people at Nassau Coliseum in Long Island, then hustled back for three sets at CB's. They really were the hardest-working act in show business, though booking agents remained unimpressed. Says Johnny, "They'd try us out at a show with a ridiculous act and we'd flop, so they'd drop us the next day."

Fields had videotaped a Ramones show at Chicago's Uptown Theater using a primitive camcorder.

"We just put the camera on a tripod and shot the show from behind the last row of the audience," says Fields. "The band got such a good reception that the audience stood up and blocked out the stage."

So Fields and Stein took the video to Premier, but since no one had video equipment in their offices in those days, they brought along their own TV and tape deck. "We cued it to the last song where everybody stood up screaming, and Premier decided to go with us."

Their agent at Premier—for the next fourteen years—was Tim McGrath, who came to the Ramones directly from booking the Nitty Gritty Dirt Band. "The first time I ever saw them, they split a bill in New York at the Palladium with the Runaways. It took me by surprise, and I remember being a little turned off. There was Journey, the Doobies, Supertramp, Yes, Frampton—mainstream stuff that was happening, and the punk scene was antiestablishment. I came to Premier from a country music agency, and seeing something like this was totally out of the ordinary."

McGrath was also put off by not being able to see Joey's face at all during the show, what with his shades and long hair covering it up. But like everyone else who stuck with the Ramones program, he came around soon enough. At first, Premier tried to break the band mainstream, packaging them with big names like the Kinks and Black Sabbath. But the agency inevitably recognized how abusive these tours proved to be for the misunderstood and underappreciated punk rockers, so it devised a new strategy.

"The Ramones hated cross-country tours, so we developed guerilla tactics," McGrath continues. "We'd hit different parts of the country. Like for the West Coast, they'd go out and do eleven shows in fourteen days, keep the costs down, and fly home. Or they'd go from Texas to Florida and then come home. Another peculiarity was if they were within a two hundred-mile radius of home, they'd come home every night. That saved a lot of money over the years in hotel bills. We then plugged away at the market until it happened for us enough to make it financially rewarding—or else we didn't go back."

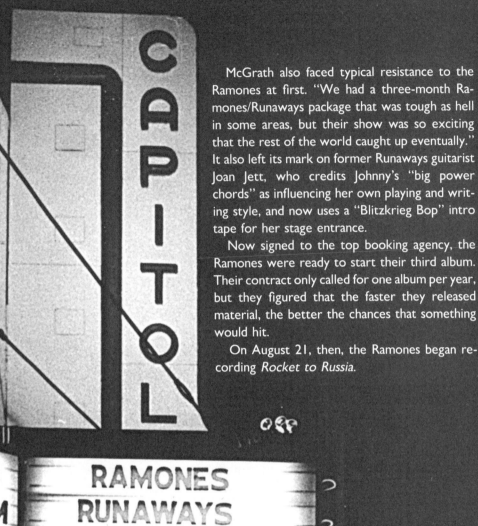

McGrath also faced typical resistance to the Ramones at first. "We had a three-month Ramones/Runaways package that was tough as hell in some areas, but their show was so exciting that the rest of the world caught up eventually." It also left its mark on former Runaways guitarist Joan Jett, who credits Johnny's "big power chords" as influencing her own playing and writing style, and now uses a "Blitzkrieg Bop" intro tape for her stage entrance.

Now signed to the top booking agency, the Ramones were ready to start their third album. Their contract only called for one album per year, but they figured that the faster they released material, the better the chances that something would hit.

On August 21, then, the Ramones began recording *Rocket to Russia*.

RAMONES
RUNAWAYS
TUFF DARTS

The Capitol Theater in Passaic, New Jer: was the home and breeding ground for rock and rollers in 1978. (Roberta Bayle

I f *Ramones Leave Home* sounded a little more poppy and fun than *Ramones*, *Rocket to Russia*, the third album, went even further in that direction.

"Cretin Hop," the opening track, at once set an overall brisk and bouncy tone—and offered a textbook Ramones song:

There's no stoppin' the cretin's
   from hoppin'
You gotta keep it beatin' for all the
   hoppin' cretins
Cretin! Cretin!

Mental illness was back in style, but as always, tongue-in-cheek. Indeed, "cretins" no doubt referred to the Ramones fans in general, who partici-

"Something's Wrong With Us Up There!"

pated at Ramones gigs by doing the then-in-vogue "pogo dance"—a crazed, pogo stick-like hopping up and down in place.

"Rockaway Beach" came next, and for many Ramones-o-philes, it remains the one song that really got away.

> Chewing out a rhythm on my bubblegum
> The sun is out and I want some.
> It's not hard, not far to reach
> We can hitch a ride to Rockaway Beach.
> Up on the roof, out in the street
> Down in the playground the hot concrete
> Busride is too slow
> They blast out the disco on the radio
> Rock Rock Rockaway Beach
> Rock Rock Rockaway Beach
> We can hitch a ride
> To Rockaway Beach.

With a driving beat, melody, and chorus worthy of the Beach Boys— well, folks, it simply doesn't get any better than this. Except that Sire Records released the perfect summer song in the dead of winter! Alas, the Ramones!

Rocket to Russia had two classic covers, "Do You Wanna Dance," previously a hit for Bobby Freeman, the Beach Boys, and Bette Midler, and the Trashmen's suitably cretinous 1964 smash, "Surfin' Bird." Other highlights included a heavier mix of "Sheena Is a Punk Rocker" than in the single version substituted for "Carbona" in the repackaged "Leave Home"; another jokey tribute to insanity, "I Wanna Be Well" (this time the culprits were LSD and the insecticide DDT!); a more serious comment on suicide ("Why Is It Always This Way?"); "I Don't Care," a cruelly concise exercise in nihilism ("I don't care about this world . . . about that girl . . . about these words, I don't care"); and the dirge-like tune about romantic breakup, "Here Today, Gone Tomorrow."

"We're a Happy Family" made both fun and misery out of the typical American middle-class family:

> Sitting here in Queens
> Eatin' refried beans
> We're in all the magazines
> Gulpin' down Thorazines
> We ain't got no friends
> Our troubles never end
> No Christmas cards to send
> Daddy likes men.

Backstage at
CBGB's when punk was
roaring (Roberta Bayley).

(Sire Records)

The joke was all the more chilling when Dee Dee barked out the chorus, "We're a happy family/Me, mom, and daddy!"

In the days of vinyl, that ended side one. Side two opened with a bare-boned drum rhythm, followed by Joey's now-famous chant: "Lobotomy, lobotomy, lobotomy, lobotomy!"—exclaimed with increasing volume as the guitars chimed in with brutal ferocity.

> DDT did a job on me
> Now I am a real sickie
> Guess I'll have to break the news
> That I got no mind to lose.
> All the girls are in love with me
> I'm a teenage lobotomy.

Who in their right minds, so to speak, couldn't relate? "I don't know ... something's wrong with us up there," Johnny told rock critic Kurt Loder.

Most of the songs were collaborations, though Janis Schacht, whose favorite part of her publicity job was getting to hear Joey's songs as they were written ("he wrote everything on a two-string guitar"), singles out Dee Dee's melodic contributions, especially on "Rockaway Beach": "He'd act so dumb, but he had such depth and ability." The production was again quick and relatively cheap, in the $25,000–$30,000 range; always eyeing the cashflow, Johnny well knew that the $150 per hour studio cost came out of the band's pockets, so everyone was well prepared going in.

Rocket to Russia was recorded in midtown's Media Sound Studio, with the same production/engineering team, plus a female engineer (on the first day) named Ramona, though not the inspiration for the song "Ramona" on the album. "It was a bigger room," recalls Ed Stasium. "We put in much more backing vocals—a lot more 'ooh's. So it was a little sophisticated for the Ramones, and more experimental. On 'Why Is It Always This Way?,' Johnny played a cleaned-up guitar instead of chain-saw guitar, using Steve Miller as a reference."

The album was mixed at the Power Station, a new studio being built by Tony Bongiovi, who had just finished the "Star Wars Theme" disco smash by Meco. Stasium remembers that they had to use a stairwell as an echo chamber; Bongiovi hasn't forgotten that the mixing equipment was pushed to the limits, abusing "every law of recording science" to get it to work.

Stasium was also responsible for a discernibly new twist to Ramones records—guitar solos. As *Village Voice* critic Tom Carson noted, the solo on "Here Today, Gone Tomorrow" had almost the same impact of the first guitar solo ever played, "because for the first time in fifteen years, you weren't expecting one."

Rocket to Russia, the title for which started out as a song which was somehow transformed into "Ramona," was released in November. It featured Danny Fields' grainy black-and-white cover photo of the band standing against a brick wall, which more closely resembled Roberta Bayley's "Ramones" cover photo than Moshe Brakha's unsatisfying color cover of the band on a Manhattan rooftop. But more important, it featured John Holmstrom's magnificent back cover cartoon of the Ramones pinhead mascot riding a just-launched rocket to Russia, with the globe below full of funny little characters representing various countries. Inside, Holmstrom illustrated the lyric sheet with smaller, equally hilarious cartoons, many of which became future Ramones T-shirt artwork.

In *Rolling Stone*, Steve Pond called *Rocket to Russia* one of the essential albums of the seventies. In the *Village Voice*, Robert Christgau gave it a straight "A": "Having revealed how much you can take out and still have rock 'n' roll, they now explore how much you can put back in and still have Ramones. Not that they've returned so very much—a few relatively obvious melodies, a few relatively obvious vocals. But that's enough."

Billy Altman in *Creem* cited the album's "dynamite" production: "more crunch to the guitars, more presence to the drums, more boom to the bass, great percussion (love those sleigh bells), and everything about it is just superb. This is the best album the Ramones have done and that's saying a lot, 'cause I dare say none of these nouveau-rockoid aggregations deserve more than one LP anyway ... and I bet most of them will be dead and gone within two years, and already the Ramones have made three solid LPs, and if I don't stop soon I'm gonna have to throw cold water on my typewriter."

Rolling Stones's Dave Marsh called *Rocket to Russia* the year's best American rock 'n' roll and perhaps the funniest rock album of all time. Comparing the Ramones growth to that of the Who between "My Generation" and "Happy Jack," he singled out "We're a Happy Family" and "Why Is It Always This Way?" for their mix of humor and truth: "The Ramones explore the dirty truths that pop music and rock designed to 'entertain' have to cover up."

In the annual *Village Voice* "Pazz & Jop" critics poll, *Rocket to Russia* placed sixth behind *Never Mind the Bollocks, Here's the Sex Pistols*, Elvis Costello's *My Aim is True*, Television's *Marquee Moon*, Fleetwood Mac's *Rumours*, and Steely Dan's *Aja*, and just ahead of *Talking Heads '77*. *Ramones Leave Home* came in at No. 25.

Thus ended a sort of trilogy for the Ramones. According to Johnny, most of the songs now recorded had been written prior to the first album, pretty much in chronological order.

"The structures were slightly different by the second album, but there was a natural progression from album to album, and we didn't blow our best fourteen songs on the first album and come back with a weaker second one—which is what always happens with bands.

"And we didn't make any *changes*, either. It always seems like bands have to change, but besides the Beatles, they never change for the better. Bands mostly change for the worse, because they get bored, or forget what they set out to do. They overindulge. Like the Rolling Stones were my favorite band before 'Satanic Majesties Request,' before they started doing disco songs and rap songs. But we always tried to keep in mind what the fans want, what they think is good and not good. Not what the people around you think, because they bullshit you about everything, telling you it's great when it isn't. I see why someone like Elvis was so fucked up, why he was wearing those stupid outfits and making stupid movies instead of being a strong man to a bunch of yes men."

But the release of *Rocket to Russia* was notable for another reason.

It was the first new Ramones album to come out under Sire's new distribution agreement with Warner Bros., which had taken over "Leave Home" after ABC had already released it, with and without "Carbona." So the album enjoyed full record-company support, symbolized by an almost full-sized album cover stand-up display for record stores.

Meanwhile, the Ramones media visibility was steadily increasing. On "Don Kirshner's Rock Concert," they blasted through a dozen songs in the best TV showcase of punk/new wave rock thus far. And print journalists were beginning to see beyond the twin illusions of the band as a single entity and the music's dangerousness. Roy Trakin's "Ramones Redefined" cover story in *New York Rocker* (which also featured stories on the likes of Helen Wheels, Sic F*cks, Patti Smith, the Shirts, Chris Stamey, Walter Lure, the Feelies, Richard Hell, and the Erasers) described the guys as "four less-than-average Joes from Forest Hills, who, through a combination of luck and desire (you better believe it!) are climbing to the head of a pack that promises to include a lot more bands before the wave subsides. . . . What they say, the words they use, becomes secondary to how they say it. Joey's two-word witticisms, Dee Dee's dumb earnestness, Tommy's perceptive objectivity, and Johnny's verbal aggressiveness all work to make an interview a hilarious, yet trying experience. The Ramones are four different personalities who barely understand one another, yet join together to form a team which looks more and more, as time goes by, [like] the seventies answer to the Marx Brothers, or at least the Three (Four?) Stooges."

Trakin keenly observed that the guys were nowhere near as mean as their on-stage personas. "We put all our meanness into our music. . . . One thing that people don't realize about the Ramones is that we try to do as much as possible naturally. . . . That's why it works. . . . It's just us."

Joey offered a similar explanation in *Melody Maker*: "The songs are just like us. We're not doing something we're not. We *are* what we sing." As for their violent lyrics, Johnny added, "We might read a story about thirty people being murdered, and we'll laugh. It might be sick, but that's just the way we see things. You can't read about things and get depressed."

As Tommy told *Drummer*, "We're not trying to compete with Bruce Springsteen."

With a new album out, the Ramones went back to their typically heavy tour schedule. "Ramones luck," however, struck again in November at the Capitol Theater in Passaic, New Jersey.

Joey was preparing to steam his throat backstage, by heating water in a teapot, (a self-fashioned makeshift humidifier, atop a hotplate—the whistle of which he had removed and replaced with a piece of plastic with a hole in the middle, which he stuck on with a rubber band). A new roadie accidentally filled the teapot up to the top and when the hotplate was turned on, the pressure caused the device to blow up in his face and shoot scaulding water down his throat and neck, giving Joey second- and third-degree burns. He was rushed to the local emergency room. Ever the trouper, he came back and did the whole set, never missing a note, though it was reported that the salve they applied to his face melted under the stage lights, giving him a weird, wax-like appearance and further complicating his injuries.

"He must have been in agony, but it was one of the best shows I ever saw," says John Holmstrom, who was unaware of the accident. "That kind of thing always happened to the Ramones."

Joey *was* in agony, according to Janis Schacht. "It was the bravest performance I've ever seen."

Joey must have been cheered by the "Get Well, Joey Ramone" message that lit up Broadway from the famous Times Square sign.

The Ramones closed out the year back in England, with a New Year's Eve show at the Rainbow Theater. During their stay there, Joey worked on "Sedated." Recalls Linda Stein, "We were backstage in Canterbury, and he came to me and said, 'Listen, Linda: "Put me in a wheelchair and get me on a plane before I go insane." ' I mean, that was it! Canterbury, Keats and Shelley, and the Ramones!" Says Joey, " 'Sedated' " has become the epitomized Ramones anthem—(circa 1977) on both coasts, America and England. A song about being on the road too long . . . 365 days a year."

A review in *Melody Maker* proved that Joey was definitely back: "[He's] pushing the mikestand in front of him like a shield, as if he's warding off some giant insect, though sometimes it just appears as though he's standing on a hotplate like a dancing chicken."

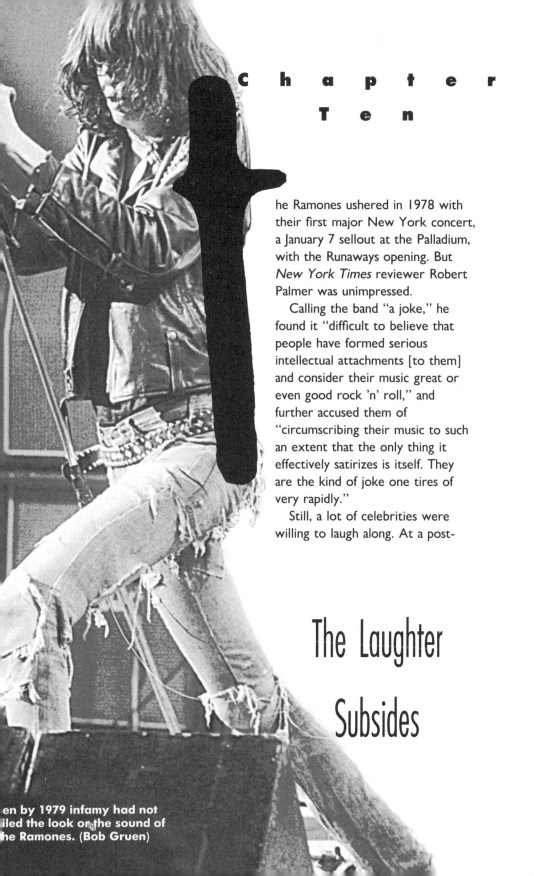

Chapter
Ten

he Ramones ushered in 1978 with
their first major New York concert,
a January 7 sellout at the Palladium,
with the Runaways opening. But
New York Times reviewer Robert
Palmer was unimpressed.

Calling the band "a joke," he
found it "difficult to believe that
people have formed serious
intellectual attachments [to them]
and consider their music great or
even good rock 'n' roll," and
further accused them of
"circumscribing their music to such
an extent that the only thing it
effectively satirizes is itself. They
are the kind of joke one tires of
very rapidly."

Still, a lot of celebrities were
willing to laugh along. At a post-

The Laughter

Subsides

en by 1979 infamy had not
iled the look on the sound of
he Ramones. (Bob Gruen)

concert party a couple doors down at Julian's Billiard Academy, the guest list included Daryl Hall, Carl Bernstein and then-wife Nora Ephron, Southside Johnny, Richard Hell, Annie Haslam, Roy Wood, the Dictators (Handsome Dick Manitoba challenged Southside Johnny to a drinking contest, but Southside was already too drunk to get in), Rick Derringer, Lenny Kaye, David Johansen, and Joey's dad, Noel Hyman—enjoying one of the proudest nights of his life.

A February 1 date at Bunky's in Madison, Wisconsin, was also noteworthy, for two reasons. An article in *Variety* titled "Ramones Give Punk a Better Name in Madison Nitery" reported that although a political group called the Committee Against Racism picketed the club for what it viewed as the Ramones "fascist ideology," media interest was high and the show was successful compared with the band's flop at El Tejon six months earlier.

But as successful as the Ramones were on the road, they were still poorly paid—only $750 to $1,000 a show. "We were playing all these big places and all the money was going back into the band," Dee Dee wrote in *Spin*. "I was only making one hundred and twenty five dollars a week and had a one hundred dollar-a-day dope habit."

But Dee Dee wasn't the only Ramone with problems. Touring was a grind, and Tommy was pretty much *grounded*. "I was having a very good time and enjoying making records and feeling that with every album we made we were making progress and doing something valuable. But I started to get claustrophobic about touring and since I loved the studio, I decided to just produce albums and quit the road."

The Ramones had recorded their New Year's Eve show in London, and when Tommy finished mixing it, he gave up the Ramones drum stool to co-produce their next studio album with Ed Stasium. Those considered as replacements included Johnny Blitz (the Dead Boys), Blondie's Clem Burke, Sex Pistol Paul Cook, and the Dolls' Jerry Nolan. But the guy who got the gig was the one Nolan had beat out for the Dolls slot vacated by Billy Murcia, who had OD'd.

"We knew of Marky from the Voidoids," says Johnny of Marc Bell, who came to the Ramones via Richard Hell and the Voidoids. "I thought he was a good rock drummer, but he was too jazzy in the Voidoids and he was wasted in that band. We didn't want to steal a drummer from another band, but he was better with us."

Brooklynite Marc Bell was born July 15, 1956, and was quite different from the other Ramones. Son of a decidedly liberal, pro-union longshoreman (who also graduated from Brooklyn Law School and now works for a law firm), Marky as a youngster participated in the 1964 civil rights march on Washington, D.C., having also marched at the U.N. two years earlier to protest the Bay of Pigs invasion. Growing up in Flatbush, he graduated from Ditmas Junior High School and Erasmus Hall High School, where, at age sixteen, he recorded two albums with the rock 'n' roll trio Dust (which also included bassist Kenny Aronsen—of Billy Idol, Joan Jett, and Bob Dylan fame—and Richie Wise, who later produced Kiss). But like the Ramones, Marky also felt alienated in high school, since he wore his hair long and dressed differently.

Although Marky's mother ran the Brooklyn College music library, he was greatly influenced by seeing Ringo on TV. But his drumming idol was Mitch Mitchell of the Jimi Hendrix Experience. "He had a jazz style combined with a rock feel. I used to watch jazz drummers like Buddy Rich, and liked the way they held their sticks, the way they played with their wrist instead of their arms, and still got a lot of volume. They didn't have to make it look hard. So I did different jazz drummer styles and time signatures."

Dust broke up in 1972, and the following year Marky did studio work for Andrew Loog Oldham, the Rolling Stones producer. He also recorded a blues album with blues guitar greats Johnny Shines and David Bromberg. In 1974, he started hanging around Max's Kansas City; the Dolls had just broken up, but the New York underground scene was just beginning.

After a stint with Wayne County and the Back Street Boys (he is on County's contribution to the "Max's Kansas City 1976" compilation), Marky joined Richard Hell's Voidoids, having met Hell at Max's. Shortly after the first Ramones album was released, Hell and the Voidoids also signed with Sire, releasing "Blank Generation" in 1977.

"When *Ramones* came, most of the CB's bands were envious of them," says Marky. "They were the ones that really stood out. Blondie was an early sixties girl group, and Talking Heads were avant-garde Bohemians, but the Ramones were the true meaning and balls of New York.

"I went on tour with Richard and supported the Clash in Europe in November, and by the time we got there the punk scene was happening all over—the Clash, Sex Pistols, Siouxsie and the Banshees, the Adverts, Sham 69, Generation X. But they all in one way sounded like the Ramones, whose album I'd got in seventy six before I was with Hell. When I played it, I knew it was the start of a new thing, that I'd never heard anything like it. I was so into drum fills and time changes and being technical, and this was something totally off the wall. I'd love to play with these guys!

"I knew Dee Dee from CB's, and one day at CB's he asked if I would play with the Ramones. Then Johnny came up and asked if I'd join the band. I went to a rehearsal, and it was one of those sneaky things. Tommy said we'd meet at the rehearsal studio, and ten other drummers were waiting around. I knew they wanted me anyway, but let the other guys play out of respect. This was in March 1978. I respected Richard's songwriting, but we didn't get along and I wanted to go into this other thing. It took a week or two to get it together."

"It worked out real well," continues Tommy, who would later return to produce "Too Tough to Die," and also produced the likes of the Replacements and Red Cross before putting together his own band, Uncle Monk. "Marky liked my playing, and combined my style with his talent."

The Ramones were scheduled to start recording their fourth album, "Road to Ruin," in just three weeks, so Marky had little time to learn the Ramones live set *and* the new album. The pace was excruciating at first, but he rehearsed constantly with a drum pad, while listening under headphones to a live Ramones tape.

"Tommy basically played eighth-notes across, with the 'one' on the bass and 'two' on the snare, constant eighth-notes on the high-hat. A lot of people try to duplicate it but they don't realize that it's harder to play eighth-notes than quarter-notes and create the wall of sound we have—with only three instruments. Bopa-bopa-bopa-bopa. All mass and no space. That's when you get the wall. Quarter-notes, spaces. Playing fast with eighth-notes constantly—a lot of people try it, but they get sloppy and can't keep up. Go back to quarter-notes and they always do old drum fills that Keith Moon and John Bonham were doing twenty five years ago. And then you throw ten drums in front of somebody and they're bound to hit them, when you only have to hit one or two in the whole song. So it's a lot of show and bullshit and I have no time to do that because I'm playing so quick I don't have time to whirl a stick!

"So I like a regular setup with five drums instead of ten, which is a lot harder because you have to hit all of them and make them work. I listen to my competition and I'm not impressed because all they do are rolls that have been done already and done better and with more feeling."

Marky started using Tommy's oversized white Rogers kit, because at first he didn't want to change things too much. Eventually he switched to Tama, then Pearl, because of its tone and roadworthiness. Having learned marching military snare drum work in high school, he stayed with the bigger military model sticks, which don't break as easily, since he plays on the skin and rim at the same time. He uses a jazz/swing trap set-up, with each tom-tom having its own separate tone, and tunes his snare tight. He would have preferred going by Mark Ramone, but was fond of the Marky cartoon character from the old Maypo cereal commercials. Besides, that's what his grandmother called him. He had three rehearsals with the Ramones, learning thirty-one classics and nine new songs. On May 31, the new lineup began recording "Road to Ruin," and June 29 marked Marky's first live date as a Ramone.

Tommy Ramone's last gig with the band was at CB's on May 4. "People thought everything was an accident," he reflected in *NME*. "These four morons are really cute and they're doing something really neat, but obviously it's all an accident. First of all, it wasn't four morons; second of all, none of it was an accident; and third of all, it's four talented people who know what they like and who know what they're doing."

But at this point, no one knew where they were going. The bottom line was this: The first three Ramones albums, despite all the new-wave hoopla, had barely rippled the surface at retail, and unless you make money, you don't get any. The English punk scene had stolen the thunder from the New York underground; the Sex Pistols album had come out on Warner Bros. in October 1977, and now the Ramones had to fight for an equal advertising budget. The Pistols infamous American tour in January didn't help, either. Johnny blamed a low turnout at a Ramones gig in Tulsa on the Pistols dismal showing there which had shortly preceded it.

But the worst thing that happened was that, for whatever reason, "Rocket to Russia" had flopped. Recalls Seymour Stein, "Warner Bros. had been so geared up in all departments, and when it didn't live up to everybody's expectations, the Ramones became somewhat indelibly stamped in the minds of Warner Bros. that they were a cult band, that wasn't for everybody."

So with the personnel change and a growing frustration with the music industry, the Ramones took a turn from the primarily fun, if tilted, pop of its first records, to a harder, meaner edge, evident in *Road to Ruins*'s first two self-explanatory tracks, Joey's "I Just Want to Have Something to Do" and Dee Dee's "I Wanted Everything."

But the third song (and first single) came as a shock. "Don't Come Close," with its spritely, tuneful melody and lilting, layered guitars (don't blame Johnny!), was—can it be true?—a *country* song. My God, you could almost hear a pedal steel guitar! It must have been a mistake, because they got back on track immediately with a standard Ramones cruncher, "I Don't Want You," followed by a stronger version of the Searchers 1964 smash "Needles and Pins" (the second single), letter perfect right down to the "needles and pin-za."

Then came a blazing "I'm Against It"—"it" being politics, Communists, games and fun, sex and drugs, anyone and everything—even Burger King! Then "Ruin"'s one true classic, complete with a repeated one-note solo, "I Wanna Be Sedated":

> Twenty-twenty-twenty four hours to go
> I wanna be sedated
> Nothing to do
> Nowhere to go
> I wanna be sedated

Keats and Shelley and Joey Ramone! "Go Mental" followed, extolling the pleasures of "staring at my goldfish bowl, popping phenobarbitol," but then—it can't be true!—*another* country song? Dee-Dee's "Questioningly" not only gave English a new word, it gave Ramones fans further pause. It had another brightly shimmering guitar intro, but this time there was a heartbreaking poignancy to the melody and lyrical despondency over a girl "that I once may have knew":

> In the morning I'm at work on time
> My boss he tells me that I'm doing fine
> When I'm going home
> Whiskey bottle movie on TV
> Memories make me cry

That left "Bad Brain," an ode to Bowery bums, "It's a Long Way Back," with its terse longing for Germany, and "She's the One," which was the only really "up" number on a downer album. The songs were longer, so due to the technical limitations of vinyl, the album was shortened to twelve selections to make sure it could still be played loud.

"Road to Ruin" (Johnny, a movie buff, got his inspiration for the title from the Bob Hope/Bing Crosby *The Road to . . .* series) was produced by T. Erdelyi and Ed Stasium and recorded at Media Sound. "It really was a milestone for the Ramones," says Stasium, the Ramones silent soloist. "We spent a couple months doing it, and tried to make—for lack of a better word—a more *commercial* record to appeal to a broader market. That's why we put in the guitar solo bits, the acoustic guitars, the infamous one-note solo on 'Sedated,' the clean guitar on 'Don't Come Close,' the chimey guitars on 'Needles and Pins,' the ballad 'Questioningly.' "

The front cover art was a beautiful color cartoon by John Holmstrom, with the back showing a standard black-and-white portrait shot by Danny Fields. When the album was released in September (along with a "Road to Ruin" promotional push-pin box), critical response was mixed.

Kurt Loder, writing in *Circus*, realized that for the Ramones, "it was either grow or court boredom." But he felt that the album's broadened "stylistic flexibility" had come at the expense of "the sheer heart attack that so ferociously animated their first two albums." Loder's verdict was that "Road to Ruin" was a "graceful and good-natured holding action."

But in *Trouser Press*, Scott Isler denounced the record's use of acoustic guitars and country music as blasphemous. "What's saddest about 'Road to Ruin' is that it marks the Ramones fall from grace. By rejecting the role of new wave idiots savant, they become just another loud rock band. True, they've improved technically—Joey is actually singing, after a fashion—but the Ramones have entered a world where quality, not concept, counts. This LP, besides lacking the non-stop blitzkrieg approach of earlier albums, even breaks with the seven-cuts-a-side practice. They're serious now."

At *Rolling Stone*, Charles M. Young saw it as more a compromise than a sellout, and Robert Christgau in the *Village Voice* gave it a qualified "A": "Like any great group, this one is always topping itself," he wrote, singling out the "candidly lyrical slow ones," especially "Questioningly" ("the guitar breaks bring tears to my personal eyes"), even suggesting that the great country singer Gary Stewart cut a cover of it.

Also in the *Voice*, critic Tom Carson noted that "Questioningly" (which Johnny absolutely hated) would give the "punk is dead" people a lot of fresh ammo. Still, he felt it was the best Ramones album. "What once seemed like a one-joke dead end is now an endless vista," Carson wrote, and while he didn't know what to expect from them next, he was hoping for the "inevitable" Ramones version of "Sergeant Pepper's Lonely Hearts Club Band."

Which is exactly what he got.

(Arturo Vega)

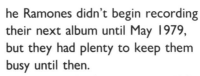

he Ramones didn't begin recording
their next album until May 1979,
but they had plenty to keep them
busy until then.

First they had to complete "It's
Alive"—named for the horror
movie—a live double album which
was recorded at a New Year's Eve
show in London and contained
twenty-eight songs (including three
encores totalling nine songs). While
four concerts were recorded, the
show on New Year's Eve—when
ten rows of seats were thrown on
stage—was considered the best.
Production credit again went to T.
Erdelyi and Ed Stasium. The set
wasn't actually released in England
and elsewhere (it was a single disc
in Japan) until April 1979, except in

"I Don't Care

About History ..."

The apocalyptic end of Rock 'n' Roll High School.

America. Though hailed as one of the high points of the punk movement, it was rejected for release here because Warner Bros. wanted a new studio album instead.

The Ramones returned to tour the U.K. in autumn of 1978, but a far more important career point was a three-night, mid-August stint at Hurrah's in New York, set up as an audition for filmmaker Allan Arkush.

Arkush was preparing to direct *Rock 'n' Roll High School* for Roger Corman, the king of the B-movies. Noteworthy among Corman's two hundred-plus productions: *Death Race 2000*, *Eat My Dust*, *Piranha*, *The Day the World Ended*, *Little Shop of Horrors*, *The Fall of the House of Usher*, and *The Wild Angels*. Among the famous actors and directors to cut their teeth on Corman flicks were Jack Nicholson, Bruce Dern, and Ron Howard, while the venerable Vincent Price starred in several of Corman's Edgar Allan Poe adaptations. Film fan Johnny especially appreciated Corman's flicks because of their violence and action; *Attack of the Crab Monsters* was among his favorites.

A youthful member of Corman's production team, Arkush grew up in Fort Lee, New Jersey, and had been a major rock fan since high school. "I used to daydream in class all the time, about having go-cart races in the hallway and blowing up the school. And I imagined getting a rock band like the Yardbirds to play there."

Putting his fantasies to paper, he and fellow Corman protégé Joe Dante (who would later direct films including *Gremlins*) wrote a treatment for a high-school rock movie, which he called *Heavy Metal Kids*, after the Todd Rundgren song. Unfortunately, Corman was anything but musically hip; he preferred something more on the order of *Girls' Gym*, which would have a lot of nude gymnastics, or *Disco High*, as disco was still the rage.

Meanwhile, Arkush had learned of the Ramones through Robert Christgau in the *Village Voice*. But after buying their first album, he decided that people in New York were nuts! "Every song sounded alike, and I wasn't into the punk culture, so it didn't make sense. I'm a huge record collector, and when people came over, I'd go, 'You won't believe that people say this is a good band!' But after five or six times of doing this, I started liking the record, and when they came out with 'Sheena' it all came together!"

Unbeknownst to Corman, Arkush was secretly laying the groundwork for what became *Rock 'n' Roll High School*. Further solidifying the Ramones among his choices for the movie's rock heroes was *Punk* magazine's special "Mutant Monster Beach Party" issue, which showcased Joey as a New York surfer boy come to rescue Blondie's Deborah Harry from the clutches of a Mutant Monster—a veritable take-off on traditional Corman themes.

So Arkush flew to New York to see them at Hurrah's and was completely blown away by the band and the entire scene. At this point, Arkush had made an offer to Rundgren and been declined (much to Rundgren's later regret), and it was either the Ramones or Cheap Trick who would Star. "I knew [Trick's] 'Live at Budokan' would be a big record, but Roger [Corman] didn't get it. Then I had to tell him that the Ramones weren't a disco band, and that it had to be *Rock 'n' Roll High School*, that it had to work out of frustration and anger—not people with money. It was about how rock music functions in every teenager's fantasy life."

Meanwhile, the Ramones hit the road. Premier had flexed its muscle and got the guys on a tour with Black Sabbath, but the November 1 date in San Bernardino, California, would go down next to the disastrous Johnny Winter concert. Johnny Ramone knew they were in trouble when the gig was billed as "The Kings of Heavy Metal *vs.* the Kings of Punk." "Six songs into the show and the equipment was all covered with garbage. There was this motorcycle gang of redneck farmers on wheels—and everybody was pouring whiskey down and throwing the bottles at you."

It wasn't only bottles, but spark plugs, carburetors, and an ice pick, which landed next to Johnny's foot! Joey added when he left the stage an eighty-year-old stage manager said to him, "the last time I saw a reaction like this is when the Rolling Stones first played America."

"Premier said, 'We've been in this business a long time, we know what we're doing more than you,' but they didn't know what the kids like," Johnny continues. "Then they put us in Toronto, opening for Aerosmith and Ted Nugent. They said 'Canada's different, you were right about America.' 'It ain't gonna be no different!' Sure enough the whole crowd stood up and I thought it started raining, but it was sunny. It was really weird. They were throwing stuff at us and they all stood up at the same time. I broke two strings on one strum, and said, 'That's it. It's a sign from God. Get out of here!' And I gave them all the finger and walked off, and the rest of the guys played a few seconds and got out of there. It was the last time they ever suggested playing with these bands again."

The Ramones played about 154 dates in 1978. In December, they began filming *Rock 'n' Roll High School*.

Arkush saw the film as an homage to the Beatles films and *The Girl Can't Help It*, a classic 1950s rock 'n' roll movie starring Jayne Mansfield and featuring Fats Domino, Little Richard, Eddie Cochran, and Gene Vincent. He said it was also a combination of *The Bandwagon* and *Freaks*, with a little of *High School Confidential* (featuring Jerry Lee Lewis) thrown in.

But as the radio jock in the movie put it, the theme really portrayed the classic confrontation between mindless authority and the rebellious nature of youth.

The comic plot revolved around perky Riff Randle, a good-hearted girl student who hates Vince Lombardi High School and loves the Ramones. She also hates Miss Togar, the evil principal, who has found that when mice are subjected to Ramones-decibel rock music (specifically, "Teenage Lobotomy"!), they *explode*. So when Riff hijacks the school intercom to crank out "Sheena Is a Punk Rocker," she doesn't win any Brownie points.

Besides the classic gym-class scene where the girls jiggle to Riff's version of the movie theme song and one in the boy's room where the class entrepreneur takes care of business, the key sequences in the movie all belong to the Ramones. Riff is in love with Joey ("I just love the way he holds the pizza dripping above his mouth, he just slithers and slides it into his mouth. . . . It's so *sexy*."), and has written a song ("Rock 'n'Roll High School") which she hopes to give him when the Ramones arrive for an L.A. concert date. Their entrance is truly climactic: As dozens of fans are camped outside the theater (the Mayan, an old porn house) hoping to be second in line for tickets behind Riff (rock critic Billy Altman was among those in front), the Ramones drive up singing in a Cadillac convertible driven by Rodney Bingenheimer and bearing "Gabba Gabba Hey" license plates. Joey tears into a chicken leg and tosses it out after the line "eating chicken vindaloo" in "I Just Want To Have Something to Do."

The band later appears in a dream sequence. Riff sits in her bedroom, lights up a joint, and suddenly, Joey and Johnny are there too, performing a new acoustic ballad, "I Want You Around" (an Ed Stasium production much like the "cleaner" songs on *Road to Ruin*, and which likewise contains a solo break). She smokes a little more, then watches as Joey gets out of his chair and comes over to her bed and sings directly to her—leather jacket, ripped jeans, and all. Now bikini-clad, Riff gets up during the guitar solo, goes to the window and spies Marky playing drums in the back yard; in the bathroom she finds Dee Dee in the shower (Arkush knew that Dee Dee liked to take four showers a day), playing bass and getting sopped. Next all four Ramones are in the bathroom, and Riff swoons onto Marky's snare drum at the end of the song.

The next scene for the Ramones was performing the show itself, filmed before three live audiences in a daylong shoot at the Roxy. The 8 A.M. show was free, one in the afternoon cost a dollar, and the evening gig, five dollars. For eighteen hours the Ramones played the same songs over and over; the movie soundtrack LP contained an eleven-minute medley of "Blitzkrieg Bop," "Teenage Lobotomy," "California Sun," "Pinhead," and "She's the One." But when the crew finished shooting at 1 A.M., the Ramones kept playing. Says Johnny, "It wasn't fair to the kids who paid five dollars for the same four or five songs sung ten times each. After six or eight more songs, they unplugged us."

When it started the crew didn't know the band, but when it was over everyone was singing "Pinhead."

Arkush had once worked as an usher at the Fillmore East in New York, and so cast himself as an usher at the Roxy, wearing his original Fillmore T-shirt. "If you're very interested in both film making and rock 'n'roll," he says, "you can't see four hundred concerts and not have strong feelings about how they should be filmed."

At this point in the film, Riff finally gives her song to Joey in the dressing room, where stacks of pizza boxes are being delivered and everyone chows down to Dee Dee's immortal lines: "Hey, pizza! It's great! Let's dig in!" (Everyone, that is, except Joey, whose face the band's manager is now stuffing with wheat germ and organic alfalfa!)

Then, after hearing Riff's high-school horror story, the Ramones decide to visit the next day. They pull up to the building just as Miss Togar has set fire to a pile of Ramones albums and other musical classics, including the Stones "Sticky Fingers" and Dylan's "Highway 61 Revisited."

"Things sure have changed since we got kicked out of high school," Joey says as the Ramones enter the building. "Do your parents know you're Ramones?" asks Miss Togar.

The rest of the movie is Arkush's dream come true. The kids trash the halls, and pelt the bound and gagged kitchen ladies with gobs of "Tuesday Surprise" to cries of "We only followed the recipe!" Mr. McGree, the music teacher who has tried to "turn the students on" to classical music, dances with Riff and tells the Ramones, "People say that your music is loud and destructive and lethal to mice, but I think you're the Beethovens of our time."

The Ramones push a laundry cart carrying two Gestapo hall monitors out a second-story window, then play "Do You Wanna Dance?" with Marky on a moving platform rolling down a hallway full of graffiti, with drum majorettes and football players leading the way. "Boy, when you have recess you really go all out," Johnny deadpans.

It all ends with the band outside playing the movie's theme song:

> Well I don't care about history
> 'Cause that's not where I wanna be
> I just wanna have some kicks
> I just wanna get some chicks
> Rock, rock, rock 'n' roll high school

The music mixes the Beach Boys "Fun, Fun, Fun" with Danny & the Juniors "At the Hop," and as the verse repeats, the school explodes. "Those Ramones are peculiar," Miss Togar says, before going insane. "They're ugly, ugly, ugly people," says the police chief. Rock 'n' roll wins, but of course, it's only a movie. Some theaters refused to show it because of the ending, which was filmed at an old Catholic school in Watts at 2 A.M. on a colder-than-average winter's night. But the explosion was five times bigger than anticipated (Johnny was actually quite startled) and for a few seconds the outside temperature jumped from the thirties to seventy degrees, vaporizing the school's flag and causing the miniskirted cheerleaders' legs to "sunburn."

In all, the twenty-one-day shoot cost three hundred thousand dollars, not even pocket change compared to today's film budgets, but Corman wanted it done for under two hundred thousand. Recalls Arkush, "He said he never dreamed it would cost so much money. And he thought there was too much Ramones. It was all I could do to convince him that that was the basic reason why people would see the movie. I remember when Dee Dee saw the dailies, he complained, 'We look like Martians!' Which was exactly right, and why they were the best choice. Ultimately, what the picture was about was how you like music because of who you are and what you'd like to be."

The movie soundtrack also included new-wave cuts by Nick Lowe, Devo, and Eddie and the Hot Rods, plus obvious school-rock favorites by Chuck Berry, Alice Cooper, and Brownsville Station. But most noteworthy was its cover of Ritchie Valens's "Come On Let's Go," which was credited to the Paley Brothers/Ramones, because the Boston power poppers Paleys did the singing. "Joey was sick, and we were cutting our own album," explains Andy Paley. "We were big fans of theirs, and it was really fun. I played organ and my brother Jonathan played guitar, and we switched lead vocals and harmonies, like the Everly Brothers. It was the only time anyone but Joey sang lead with the Ramones."

Rock 'n' Roll High School suffered from poor distribution when it was released sporadically in April 1979 (the soundtrack album came out in May, accompanied by school-related *tshatshkas* like notebooks and hall passes), and died quietly—though it still lives on in cult stature. It did well in Chicago, thanks to a favorable review from Siskel & Ebert and pairings with either *Grease* or *Dawn of the Dead*, and it sold out the 8th Street Playhouse when it opened in New York. "It was one of the greatest nights in my life," says Arkush. "They played it loud, and people stood on chairs and screamed."

"If the film had been properly promoted and distributed," wrote Martha Hume in the *New York Daily News*, "it might have turned [the Ramones] into a major, nationwide draw."

In the *Madcity Music Guide*, Yours Truly wrote, "This sometimes silly, often hilarious film is a must-see not only for Ramones fans and all who identify with the rock 'n' roll high school frustration that they so brilliantly capture in their songs, but also for any moviegoer sick of all the big pictures by big directors with big stars and bigger budgets that cannot cover up big disappointments. True, *High School* hardly strives for greatness. But by combining nonstop fun with a classic rock soundtrack it succeeds perfectly on its own unpretentious terms. . . . And while movie sequels rarely live up to the originals, *Rock 'n' Roll High School* practically begs for *Rock 'n' Roll University*. Just imagine the Ramones at commencement!"

Of course, there was a sequel, but the Ramones weren't in it. As for the original, the Ramones proved big hits with the cast. "The whole time I was there they ate nothing but tacos," said Mary Waronov, an Andy Warhol starlet who played Miss Togar (Waronov's husband Paul Bartel, the director of *Death Race 2000* and *Eating Raoul*, played Mr. McGree). "It was refreshing, too, because they weren't putting on some big act—which is also rare in L.A."

P. J. Soles, who played Riff Randle (and was the ill-fated babysitter in *Carrie*) didn't know what to make of the Ramones at first, but when she realized they were for real, invited them home for a holiday turkey dinner. "They came all dressed up, like little gentlemen! They were very sweet and my family enjoyed them very much."

Since the entire band received only five thousand dollars for their roles in the movie, they couldn't even afford their bills at the Tropicana Hotel. So they had to play gigs during days off—including one night in Phoenix, even though they had to be back on the set the next morning at 6 A.M. But luckily, they did three nights at the Whiskey over Christmas, earning $2,500 because it was a big date.

They also had time to better get to know the man who had remixed the two new Ramones tracks on *Rock 'n' Roll High School* and was to produce their next record—one of the most influential and controversial individuals in rock 'n' roll history.

When rock 'n' roll historians mention the Beatles, the Rolling Stones, and Bob Dylan, the next name that usually comes up is Phil Spector. And when they talk about the Ramones "Wall of Sound," they're borrowing a practically trademarked phrase describing Spector's awesome, heavily orchestrated, near-symphonic arrangements and productions.

Indeed, from 1962 through 1965, Spector produced twenty-one Top 50 hits, including the Crystals "He's a Rebel" and "Da Doo Ron Ron," the Ronettes "Be My Baby" and "Baby, I Love You," and the Righteous Brothers "You've Lost That Lovin' Feeling" and "Unchained Melody." He would go

"Do You Want To Make a Good Album, Or a Great Album?"

on to produce albums for the
Beatles, John Lennon, George Harrison—
and commencing on May 1, 1979, the Ramones.

Books have been written about Spector's influence, artistic brilliance, and allegedly bizarre behavior. As with everything in his career, his collaboration with the Ramones was fraught with confrontation, controversy, and the stuff of legend. In some ways, it was a marriage made in heaven: the two Walls of Sound meeting at the corner. In other ways it was quite the opposite.

There's the oft-told story of Spector's spending ten hours listening to the opening chord of the re-recorded "Rock 'n' Roll High School" over and over, an understandably unnerving situation for the quick-in, quick-out Johnny. Of course, the idea of a band used to making albums in a day or two hooking up with a guy who might not even finish a single *track* per day must have given someone pause.

"Maybe I didn't think it through quite enough," says Seymour Stein, still smarting over the consequences. "I think it was my idea, but also Joey's. Phil was producing a couple singles for the Paley Brothers, who were signed to Sire at the time, and the Ramones did the song with the Paleys. But all kinds of terrible things happened during the making of the album. Johnny's father died, for one thing. Then he called me up telling me that Phil was treating them badly, making them do twenty-three takes of one little thing. Before, they'd be fighting with each other if they hadn't completed seven songs the first night!"

Joey recalls first meeting Spector after a backing vocal session he did for Rodney Bingenheimer (the Ramones and Bingenheimer performed as

Rodney and the Brunettes; their cover of "Surfin' Safari" was released in 1984 on *Rodney Bingenheimer Presents 'All Year Party' Vol. I*). The track was produced by Dan and David Kessel—the sons of guitarist and Spector session player Barney Kessel—who often acted as Spector's bodyguards. Bingenheimer also brought Spector to see Ramones shows at the Whiskey, where on one occasion Spector invited everyone over to his house, where the hyper-shy and sensitive man who had once been called "the first tycoon of teen" had been keeping a low profile since losing his hitmaking momentum.

At this time, the Ramones, too, were at a standstill. After six years of headbanging, noted Scott Isler in *Trouser Press*, they couldn't even achieve total failure. They were nowhere near the top, nor were they alone at the bottom.

"Do you want to make a good album, or a great album?" the maestro had asked.

"He more or less came out of retirement to produce us," says Joey. "It was the two Walls of Sound coming together, and there was a clash to some degree. But for all the insanity, it was very exciting, *crazy*, but a good feeling to work with Phil."

The recording experience was definitely *unlike* that for any other Ramones album, since Spector's productions were monumental. The Wall of Sound characterized Spector's arranging technique of plastering instruments upon instruments—multiple drums, guitars, basses, vocals, strings, horns, pianos (as many as a dozen squeezed in at a time!)—as if they were bricks; what came back at you was so powerful and dense that it was almost solid, though it was way too artfully structured and controlled to be undistinguishable noise.

The biggest recording problem, aside from personalities—both Spector and the Ramones themselves were virtually immovable objects—was that the Wall took so long to build—and cost so much. "He could never finish anything, so it was the most expensive album we ever made—over two hundred thousand dollars," says Joey. "It took him six months to mix, and finally when he did finish, he wanted to mix some more. He did the same thing with John Lennon on 'Rock 'n' Roll.' He just didn't want to hand over the tapes."

But there were other problems stemming from the fact that everyone involved in the production was tightly wound and tragically insecure.

"We were based in L.A. for a month or more, at the Tropicana, shooting the movie, doing shows when we weren't filming, and rehearsing with Phil. L.A. was a good place to get into trouble, and Dee Dee was really into drugs and he and Phil got into a fight."

Published reports also said that Spector drank a lot, ranted and raved, and lived in quite a house! *Time* magazine did a major story on the making of the album, and described Spector's L.A. mansion as heavily guarded by dogs, electronic devices, and armed watchmen, with a welcome mat out front that said "Get Lost!" (Also like the Ramones, Spector had a wicked sense of humor: He once presented Joey with "a box containing nothing" as a birthday gift, which contained . . . nothing!)

"They checked us for metal and let us in, and Phil made us wait an hour before he made his *entrance*," recalls Vera Ramone. "Al Lewis—Grandpa Munster—was in the living room, drunk as a skunk. We all hung out and Phil orchestrated the whole show, going to the piano to play first and then answer questions. He played the Ronettes over and over again till we couldn't take it anymore.

"It was a funny night. He wouldn't let us go, and we had to stay and watch [the movie] *Magic*. Marky had a Ronettes T-shirt on, and Phil freaked out, since he used to be married to Ronnie of the Ronettes. 'Take my wife off your chest!' It was like he was in control of his territory. His bodyguards were there with their guns, and he wouldn't let us leave. We had to beg him to let us out of the house at 6 A.M.

"He was definitely an eccentric, and Dee Dee was eccentric too, definitely. He made Dee Dee a nervous wreck. As with many talented artists, these people were all borderline personality-wise. It was a fine line of crossing over to almost craziness, but Phil was so up there he was almost like *past* genius."

And Dee Dee, of course, was in *L.A.* "He was always insane when he got to L.A.," Vera adds. "He'd get off the plane and things would *happen*."

What eventually happened was that Dee Dee, who collected knives and liked guns, brought out the guns in Phil. As Marky tells it, "Phil was very intense and prone to tantrums and needed a release, and one night we wanted to leave and Dee Dee was stoned, maybe on Quaaludes, and Phil was high on the booze. Words were said and there was a confrontation and the guns came out, and the bodyguards. But it was really just a bunch of babies in a sandbox, 'My dog's bigger than yours.' We had to put up with a lot with Phil in the seven weeks it took to do that album. We were just coming off *Rock 'n' Roll High School*, and we got there and realized the guy had a drinking problem, and would throw a lot of temper tantrums because maybe he wasn't getting a certain sound and he'd want to listen to it over and over again. And we'd be in the studio until 5 A.M. and the sun was up already and he'd want us back in the studio! But for me and Joey, at least, we really had fun."

It was fun for Marky because he was such a fan of drummer Hal Blaine, who played on most of Phil's sessions, and thought that the drum sound they achieved together was the best ever. For Joey, it was fun because Phil taught him so much about singing, especially the importance of *timing* and of staying on the beat.

For Dee Dee, though, the experience was a dream turned nightmare. He wrote in *Spin* that at the time, he had only enough money to buy "two damn Tuinals and a beer every day," and that Spector's eccentricities—the house arrests, the guns, the repetition in the studio, the uncertainty over which of five studios to go to and when—did him in. "The worst crap I ever wrote went on that album," he said.

But he also told an interviewer that Spector could have done a good job, but the Ramones just wouldn't cooperate.

"Phil was really misinterpreted," says Vera. "He wasn't such a bad guy or crazy like Dee Dee made him out to be, just eccentric. Dee Dee couldn't tolerate a lot of people—if Phil was crazy, Dee Dee was a lot crazier. They did an interview for PBS once after a long drive after a long tour, and they had to do a show after a seven-hour bus ride, after five shows in a row. Dee Dee said some horrible things on film, and I was cringing and giving him the eye, but he wouldn't look at me.

"You know, they would do things to amuse themselves, like pick on Monte, or whatever the thing was at the moment. Johnny egged Dee Dee on and Dee Dee had a big mouth and he went off at Phil on TV. Dee Dee has a wild imagination, to put it mildly, and they all tend to exaggerate. It was just bad timing."

The goal was noble enough: to have a hit record. "[Phil's] intentions were really sincere and honest, and well meaning throughout," says Ed Stasium, credited this time as musical director (Spector brought back his own longtime engineer Larry Levine). "He was one of my idols. He had personality swings and tantrums, but he was always very cordial with me, and even when he kept you in the house, which wasn't that much with me, he loved having you around and entertaining. But when strange people came in he became introverted.

"We'd set up very late at night and he'd work all night getting the sound going. That damn guitar chord in *Rock 'n' Roll High School!* He kept obsessing over it for hours, and Johnny's patience ran out. So we set up a meeting at the hotel, and put everything on the line, and Phil agreed not to torture Johnny anymore."

Now as aggravating as all this may sound, it should be noted that Spector was pretty much following the same procedures that had changed rock 'n' roll history. As his premiere vocalist Darlene Love explained many years later in *EQ* after his classic singles were reissued in the "Back to Mono" boxed set, he really *could* hear anything he was looking for, no matter how many instruments were in the mix, be it one guitar chord or even a single note, at a time when the technology forced him to pile studios full of musicians onto one track.

And on *End of the Century*, the results were immediately striking. After a disc jockey's lead-in "This is rock 'n' roll radio. Let's rock 'n' roll with the Ramones!," the Wall of Sound takes off in all its glory. Massive drums, chiming keyboards and guitars, churning horns, all build tension until Joey comes in on top, "Rock it, rock 'n' roll, radio. Let's go!" and the horns carry it away:

> Do you remember 'Hullaballoo,'
> 'Upbeat,' 'Shindig' and 'Ed Sullivan' too?
> Do you remember rock 'n' roll radio?

> Do you remember lying in bed
> With the covers pulled up over your head?
> Radio playin' so no one can see
> We need change and we need it fast
> Before rock's just part of the past
> 'Cause lately it all sounds the same to me.

Anyone who thought the Ramones records all sounded the same was now given pause. "Danny Says," an ode to the road and Danny Fields's orders to head out to a gig in Idaho, was pure Spector: gorgeous music-box guitars and keyboards, then additional percussion to thicken the Wall almost brick by brick while Joey laments:

> Hangin' out in 100 B
> Watching 'Get Smart' on TV
> Thinkin' about
> You and me and you and me

The choice of song to cover was easy. Spector had originally wanted to make a solo album with Joey, whose voice has a similar quality and presence to that of Ronnie Spector of the Ronettes. Although he preferred that the Ramones sing Darlene Love's "Not Too Young to Get Married," the Ramones went with the Ronettes "Baby, I Love You," though theirs was a rather campy version. "Chinese Rock," one of the great heroin-addiction songs, has also a standout—the Heartbreakers used to sing it, and the Ramones still play it in concert.

> I'm livin' on a Chinese rock
> All my best things are in hock
> I'm livin' on a Chinese rock
> Everything is in the pawn shop.

Other tunes harked back to traditional Ramones themes. "Let's Go" went to war,

> Don't wanna study on the G.I. bill
> Want more action, haven't had my fill
> Mercenary, fight for anyone

Fight for money
Fight for fun

while "All the Way" went both military and mental:

I just wanna have some fun
Before they throw me in the sanitarium . . .

Well Monte's making me crazy
It's just like being in the Navy.

But the Ramones hard-edge musical sound was not glossed over by Spector's production technique. The blazing guitars and hard rock rhythms were still there; Spector just gave them an overall sheen and musicality that were new to the Ramones.

As Johnny told interviewer Joan Tarshis, "The album was heavily produced, but he didn't try to change us or anything. He just produced us the way he produces. The songs were good, but we shouldn't have done 'Baby, I Love you.' That was our idea. We said, 'We're working with Phil Spector, let's do a Phil Spector song.' All of a sudden he starts bringing an orchestra. There was no point in me even playing on it, because if you've got an orchestra, my talent isn't going to be of use."

If nothing else, *End of the Century* was the bestselling Ramones album to date. In *Time*, Jay Cocks wrote, "A producer responsible for some of the greatest vintage rock, Spector put the band through his often intricate, sometimes tortuous studio paces, and came up with an album that smooths the Ramones out without cutting them down. . . . The whole album is the kind of virtuoso feat one expects from Spector, but it is livelier and more intense than anything he's done since his work with John Lennon. For the Ramones, it's both a consolidation and a subtle change-up; a record that proves professionalism does not have to dull the gleaming amateur edge the Ramones like to affect. 'End of the Century' might even help avert the grim destiny that Johnny Ramone, during dark days, can see looming ahead. 'It'd be terrible to spend ten years being a rock 'n' roll star,' he frets, 'and then go out and have to get a job.' "

Rolling Stone's Kurt Loder, noting the fateful inevitability that the Ramones would some day collaborate with the creative force behind so many of their influences, called the album "the most commercially credible album the Ramones have ever made" as well as Spector's finest and most mature effort in years. Although the production relied on heavy overdubbing and guest players like Spector session saxophonist Steve Douglas and former Electric Flag keyboardist Barry Goldberg, Loder felt that Spector had let the Ramones do their thing, "creating a setting that's rich and vibrant and surging with power," while still spotlighting the band rather than Spector himself—as was his practice in the past.

End of the Century, incidentally, was the last album Spector made at the legendary Gold Star Studio, where he had recorded the bulk of his work. It was released in January 1980, with a cover shot of the band in colored T-shirts, no leather. Joey's compositions included "Do You Remember Rock 'n' Roll Radio," "Danny Says," "Affected," and "Rock 'n' Roll High School," while Dee Dee and Johnny wrote "This Ain't Havana" and "Let's Go."

Both "Do You Remember Rock 'n' Roll Radio" and "Baby, I Love You" were released as singles, with the latter becoming a Top 10 hit in England, where the musicians' union rules demanded that any time an orchestrated piece of music was played on television, a live orchestra had to perform on camera. So when the Ramones performed the song on "Top of the Pops," the BBC London Orchestra supported them, in full black tie and tails.

At the end of the year, *End of the Century* made *Time*'s list of best rock albums for 1980. Ironically, Ronnie Spector would soon record the Ramones "Here Today, Gone Tomorrow" on her comeback album. The Ramones were sought to do the backing tracks, but they were busy working with her ex-husband.

As for Phil Spector, he later re-entered the spotlight after taking his rightful place in the Rock 'n' Roll Hall of Fame and releasing his hugely acclaimed boxed set. Those close to him say he is generous, caring, and kind, and Joey has said on numerous occasions that he'd love to work with him again.

Phil Spector with Darlene Love, Joey Ramone, and the Paley Brothers. (Bob Merlis)

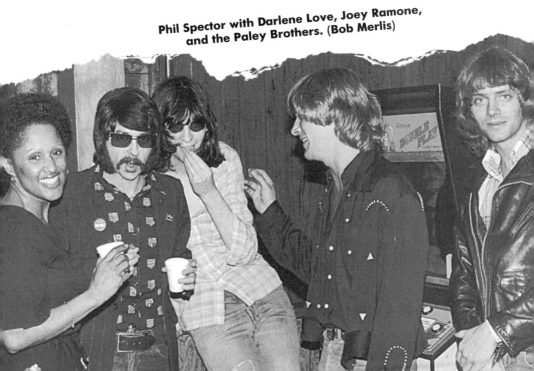

f there were ever a period the Ramones were in the doldrums, this was it. Whatever anyone had thought about "End of the Century," it did mark changes within the band—both musically and in business—not all of them good. Markey was still in, but Danny Fields and Linda Stein were out. Meanwhile, the group members themselves were on the outs.

An early 1981 concert review set forth the situation's underlying vibe. "The Ramones are a one-joke band gone stale," wrote *The New York Times'* Stephen Holden. "This protominimalist quartet, who parody teenage machismo and knowingly manipulate fascist imagery, originally made their mark

A "One-Joke Band

Gone Stale"?

as one of America's first and purest punk bands. But in today's post-punk scene, the Ramones music not only seems anachronistic but unnecessary."

After *End of the Century,* relations between Joey and Johnny grew especially strained. Early on, it was Tommy who felt the original Ramones were *his* concept, *his* myth. His departure had left a vacuum. According to Dee Dee's account in *Spin,* Johnny immediately asserted himself as the new leader, and while the others may have resented it, Dee Dee admitted that he did do things for the band that the others couldn't, such as take care of business and make money. "No manager ever got us more money than Johnny," wrote Dee Dee, also crediting Johnny with helping him get through his weakest and most self-destructive moments. Marky admits to having shared those moments, as both musicians enjoyed drinking and partying to the extreme. "He was about the only person who could drink as much as me," said Dee Dee. "We were like poison for each other." The fantasy of the Ramones as brothers, he added, was exactly that. If anything, they were four angry brothers. But as Danny Fields once said, no matter how they related to one another in private, they kept it from their audiences. The Ramones remained totally professional.

"I don't know if anybody was talking to each other around this time," concedes Johnny. "We had personal differences, but there were artistic differences, too, about what we should be doing, if we should try different

**Poughkeepsie, the night after
Marky joined the band.**

things. Constant complaining: What are we doing wrong? Maybe it's our image. So we took our jackets off on the [cover] picture in *End of the Century,* which I voted against. [There was] every possible reason why things were wrong. But the Ramones do certain things better than anybody, [and I felt] we should stick to what we do best. If we start doing things other bands do well, the other bands do it better. Any speed metal band that starts tomorrow, we can top them. The combination of punk and pop—whatever we play—we do better than anybody. But just pop music, there are other bands that do it better than anybody. But sometimes people get frustrated by lack of success."

This was certainly true of the Ramones. So after the Spector project, the move continued to get the group to make commercial-sounding records. But first, the continued frustration noted by the band brought about a change in management.

"They were a very successful touring band, but the struggle to get a hit record had come to naught," says Fields. "After five years, our contract was up, and they had the option to renegotiate or seek new management—which is what they decided to do, and I can't say I blame them. Five years and still not sold any records, but they'd played all over the world and were famous, but not on the radio."

In 1980, new-wave bands Blondie and the Knack had already had No. I hits, the Cars were currently big, and the Police, Human League, Duran

Duran, and even the Clash were just around the corner to forever bury the new wave by successfully commercializing it.

True, the Ramones finally had graduated from CBGB's, with their last appearance there an April 10, 1979, benefit for the New York City Police bullet-proof vest fund. Their recent New Year's Eve show at the Palladium, preceded by a screening of *Rock 'n' Roll High School*, had sold out and earned them eight thousand dollars—their biggest paycheck to date. They continued touring, with an annual 150-plus concert schedule, yet now they were taken for granted, passed over by the times they themselves had changed.

"They didn't have alternative radio then, so they just fell between the cracks," says Fields. "It was very sad. All they needed was one big hit and they could have sold two million albums. 'Sheena' should have done it. 'Rockaway Beach.' Maybe it wasn't Foreigner or Kenny Loggins, but it wasn't *that* much of a stretch."

At least they were financially independent enough to get their own places: Joey on the Lower East Side; Johnny, on Fourth Avenue; Dee Dee, in Queens; and Marky in Brooklyn. So by the time work began on their next album, Gary Kurfirst was in charge. Another Forest Hills expatriate who was as hardnosed as Fields had been gentle, Kurfirst had promoted bands locally in the 1960s; these included the Ronettes, the Shangri-Las, and the Vagrants, a Forest Hills rock group fronted by Mountain's future guitarist, Leslie West. Kurfirst graduated to bringing to New York such headlining acts as Jimi Hendrix, the Who, and the Yardbirds, staging the 1968 New York Rock Festival in Flushing Meadow Park with Hendrix and the Who, along with the Doors, Janis Joplin, the Vanilla Fudge, the Chambers Brothers, and the Rascals.

Moving into management, Kurfirst counted among his early clients Free, Mitch Ryder, and Peter Tosh, then picked up the CBGB bands Talking Heads, the B-52s, and finally, the Ramones.

"It was right after Spector, and the Ramones were floundering," says Kurfirst. "The other bands that they'd paved the way for were passing them by, so they had to rebuild and try to stay alive."

But Warner Bros., according to Kurfirst, still wanted to make them palatable enough for radio programmers. Seeking "song sensibility" over "energy," 10 cc's Graham Gouldman ("The Things We Do for Love") was brought in to produce the album *Pleasant Dreams*, which commenced March 30, 1981. Joey had wanted the Ramones either to produce themselves or to work with producer Steve Lillywhite, who had produced Johnny Thunders's solo album "So Alone," but the future Psychedelic Furs and U2 producer didn't have a sufficient track record for Sire, and other hard-rock producers like Tom Werman and Ted Templeman were unavailable. Also, Seymour Stein, the renowned song man, favored

Gouldman because of the latter's renowned songwriting skills—he had penned big hits for fellow Brits including the Hollies ("Bus Stop") and the Yardbirds ("For Your Love"). Gouldman had free time, too, since his partner, Eric Stewart, had been laid up by a car wreck.

On *Pleasant Dreams*, Gouldman oversaw the laying of basic tracks (which were cut at Media Sound in New York), contributed harmony ideas, and helped with chord changes. A bass player himself, Gouldman also gave Dee Dee pointers on how to play the instrument melodically.

Joey recorded most of the vocals in England with backup help from Gouldman. Additional vocal support on the Four Seasons–style "Don't Go" came from Russel Mael, of the influential L.A. brother duo Sparks. Joey, who had written much of the early Ramones material, also succeeded in getting individual writing credits—further chipping away at the band's facade of total brotherhood, perhaps, but strengthening each songwriter's personal message.

But by all accounts, compared with Ed Stasium's demos, the finished product lacked Ramones-style aggression and power. Even so, the lead track, "We Want the Airwaves," packed plenty of nasty punch. Of course, the Ramones did have a bone to pick:

> We want the world
> And we want it now
> We're gonna take it, anyhow
> We want the airwaves, baby
> If rock is gonna stay alive

They weren't reminiscing about the glory days of rock 'n' roll radio anymore:

> Where's your guts
> And will to survive
> And don't you wanna
> Keep rock & roll music alive
> Mr. Programmer
> I got my hammer
> And I'm gonna
> Smash my
> Smash my
> Radio

"Airwaves," which Joey wrote, became the first single. Not surprisingly, radio didn't take too kindly to it. The rest of the album, though, showed the kind of pop craftsmanship for which Gouldman was famous.

"The KKK Took My Baby Away" (another Joey-authored radio-unfriendly title, from 1981) was highlighted by background harmonies, as was Joey's "It's Not My Place (in the 9 to 5 World)"—which, aside from great singing (the *Village Voice* saluted Joey's ten-note vault in the chorus), owed much to the Who. Lyrically, it saluted such faves as Phil Spector, Allan Arkush, Lester Bangs, Stephen King, Vin Scelsa, New Jersey TV personality and Ramones supporter Uncle Floyd, and of course, 10 cc. It also featured a very British sounding instrumental break.

Joey's poignant "7–11" and "She's a Sensation" were pure topical ballads, whereas Dee Dee offered an upbeat actioner in the confessional "Come On Now" ("I'm just a comic book boy/ There's nothing scary to enjoy/Freak admission stroll inside/I was born on a roller coaster ride"), also exposing himself in "All's Quiet on the Eastern Front," a song in which a hopped-up city stalker joyfully walks the streets till daybreak.

"Usually my songs are some kind of expression of torment that I may have within me," he told journalist Roy Trakin, adding that since "Rocket to Russia," his songs had shifted from silliness to seriousness in keeping with a growing sense of adulthood.

None of this—neither the lyrics nor the production—represented a change in direction so much as a little veering off the Ramones path. The songs themselves were more ambitious and sophisticated, while the addition of keyboards and vocals made them sound more musical. Still, hardcore fans had to wonder, especially since this was the second consecutive album to show such stylistic growth. And just as some had questioned Spector for softening the Ramones, Gouldman now was criticized for making them sound slick.

After *Pleasant Dreams* was released in July 1981, *Musician*'s reviewer heard the rich harmonies, soaring guitars, and varied rhythm patterns and blamed Gouldman for further "diluting" the Ramones characteristic sound and heightening the impression that the band was "adopting others' styles" rather than broadening their own scope. But *Rolling Stone*, recognizing the group's striving for pop credibility, hailed the "ironically titled impassioned display of irrepressible optimism and high-amp defiance laced with bitterness ... over the corporate sabotage of their rock 'n' roll fantasies."

Holden's *New York Times* counterpart Robert Palmer, meanwhile, suggested that Gouldman had helped the band deliver an album "that *sounds* like a New York version of the Beach Boys"—which was what they likely had wanted to be to begin with. "The tempos are considerably faster, but so is life in the big city. The flavor of the lyrics is more urban, but that is to be expected, too." The *Village Voice* cited accessible melodies as fresh as Buddy Holly's, and Robert Christgau gave it an A-minus.

None of this acclaim made the boys themselves any happier. Says Joey, "As far as the album and songs go it was great, but it was at the time the Clash was happening in the U.S., and the whole new wave scene, and the album was too slick and too polished and lacked aggression. We were years ahead of our time, and now other people were catching up."

"Pleasant Dreams," by the way, was the first Ramones album cover to go without a photo. Instead, it featured a surreal, anxiety-provoking design of a sinister black figure lit up by a spotlight. "We Want the Airwaves," was represented by a promo video shot by N.Y. students mixing footage of airplanes taking off with clips of the Ramones performing in front of the World's Fair globe at Flushing Meadow Park. It also included a rooftop shot of the guys playing with a ball-sized globe and other material taken from shots of them walking about town. The video had a lot of flash cuts and strobe cuts, and wasn't particularly good.

Better were clips promoting two songs from *End of the Century*. "Do You Remember Rock 'n' Roll Radio?" had the Ramones watching themselves perform on TV, the station then switching to show old fifties and sixties rock 'n' roll dance parties, some Buddy Holly footage, and even a Ramones pinhead. A disgusted Johnny eventually sticks his guitar through the TV set.

Rock 'n' Roll High School found the boys—where else?—in detention. After the teacher steps outside, the band goes into the song, with Dee Dee alternately working on a chemistry experiment. Teacher returns just in time to see the result of the experiment blow up: Unfortunately, it was an H-bomb!

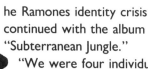

he Ramones identity crisis continued with the album "Subterranean Jungle."

"We were four individuals who were always on the road, always getting into conflicts," says Joey. "And none of us was happy about what was happening. We really wanted to try and get our edge back."

Johnny had also had enough. He had hated the reaction to "Pleasant Dreams" and the direction the band was going, and was afraid the Ramones were losing the respect from fans and critics that they'd worked so hard for over the years. He was on the verge of quitting unless things changed.

If nothing else, though,

We're a Happy

Family?

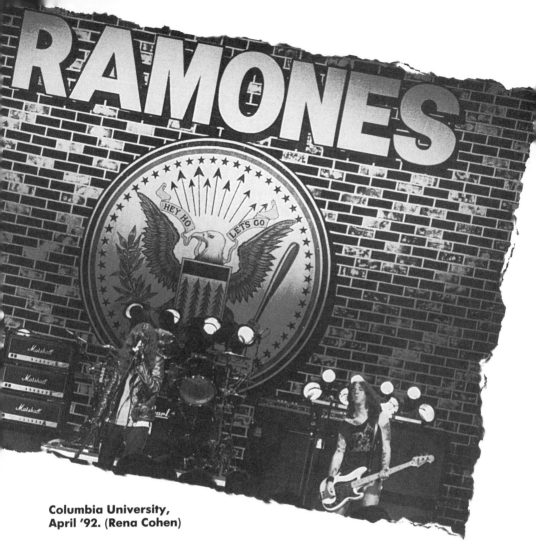

RAMONES

Columbia University, April '92. (Rena Cohen)

Subterranean Jungle would prove a small but necessary step in the right direction. Initially, the Ramones had wanted Joan Jett's manager, Kenny Laguna, to produce it, since they liked the guitar sound on Jett's records. Laguna, though, was more an arranger, and was too busy with Jett, anyway. But he did hook up the Ramones with his close associate Ritchie Cordell, who co-produced Jett's records and had worked on the great sixties pop hits by Tommy James and the Shondells, as well as co-writing and producing the 1910 Fruitgum Company's 1969 bubblegum smash, "Indian Giver." Cordell's partner was Glen Kolotkin, who had worked with Hendrix and had produced the Chambers Brothers 1968 psychedelic counterculture anthem "Time Has Come Today"; more recently, he'd worked with the likes of Greg Kihn and Jonathan Richman.

So with Cordell and Kolotkin at the helm, recording sessions for the Ramones new album began inauspiciously in October 1982, at Kingdom Sound in Syosset, Long Island, about a month after the Ramones headed the punk rock segment of the US Festival in California, performing before 300,000 people with the likes of Talking Heads, the Police, and Gang of Four. Cordell recalled that the Ramones verbally attacked him as soon as he walked in, and that he was so upset after fifteen minutes that he tried to leave—and walked into a closet. And when *Subterranean Jungle* was released in 1983, its lead track could easily have given Ramones fans even more room for doubt.

"Little Bit O'Soul" covered the 1967 smash by the Music Explosion. While the song was quite well done, and sounded more bare-knuckled than the preceding productions, this was the first time the Ramones had opened an album with a cover; in fact, they didn't even *have* one on their last album. To further muddy the picture, the next song, "I Need Your Love," was *also* a cover, by the local band The Boyfriends. There was even a third cover later on side two, though "Time Has Come Today" was a more sensible choice.

But the first song on side two was a true Ramones classic—the first in what seemed like a long time. "Psycho Therapy" was written by Dee Dee and Johnny, who hadn't written anything on "Pleasant Dreams."

> Psycho Therapy
> Psycho Therapy
> Psycho Therapy
> That's what they wanna give me
> All they wanna give me
>
> I am a teenage schizoid
> The one your parents despise
> Psycho Therapy
> Now I got glowing eyes
>
> I am a teenage schizoid
> Pranks and muggings are fun
> Psycho Therapy
> Gonna kill someone

No surprise—no airplay. But this time, the Ramones cared more about regaining lost momentum than pleasing deejays, especially now that young upstart hardcore metal bands were muscling in on Ramones territory. Johnny, for one, definitely wanted to show the kids that even now, nobody played faster than the Ramones.

The playing, actually, was *Subterranean Jungle*'s strongest suit. Cordell and Kolotkin succeeded in reviving the Ramones guitar bite, doubling the guitars for a thicker sound that didn't greatly distort it (Walter Lure of the Heartbreakers was guest second guitarist). The guitars on "Psycho

Therapy," for instance, sound terrific, especially beneath Joey's jolting repetition of the title. And the overall energy level was noticeably up.

Another high point was Dee Dee's alienated "Outsider," which was at once tuneful and disturbing, with Dee Dee singing a chorus as well as writing the song. Joey's "My-My Kind of A Girl" offered a nice bubblegum flavor to the tale of a new girl, this time standing by the juke box ("And this time I think it's forever/I hope your parents understand"). Dee Dee's "In the Park," meanwhile, perfectly captured the summer spirit ("Music playin' that portable sound/Everybody's hangin' all around"), though he followed it with the total fallout of "Time Bomb": "Gonna kill my mom and dad/I won't be sad about it/'Cause they treat me so bad. . . . Everybody, everywhere/You can all go to hell."

The album ended with Joey's "Everytime I Eat Vegetables It Makes Me Think of You." The joke was that the girl ("you") in question had been institutionalized and had become a "vegetable"—a "head of lettuce" to be exact: "She eats Thorazine in her farina."

Subterranean Jungle came out in February 1983, bearing a great cover design featuring photos of the band inside a graffitied subway car. Photography was by George Du Bose, who has designed and/or photographed all subsequent Ramones album covers.

Once again, the big critics came through. In *Musician*, Roy Trakin called the album "the missing link" between heavy metal and the Archies ultimate bubblegum hit, "Sugar Sugar." Kurt Loder's four-star review in *Rolling Stone* correctly recognized the beauty in the lyrics to "My-My Kind of A Girl": "When I saw you by the Peppermint Lounge/You were lost but you've been found, baby."

"*Subterranean Jungle* had some good things," says Johnny, grouping it with its two predecessors. "Basically, it was a good LP—but not good for the *Ramones*."

There were two videos from the album. *Psycho Therapy* was set in an insane asylum (obviously), where the Ramones feigned mental illness to the hilt, playing air guitars and drums, with Joey singing into a live snake "microphone" as a little girl with bandages around her neck looks at him blankly. There was a remarkable lobotomy scene (predictably) wherein the patient gets his head cut open and another grotesque head emerges "Alien"-like—you know, the bad alter ego. It was so realistic, in fact, that MTV demanded it be trimmed, along with a scene where the patient kicks his psychiatrist after hallucinating that the shrink is a cigarette-smoking skull.

The *Time Has Come Today* video was also well done, set in an old church, with everybody in the packed pews—even the red-robed boys' choir—rockin' and thrusting their fists in the air to every chant of "Time!"

There were also two other Ramones recordings of note that appeared around this time. "Chop Suey," which was written in the B-52s mode (and featured that band's girl singers, Kate Pierson and Cindy Wilson, as the B-52s, too, were managed by Gary Kurfirst), appeared on the soundtrack to "Get Crazy," Allan Arkush's 1983 follow-up to *Rock 'n' Roll High School.* And in mid-1982, Joey joined Holly Beth Vincent, lead singer of Holly and the Italians, in a duet of Sonny and Cher's classic, "I Got You, Babe" (he also sang backup on the band's album track "We Danced"). Reviewing it in *Trouser Press,* Jim Green called the duet "charming in a cloddish way ... It's a treat to hear Joey take on such fluffy pop—he should croon more often."

After "Subterranean Jungle" was released, the Ramones renegotiated their Sire contract to ensure that they took control over their destiny, gaining promises that things would be different in the future. That changes *would* be made was readily apparent with the album's release, when Marky Ramone became the second Ramones drummer to leave. Dee Dee's drug problems were severe enough, but Marky's drinking had become intolerable.

The incident which precipitated his dismissal was his arrest after passing out early one morning on Flatbush Avenue in Brooklyn, slumped over the wheel as he was trying to drive home.

"At one point I even missed a show," says Marky. "We were in Cleveland, and I stayed an extra night with a friend and woke up the next day partied out. We had to play that night in Virginia Beach, but I started drinking that day and hung out at the Holiday Inn with Roger Maris. I'm not really a baseball fan, but I liked Roger Maris because I had his model glove when I was ten years old. He was dying of cancer, then, and drinking and talking about this and that, and I got his autograph and got bombed. After that I was supposed to get to the airport and I was already late and they wondered where the hell I was. So I was going to rent a private plane, and they wouldn't take me because I was too drunk, and I missed the show. The crowd went crazy and wrecked the place, so we had to make it up a month or two later. That's one of the things alcohol was doing to me."

During the *Subterranean Jungle* sessions, the rest of the band had already begun thinking about finding a new drummer. They tried out Heartbreakers drummer Billy Rogers, who played on "Time Has Come Today," the only album track Marky didn't complete, but he didn't work out in the long run. The one who did was Richie Reinhardt, also known as Richie Beau, who had played in local bands (most notably Velveteen). He became Richie Ramone at a gig in Utica, New York, on February 13, 1983—in time to appear in both the videos from *Subterranean Jungle.*

Things then proceeded smoothly enough until August, when, as an August 15 tabloid headline screamed, "Battered Punk Star Fights for His Life." The report said that Johnny and another punk musician, Sub Zero Construction's Seth Macklin, had gotten into a brawl over a girl at 4 A.M.

Johnny remembers seeing the girl drunk and offering assistance, and very little else. "I got hit when I wasn't looking and woke up in the hospital. They said I'd been kicked in the head, but I never saw what happened or what led up to it. The kid got arrested and went to jail."

Johnny was critically injured with a fractured skull and underwent brain surgery. He returned with his hair shorn (he had to wear a baseball cap for a couple of months) but with his determination intact.

"After 'End of the Century,' sometimes nobody was talking to each other," he says. "It was our middle period and nobody got along, which happens to a lot of bands. You know, *egos*. It goes to your head. Maybe we were touring too much. But you look at it as a *job*. You're not doing anything of *importance*. Think how lucky you are instead of everything that's owed to you, everything that's wrong. We don't play music for everybody! I saw the Cars come out and they got big, and they were a bunch of wimps! It had nothing to do with us! Now if the Sex Pistols became big in the U.S. and we didn't, *that* would be frustrating. But it didn't happen, and if they were we would become big, too, because punk rock would become big.

"Then, with *Subterranean Jungle*, we started coming back together. We realized we had to play harder material, because that's what we do best. That's what the fans want. When we started recording the next album people were getting better. Everybody became friendly again. Bringing girls on the road was often a problem [however]: You bring your girlfriends, they never get along with each other, they're always trying to give their boyfriend advice: 'Why don't you do this? Why don't you do that? It's your manager's fault.' I go after a *fan* for advice [rather] than ask a girlfriend! So we tried to discourage it. Now we still have personal differences, but we're able to work through them usually. It might last a day or two instead of dwindling for a year!"

For his part, Joey took a more active role in getting the band back on track. "I made sure that from now on I had total control over anything that concerned me personally. A lot of people started giving up on us, but 'Too Tough to Die' reinstated us and put us back on top."

The Ramones next studio album, *Too Tough to Die*, was recorded in the summer of 1984 at Media Sound, with T. Erdelyi and Ed Stasium back at the production helm. When Dee Dee launched the opening track, "Mama's Boy," with an old-fashioned "One-two-three-four!," it was instantly clear that the Ramones had returned to punk basics. Not that it was necessarily harder and faster, just *tougher*. The guitars (again buttressed by Walter Lure) simmered and threatened, and the subject matter took on a decidedly serious tone. While "Mama's Boy" (written by Johnny, Dee Dee, and Erdelyi) was traditional, with its scolding lines such as "You couldn't shut up, got a bad bad brain," the next song, Dee Dee's "I am Not Afraid of Life," was totally un-Dee Dee-like:

There's the threat of the nuclear bomb
We know it's wrong
We know it's wrong
Is there a chance for peace
Will the fighting ever cease
Mankind's almost out of luck
A maniac could blow us up

The world had changed a lot since *Road to Ruin*—the last time the Ramones had sounded so lean and mean. Aside from their return to the musical essentials, then, the Ramones now revealed a surprising awareness of the politically and environmentally deteriorating state of the planet. After all, these were the guys who claimed that kids didn't care about politics, who said that if they wanted to spread a message, they'd have had Joan Baez open for them.

Another surprise was that most of the songs were Dee Dee's. His "Planet Earth 1988" was especially pessimistic:

The solution to peace isn't clear
The terrorist threat is a modern fear
There are no jobs for the young
They turn to crime turn to drugs
Battle ships crowd the sea
Sixteen-year-olds in the army
Our jails are filled to the max
Discrimination against the blacks

"Danger Zone," which Dee Dee co-wrote with Johnny, had a similar message:

New York City is a real cool town
Society really brings me down
Our playground is a pharmacy
Kids find trouble so easily

Even Richie got into the act. His sole songwriting credit, "Human Kind," was a straight-ahead rocker which questioned why people were so rotten. It was like the Ramones had suddenly grown up. And in "Durango," they even had their first instrumental!

There were other highlights. Dee Dee's and Johnny's thrashing "Wart Hog"—the lyrics of which the record company deemed too offensive to be included on the album sleeve—remains a concert favorite:

I shot some dope
I feel so sick
It's a sick world, sick sick sick
Drugs and bitches and junkies and fags
Artificial phonies, I hate it, hate it
Wart hog, wart hog

Joey's and Dee Dee's forceful declaration of independence "Chasing the Night" ("Live my life as I choose/I paid the price, paid my dues/You know I need no alibi") was set to the music of Talking Heads sideman Busta Jones, with Head Jerry Harrison pitching in on keyboards.

There was one outside production on the album, "Howling at the Moon (Sha-La-La)," which was produced by David A. Stewart of the group Eurythmics, another Kurfirst client. Also written by Dee Dee, this ambitious tune had a Robin Hood "steal from the rich and give to the poor" theme, and featured keyboards by Ben Tench of Tom Petty and the Heartbreakers. It was also made into a concept video, centering around a modern-day Robin Hood who gives away unusual merchandise to the needy. For example, a baby in a carriage was handed over to a pair of punk chicks, and the Ramones themselves were delivered in a crate to a rich elderly lady.

Released in October 1984, *Too Tough to Die* featured a cover shot outlining the quartet at the end of a dark tunnel. Its musical contents were celebrated along with the Ramones tenth anniversary.

Jim Farber in *The New York Daily News* hailed it as the band's most thrill-filled album since *Road to Ruin*, as well as one of the most high-charged albums of the year. *Rolling Stone*'s Kurt Loder called it both "an exhilarating summation of all they do so well" and a "significant step forward for this great American band." In *Creem*, Billy Altman said the album "reaffirmed their faith in the almighty power chord crunch," and rationalized away the long interval between it and "Road to Ruin": "That it took them four albums and almost six years to finally make the spiritual followup . . . because the world kept telling them that they had to try to 'fit in' better if they wanted to survive is, ultimately, just so much glue under the bridge. . . . We are speaking, after all, of probably THE MOST INFLUENTIAL ROCK 'N' ROLL BAND OF THE LAST TEN YEARS."

In 1984, ten years after it had all started, people were again predicting that the Ramones were going to make it. That year they played in Europe before a quarter of a million people in Amsterdam Park.

he Ramones new interest in world
issues reached its zenith in mid-
1985, when Joey, Dee Dee, and
former Plasmatics bassist Jean
Beauvoir wrote and recorded
"Bonzo Goes to Bitburg" as a
protest against President Reagan's
controversial wreath-laying
ceremony at a German cemetary
which contained the graves of Nazi
storm troopers. The Mohawk-
topped Beauvoir, a member of
Little Steven and the Disciples of
Soul, produced the song for rush-
release as a U.K. single; Little
Steven, once Bruce Springsteen's
guitarist, was so impressed that he
enlisted Joey to join Springsteen
and some fifty other musicians in
Artists United Against Apartheid,

"Ramones Aid"

**Publicity photo with
new but short-lived
band member Clem Burke.**

which recorded an album. Joey even got to sing a line *solo* on the single "Sun City," and joined in the chorus alongside such fellow legends as Bob Dylan and Miles Davis.

As for "Bonzo," remember that this was a basically apolitical band that not only peppered their early albums with admittedly jokey Nazi references, but some band members were for the most part much closer to Reagan-style conservativism than anything else.

> You're a politician
> Don't become one of Hitler's children
> Bonzo goes to Bitburg then goes out for a cup of tea
> As I watched it on TV somehow it really bothered me
> My brain is hanging upside down

"What Reagan did was fucked up," Joey told a reporter. "Everyone told him not to go . . . and he went anyway. It embarrassed America, and it was a real slap in the face. How can you fuckin' forgive the Holocaust? How can you say, 'Oh well, it's okay now?' That's crazy."

The import twelve-inch single, by the way, had a couple of non-LP

"Ramones Aid"

B-sides, including "Go Home Ann," which was mixed by Lemmy of Motorhead.

"Bonzo" was retitled "My Brain is Hanging Upside Down" when it appeared on the next Ramones album, "Animal Boy," which Beauvoir produced in December 1985 at Intergalactic Studios in New York. Joey wrote only two other songs on that album, including "Mental Hell," which summed up all the bad feelings he had held about the band during its most miserable period. Things had gotten so bad, he said, that he had thought of quitting, or at the very least, doing a solo album. After making "Animal Boy," however, he was confident that the worst times were over.

"What this band is all about goes beyond your own personal things," he told *East Coast Rocker*. "When we go out and play live, that's when you see it. It feels like we're *the best*; it's so exciting, and it topples all the other obstacles. We can hate each other's guts, but we go out there and we play as a unit, and it's fucking *great*. Were a band, and we're united and everything else just seems small."

"Animal Boy" opened with Richie's second Ramones composition, "Somebody Put Something in My Drink." The throbbing, hard-guitar rocker was inspired by a true incident, when someone slipped some acid into Richie's Tanqueray gin and tonic at a club, and he freaked out so badly he was taken away in a strait jacket. That's why the Ramones insist on canned soda in their dressing room!

The title track followed, and, after "Bonzo," is probably the second-most noteworthy song on the album. Another power-chord cruncher, the Dee Dee/Johnny copyright pointedly captured the alienation theme forever at the core of the Ramones reason for being.

> I'm not an imbecile
> Don't treat me like an animal
> I'm not a creature in the zoo
> Don't tell me what to do
>
> You don't know what it's like
> You don't know how I feel
> I don't have a monkey's brain
> I'm not an animal

Dee Dee also wrote "Apeman Hop," but that was more a cretin-hoppy tune about a "missing link" who didn't have much fun living in the jungle. His thrashing "Love Kills," though, was a tribute to his late friend Sid Vicious, and was written for the movie "Sid and Nancy," though it

Columbia University, April '92, pulling out all the stops. (Rena Cohen)

wasn't used. But "She Belongs to Me," which Dee Dee co-wrote with Beauvoir, was an almost lush, surprisingly pretty ballad; their "Something to Believe In" collaboration was Spector-like in its orchestration, especially the glistening keyboards which opened the very moving song:

> I wish I was someone else
> I'm confused I'm afraid I hate the loneliness
> And there's nowhere to run to
> Nothing makes any sense but I still try my hardest
> Take my hand
> Please help a man
> Because I'm looking for something to believe in
> And I don't know where to start

"Something to Believe In," which closed the album, was also made into a spectacular video. Spoofing all the superstar "cause" collaborations like "We Are the World" and "Live Aid," the video began with spokesman Ken Senomar (spell it backwards!), explaining what "Ramones Aid" was all about. "It's about people—people who care. We think the time has come for caring people who care about people to stand up and be counted. The Ramones are standing tall for every cause, so please, reach deep into your hearts and deep into your pockets. Let's make this the most significant event of the eighties."

The rest of the clip was a splendidly silly takeoff on "Hands Across America": There were a "Hands Across Your Face" banner, Michael Jackson and Lionel Richie lookalikes, a celebrity studio singalong, a chain of people holding hands with the Statue of Liberty in the background, guys holding hands at urinals, Monte Melnick handcuffed to a cop as they are swaying and singing together, and a little girl pleading, "Won't you please lend a hand?" Even a skeleton and a guy with a hook participated! "Ramones Aid. Let's make it a reality," concluded Senomar. "Senomar" was really music business attorney Elliot Hoffman, who was joined in the effort by a host of notables: the B-52s, Afrika Bambaataa, Toni Basil, Berlin, Rodney Bingenheimer, Cheap Trick's Tom Petersson, Fisher and Preachman (the clip's directors), Holly Beth Vincent, ex-Plasmatics member Richie Stotts, Ted Nugent, Penn and Teller, the Rattlers (which was Joey's brother Mickey Leigh's band, most notably, guest backing vocals on the single "On the Beach"), Sparks, Spinal Tap, Gary U.S. Bonds, Mary Waronov (who gave back five dollars she owed Joey), X, Weird Al Yankovic, Fishbone, and the Circle Jerks.

Animal Boy came out in May 1986, with a front cover photo, appropriately enough, picturing the the band standing in front of an occupied gorilla cage, with Richie holding a chimp. Noting the album's more serious tone, *The New York Times'* Jon Pareles picked it as "rock album of the week." He wrote, "They speak up for outcasts and disturbed individuals ... and worry about drug users and politics.... Whether or not they sneak into the Top 40, the Ramones aren't geared to sell out." But the *Village Voice*'s Robert Christgau felt the songs were "too defensive," and that the album was "ominously hit or miss" compared with the "consistency that has made them great."

For Christgau, unfortunately, the next Ramones album *Halfway to Sanity* lived up to the "ominous" quality he found in "Animal Boy." "It kills me to say this," he wrote upon "Sanity" 's September 1987 release, "but a great band has finally worn down into a day job for night people."

But others saw it differently, especially the Ramones. Joey thought *Sanity* was their best album ever, while Johnny said it was the best one since *Rocket to Russia.* This second school of thought held that *Halfway to Sanity* reflected the band's early days, as it was full of fresh, exciting hardcore hard rock. And it reinforced a renewed sense of unity in that it was produced by the band themselves, along with guitarist/songwriter Daniel Rey.

Rey's is another typical Ramones fan's story. A teenager in Red Bank, New Jersey, when *Ramones* came out, Rey and his pals would get together every Friday night at one of their homes for a "listening party," as one of the guys worked at a record store and would bring over some new releases. "I was fourteen and into the MC5 and the Stooges, and one day my friend came home with a stack of albums—Uriah Heep, Head East, REO Speedwagon, Dictators' 'Go Girl Crazy,' and stuck in there was the Ramones album. We looked at the cover in awe and amazement and put it on—and took it off and started laughing! No leads, no solos, it all sounded the same—like New York Dolls sped up. So we listened to some other stuff, and then put *Ramones* back on—and laughed *again.* But by the following weekend, we couldn't listen to anything else! In the course of a week, two-thirds of my album collection became obsolete!"

Discovering the CBGB's scene, Rey started hanging out there and got to know the band. He also became a member of Shrapnel, a punk band which was managed by *Punk*'s Legs McNeil and which eventually opened for the Ramones dozens of times over the next few years. During this time Rey became friendly with Joey and assisted him with songwriting. He also produced numerous demos for New Jersey punk bands, which impressed Johnny.

Rey says, "He figured he could save money by getting a young kid to produce instead of spending twenty thousand dollars on a big-name producer. But that's how he is—very thrifty and pragmatic. He keeps things simple and doesn't let costs get out of hand, and stays loyal to what Ramones fans would think."

Rey also became Dee Dee's writing partner, and the two co-wrote *Halfway to Sanity*'s lead track, "I Wanna Live"—another hard-edged kickoff, about doing what you gotta do. Their other collaboration on the album, "Garden of Serenity," surrealistically explored Dee Dee's demon world:

> Meet me in the graveyard
> We'll walk among the dead
> On a midnight odyssey
> Riding in my head
> In the garden of serenity

Both songs showcased a stripped-down guitar sound that was at once crystal clear and completely commanding. The rest of the album followed suit. Dee Dee's and Johnny's power-chord rocker "Bop 'Til You Drop" was a little on the down side:

> You tried and tried
> But you're a flop
> You're thirty-five
> Still pushing a mop
> No time to cop
> Do the cretin hop
> Bop 'til you drop

So was their pounding "Weasel Face" (about a lonely guy whose only friend is his TV set; Dee Dee said it was written after the van hit a weasel on the road in Louisiana!), and the self-explanatory "I Lost My Mind." Dee Dee's "Worm Man" portrayed another pitiful, self-hating character, but his "Go Lil' Camaro Go" took a 180-degree turn. Another perfect summer song, the upbeat rocker promised "Girls cars sun fun/Good times for everyone," and featured the singing of fellow Gary Kurfirst client Deborah Harry, to boot!

Joey, meanwhile, offered his own Beach Boys-style rock 'n' roller on "A Real Cool Time," a song about meeting a girl at the Cat Club, New York's heavy-metal headquarters, where Joey frequently spun records and presented new-band showcase extravaganzas that featured celebrities and offbeat events in addition to music. His "Bye Bye Baby" was of epic length (4:33!) and was full of classic Spector touches.

Richie wrote two songs this time. "I'm Not Jesus" was a hardcore rocker using Christian metaphors to state the obvious, and "I Know Better Now" expressed bitterness over being forced to conform to parental rules. That Richie had outgrown the authority of the *Ramones* was made shockingly clear when he bolted from the band without warning.

"Things were going fine, then all of a sudden he left his old girlfriend and found a new one and right away got married," recalls Johnny. "She tells him he should be paid more than the rest of the Ramones, his wife shows up in a limo outside the show and tells Monte he's quitting, and he just left. He heard we threw him out anyway, which wasn't true."

Not surprisingly, none of the remaining Ramones speak favorably of Richie, who in fact split after an August 12 gig in East Hampton, right before a series of important shows connected with the new album's release. For their part, neither Richie—now a golf caddy in L.A.—nor his wife will say *anything*. "After he got married he had a total different personality," says Monte Melnick.

Joey told *Creem* that Richie wanted a pay raise, but instead of bringing it up with the band, he went to management directly. "I just felt screwed," said Joey. "It was the way he went about it. . . . Now, me and Richie were friends, which is why I have mixed feelings about this. He was more than just the drummer in the band. But he was just out for himself. He said he would do the New York shows for five hundred dollars a night. I'm sure he felt he had us by the balls—our album was coming and there was a lot of press coming."

A pair of important dates at the Ritz had to be postponed, but the Ramones neither caved in to Richie's demands nor buckled under the pressure of not having a drummer on the eve of a new album. Within twenty-four hours they tapped Clem Burke, formerly of Blondie and Chequered Past, and his first gig with the band was on August 28 at The Living Room in Providence, Rhode Island. But Burke, who was all set to become *Elvis* Ramone, only lasted two shows before bowing out due to "personality differences."

"The two shows with Clem were a disaster," says Johnny. "He was interested, but his drumming style wasn't right. It was very loose, like in Blondie, not as rigid as we need. Double time on the high-hat was totally alien to him. Then all of a sudden Marky comes back, which was enough to make you start doubting yourself and think of giving up! But I heard he hadn't been drinking, and it was better to get an old Ramone back in for the fans to relate to."

Sure enough, Marky, gone since 1983 because of his alcohol problem, *had* quit drinking. "Don't get me wrong!" says Marky. "I believe people should party till they drop—unless they have a problem. I'd been a binge drinker for maybe a week at a time, since I was twenty, twenty-one. But it started getting bad at the end, and after eighty-three, I put myself through detox three times. It started taking over me, and I didn't want my life and career to end so I decided to stop and get better and I've stopped for nine years so far and I feel great. Being straight is so much better: For eighty minutes you have to play sixteenth notes constantly on the high-hat and be ready for the 'One-two-three-four!' counts that the bass player screams out, and it's all playing—not a lot of conversing. And I party better now because I remember what I did, which, for a decade, was like the twilight zone."

Besides drying out, Marky had spent his time away in Richie Stotts's heavy-metal band King Flux, and, when they couldn't get a record deal, in his own band, M-80. Returning to the Ramones fold, he barely skipped a beat. "We set up rehearsal with me and Mark to see how Mark was," continues Johnny. "One song and it sounded just like the Ramones were supposed to sound. I called Joey and said 'Mark's great!' and he agreed. Less than a week after Clem, Marky was back in the band. It took him five days to get ready, without cancelling any shows."

Monte Melnick originally had his doubts as well. "It's hard to believe anybody can turn his life around, but Marky was like another person. He [had] had a tremendous drinking problem. I saw him drink sixteen double martinis in Cleveland, then the next day he was doing interviews and every ten minutes he had to stop and throw up! So I really give him credit. Clem was great. He had Continental tastes, but I think he secretly always wanted to be in the band. But it didn't work out. People think anybody can play these fucking songs because they're just three chords, but no way! It's a technical thing."

Marky analyzed his musical objectives for Rick Johnson in *The Record Exchange Music Monitor*: "Tommy was good and everything, but that was the best that he could do. Richie was very jazz. Too many jazz drum fills. It was ridiculous. I mean, this isn't a heavy-metal band. I could put fills all over the place if I wanted to. But you've got to put them in the right place. The roll in 'Sedated' after the guitar break, the little roll there, it's short and sweet, but it's to the point. It's not there because it's a roll, its there to link the end of the break to the next part of the song.

"You just do it. You go up there and say to yourself, What has to be done to make this song the way it should be? You've got to look at everything and see what fits the best. No matter what you're playing— the high-hat, the bass, the snare, cymbal crashers. And once you realize that, that you're not playing for yourself, that you're playing for the whole band, then you can really do the best you can."

One of Richie's complaints about playing with the Ramones had been that they only had two tempos: fast and faster. "Yeah, it's fast," Marky once said, pointing to the relentless pace of New York City. "That's part of the deal." What did Richie want to play? asked Joey rhetorically. Mambo music or *swing*?

Now, with Marky back behind the skins, the question of filling the Ramones drum slot was put to rest.

ichie Ramone had at least made the cover photo of *Halfway to Sanity*, standing with the band in front of a Chinese establishment, a "Born American" sticker aptly fixed just to the right of Dee Dee. Christgaus' complaints notwithstanding, the critical consensus supported the Ramones contention that it was their best since *Rocket to Russia* or *Road to Ruin*. *Stereo Review* said that besides the usual Ramones pleasures, the album offered a couple of new wrinkles, the most startling of which was Joey's deepened vocal: "His endearing nasal whine has mutated into a creepy bullfrog baritone [at times sounding like] Mick Jagger doing his imitation of an eighty-year-old

Like Fleetwood Mac—Or Something

**It never stops or varies,
but why mess with a good thing? (Ian Harper)**

sharecropper." The band as a whole, the review stated, clung to adolescence with such determination that the Beach Boys looked mature.

Billboard recognized Joey's new lyrical ambitions next to Dee Dee's suitably cretinous tunes, but criticized Sire for not releasing "Go Lil' Camaro Go" as a sure-shot summer single. Surprised by the album's freshness and maturity, *The New York Post* exulted: "Our boys may be halfway to sanity, but they've definitely crossed the line in turning out another great album"—one which made numerous Top 10 critics' lists at the end of the year.

"Justice is finally being served," Joey told *New Times*. "For a long time we got fucked, but things are happening. I mean, I'm proud of everything we've been through. But this is justice. We're fourteen years old as of February. Man, it's like we were Fleetwood Mac or something. . . . Hey, a lot of the initial people got old on us . . . [but] the best are still here. The Ramones are still here."

In *The New Paper*, he explained that the years of rivalry and jealousy and infighting had come to a head during the "Animal Boy" tour, and it was then that the band had resolved, *successfully,* to set aside their differences. There was a new communication now, even a looseness backstage that was making things fun again.

That the band was in top form was further evidenced by the "I Wanna Live" video—which admittedly was based on Bon Jovi's on-tour video "Wanted Dead or Alive," and was shot during a performance at the Ritz. To obtain novel concert shots, a camera was wrapped in foam and thrown into the audience to approximate the point-of-view of a kid diving off the stage. Another shot had the crowd passing director Preacher Ewing back hand-over-hand from the stage as he filmed. Down in the "mosh pit," the directors physically had to push slam-dancing kids away from a camerawoman. Up in the balcony, a "Thrill Cam" slid down a rope extending to Joey's stage microphone, while another shot used a camera rig made to look like a guitar, so that Johnny could "strum" it while the camera shot footage through the strings and out into the audience. Additional material included a shot of the illuminated billboard in Times Square flashing "We Love the Ramones" and their full names, followed by "No Melnicks."

Actual album tour highlights included a sellout in Paris, where fire marshalls limited admittance to 2,000 riot police tear-gassed the rock-throwing fans who couldn't get in. But a concert at which the Ramones *didn't* play caused an even bigger incident, when the Boston University Concert Committee's request for a November Ramones concert was turned down by the school's administration. Among the reasons given were that the proposed venue only held one thousand fans, and that the Ramones "attract a particular audience and atmosphere" prone to "inappropriate behavior" including "rowdiness, destructiveness (both on a personal level to the individual audience participant and to the facility), and drug use."

In response, the University's Program Council and Civil Liberties Union staged an anticensorship rally at Marsh Plaza, at which Joey and Marky addressed a crowd of over one thousand people (the largest group assembled there in eight years) before leading a march to the Student Activities Office.

"We're here to uphold the honor of the students and the Ramones," said Joey. "We've played all kinds of colleges, major colleges ... small rooms, student unions as well as larger situations without ever any incidents, without ever any brutalities. We've always been asked back...." Said Marky, "B.U. students aren't kids anymore, that's why they're in college. If they're old enough to get dressed, then they're old enough to see our concert."

The Ramones were then made honorary B.U. students, and the protest organizers were made honorary Ramones. That night, the band played a club gig at the Metro in Boston.

Also in late 1987 came the first recording since Marky rejoined the band, Joey's "Merry Christmas (I Don't Want to Fight Tonight)," which was a British B-side to "I Wanna Live" and an entry on the Warner Bros. "Yulesville" Christmas promo album. A Christmas present to a girlfriend, the song and its production were straight out of Spector, with wonderful lyrics like "Where is Rudolph, where is Blitzen, baby?" and "All the children tucked in their beds/Sugar plum fairies dancing in their heads/ Snowball fightin'/So excitin', baby."

Dee Dee's first solo record was also released at this time: the rap twelve-inch-single "Funky Man," on Rock Hotel Records. A sample:

> For the last ten years I been doin' 'the Bop'
> I'm still not tired, I'm never gonna stop
> I like what I'm doin,' I'm having fun
> Here's some advice for everyone
> Try to make the most outta every day
> And remember that drugs don't pay

The punk-rap attempt was accompanied by a video, which opened with a shot of Dee Dee and Vera in bed, then cut to a neat "scratch" of subway doors opening; out bounds Dee Dee to traipse around Greenwich Village with his disciples, affecting a tongue-in-cheek rapper macho swagger. It's pretty much a fun piece of fluff.

Dee Dee said at the time that he was listening mostly to rap, his faves including L.L. Cool J., Doug E. Fresh, Whodini, Run-DMC, and the Beastie Boys, though he also cited hard rock/punk bands like X, Chesterfield Kings (for whom he wrote material), and Suicidal Tendencies, whose rap-like "Institutionalized" inspired "Funky Man." Drawing similarities between rap and punk, he told *The Miami News*, "they're both a rebellious type of music of the streets." Rodney Dangerfield's "Rappin' Rodney" parody also influenced both the record and the accompanying video.

At an AIDS benefit in mid-December, Joey joined Deborah Harry's group Tiger Balm in singing three Ramones songs, including "Go Lil' Camaro Go."

In May 1988, more than fourteen years after it all started, Sire released "Ramones Mania," a compilation of the greatest Ramones non-hits and rarities, which proved for anyone still in need the diversity and range of this so-called one-joke wonder. The thirty tracks included the single versions of "Sheena Is a Punk Rocker," "Needles and Pins," and "Howling at the Moon (Sha-La-La)"; the previously unreleased stereo movie mix of *Rock 'n' Roll High School*; and the respectful cover of "Indian Giver" which had been released only as a British B-side. Billy Altman wrote extensive liner notes for the collection, and its cover collage featured old

Ramones album covers and memorabilia, including the miniature baseball bat from the group's first album and the combination pen knife/letter opener *tshatshka* from the second album. "I Wanna Be Sedated" was then released as a single, backed by a fabulous "Ramones-on-45 Mega-Mix" of "Sedated" and several other Ramones faves intermixed with the classic "Hey, ho! Let's go!" chant.

A remarkable "Sedated" video was also filmed, setting the boys at a breakfast table at the end of a hallway in what looks to be an insane asylum. Essentially done in a single take, the clip has the Ramones appearing in real time, pouring cereal while Joey sings. But the action around and behind them is filmed in double-time with all sorts of energetic oddballs entering in and out of the frame—including an abducted nun, a bride, a man walking on his hands, a ballerina, a bagpiper, a pinhead, a unicyclist, a video cameraman, and Monte Melnick. A doctor with a stethoscope gives the band a checkup, a nurse administers medication, and someone wraps up the entire group in a bandage as they sit there eating, reading, and looking altogether bored. Among the "extras" were various L.A. club types, including Rodney Bingenheimer (as the pinhead), and Dorothy Lyman of Joey's favorite soap opera, "All My Children."

Other highlights of 1988 included Joey's and Marky's cameos (along with the likes of Mickey Mantle, Grace Jones, Christopher Reeve, and Donald Trump) in the video for Bobby Brown's theme song for the movie *Ghostbusters II*, "We're Back." In this clip, Joey, as a street musician, played the tuba and Marky collected the money (they actually pocketed seventy-five cents!). Gigwise, the band played in Puerto Rico at the World Surfing Championships, an event which drew some two thousand surfers from sixty-four countries. A show at the John Anson Ford Theater in Los Angeles, meanwhile, drew complaints when "I Wanna Be Sedated" drowned out "Alexander's Ragtime Band" at a birthday celebration for Irving Berlin across the street at the Hollywood Bowl. "It was just our way of saying 'Happy birthday, Irving!,'" said Joey at the time. And in Europe, the co-presidents of the Ramones Italian fan club drove 315 miles from Milan to Munich to greet the band at the airport and present them with plaques commemorating the release of "Ramones Mania."

In April, the Ramones had received another honor when the Board of Directors of the New York Music Awards bestowed upon them its Lifetime Achievement Award, prompting Joey to comment, "It makes me feel like Sinatra." The band had previously won the award for Best Rock Band three times, as well as for Best Single (for "Bonzo Goes to Bitburg") and Best Album (for "Animal Boy)."

In March 1989, after the Ramones had rung in the new year by closing down the venerable Irving Plaza venue, Dee Dee's solo album *Standing in the Spotlight* was released on the Sire/Red Eye label, under the name

Dee Dee King—after B. B. King, and because he felt like the "king of rap." Calling the album "rap 'n' roll," Dee Dee rapped to a hard-rock backup, which included a performance by ex-Blondie guitarist Chris Stein on the autobiographical song "German Kid." Blondie's Deborah Harry sang background on that cut (part of which was in German) and on the lead track "Mashed Potato Time," which turned Dee Dee Sharp's 1962 hit into a lazily boastful rap ("I'm as cool as they come . . . I'm as strong as Sly Stallone").

Other cuts were similarly lighthearted, including "2 Much 2 Drink" (where he swears off drinking after a binge), the surfer rap "Commotion in the Ocean," and "The Crusher," about wanting to be a pro wrestler. There was also the straight punk rock of "Poor Little Rich Girl," and a very tender ballad, "Baby Doll," his pet name for his wife Vera.

Affecting a punk/hip-hop pose, Dee Dee King slicked his hair back and wore earrings, shades, studded bracelets, a gold chain, top hat, and "D. D. King" jacket, in addition to standard Ramones sneakers and torn jeans.

Dee Dee claimed he'd been influenced into cleaning up his act by former Sex Pistols guitarist Steve Jones, and had found that instead of leading him to experience writer's block or go soft, clean living had changed his lyrics from macho-style crazy subjects to those about real-life experience—with a hard edge. Dee Dee wrote all the songs with Daniel Rey, who also produced the album.

Recalls Rey, "Dee Dee had gone into the hospital a couple weeks for 'servicing,' and the kids would call him Doug E. Fresh, because his real name is Doug. When he came out he was Dee Dee King, the rapper, and to be supportive, we wrote rap songs and I produced the solo album. I never felt right about it, since he was a Ramone and shouldn't be doing that stuff. But I also knew he needed to create and produce things to keep him busy."

Billboard called Standing in the Spotlight a great party album, and said that Dee Dee's hilarious white raps put the Beastie Boys to shame. Other reviews were mixed; no one suggested that he quit the Ramones. "He's changing colors!," Joey told a reporter. "I don't think that will have any effect on the rest of the band, though. If one of us left, things just wouldn't be the same—each one of us has his own special personality, and none of us could be easily replaced or anything. If Dee Dee left the band, for example, [and] someone else joined instead, things would never be the same again, y'know."

On Brain Drain, the next Ramones studio album, Dee Dee seemed to be more involved than ever. He wrote or co-wrote six of the twelve songs, including the powerful but optimistic lead track, "I Believe in Miracles":

Tattooed your name on my arm
I always say my girl's a good-luck charm
If she can find a reason to forgive
Then I can find a reason to live
I believe in miracles
I believe in a better world for me and you

"All our albums are autobiographical," Dee Dee explained to a reporter. "We've all had a hard struggle and feel we've come out on top. When we sing 'I believe in a better world for you and me,' we really mean it. If you struggle through life and do the right thing, you'll have a good life, not necessarily in a materialistic sense, but in being happy with yourself."

Except for "Merry Christmas (I Don't Want to Fight Tonight)," which had been produced by Beauvoir and Rey, "Brain Drain" was produced by the acclaimed Bill Laswell, who had worked with the likes of Public Image, Ltd., Motorhead, and Iggy Pop, as well as on his own projects combining all kinds of world music. Laswell was the first "outside" producer the Ramones had used in a while, but he sacrificed none of their customary strengths. The album's opening track showcased incredible vocals from Joey, and a very powerful, *down* sound from the band, marked by especially fierce guitar playing.

The album also continued in a more politically and socially aware vein. "Ignorance Is Bliss," a speed-metal attack written by Joey and ex-Dictator Andy Shernoff, addressed the "disintegration of humanity" and "destruction of the environment" and resulted from the band's participation in a rain forest benefit.

Dee Dee, Johnny, and Rey teamed up with Marky in the telling "Learn to Listen," in which the voice of experience teaches that "happiness is something you got to earn" and cautions against making the same mistakes the songwriters made: "I lived your life for so many years/All I got was self pity and tears/.... Learn to listen, listen to learn/Before you get burned."

" 'Learn to Listen' gives advice to our younger fans," said Dee Dee after the album's release. "We want to save them from the anguish of having to go through the school of hard knocks which the Ramones had to go through." As Joey explained to *Metal Hammer*, "Our songs have all got a statement that everyone can identify with. They're about relationships, about dissatisfaction with the whole system, daily life, and the frustration that goes with it—all these things that affect each and every one of us, except we try hard not to preach to anyone, but try and judge the whole situation from the same angle as the people who listen to our music."

But the Ramones didn't give up their more traditional subject matter, like sci-fi ("Zero Zero UFO"), girlfriend tell-offs ("Don't Bust My Chops"), or old-fashioned romance, as in Joey's "Come Back, Baby," which artfully mixed a bubblegum chorus with lean-and-mean verses and an anthemic rock-guitar break. And there was a classic cover in Freddy Cannon's 1962 smash "Palisades Park," a perfect Ramones vehicle with its girls standing by the amusement park rides and hot-dog stands.

"What we like to do is take a song that we all like and that we feel we can do a little better," Joey told the Tennessee paper *Metro*. "Some songs are classics, but most people don't know this ... which is why Tiffany will tackle 'I Saw Her Standing There' or some shit and butcher it to death. It's cool, too because you're turning the kids on to new stuff that they didn't know and now they'll venture backward in music.... There's so much good stuff to delve into ... life doesn't just consist of Poison, you know. I listen to everything from Patsy Cline to Motorhead ... there's no reason that you can't like 'em both."

Brain Drain also included the second Ramones movie theme song, "Pet Sematary," written for the Stephen King fright film. King was a big fan of the band, having promoted a 1984 concert near his home in Bangor, Maine, starring the Ramones and Cheap Trick. ("Sheena Is a Punk Rocker" made the film's soundtrack as well.)

Dee Dee wrote "Pet Sematary" with Rey in a tribute to King's style. "One thing that really inspired me about the book was the quality of King's writing," Dee Dee said. "He's almost musical.... You can read a couple of paragraphs in the book and get visual images flashing in your mind."

Dee Dee waxed particularly poetic in the opening verse:

> Under the arc of a weather-stain board,
> Ancient goblins, and warlords,
> Come out of the ground, not making a sound,
> The smell of death is all around,
> And the night when the cold wind blows,
> No one cares, nobody knows.
> I don't want to be buried in a Pet Sematary,
> I don't want to live my life again.

Notorious New York radio personality and Ramones supporter Howard Stern picked "Pet Sematary," which was released as a single, as his Song of the Year. "It summed up 1989," he proclaimed. "It was a phenomenal song and should have been a bigger hit."

At least the video garnered attention. Shot at the Sleepy Hollow cemetery in Tarrytown, New York (setting for the Washington Irving stories "Legend of Sleepy Hollow," "Rip Van Winkle," and "Legend of the Headless Horseman"), the clip was filmed under a full winter moon, with the Ramones walking through the graveyard, later to be slowly buried alive in a freshly dug hole while playing the song before numerous celebrity mourners including Deborah Harry, Chris Stein, the Cycle Sluts from Hell (with their dogs, the Cycle Mutts from Hell), Daniel Rey, Richie Stotts, Cheetah Chrome, Andy Shernoff, and Raging Slab. The video ends with the laying of a tombstone flashing the band's name in blue lights. "It made us very uneasy to be experiencing what's coming in the future," said Joey.

Brain Drain was released in May 1989, adorned with a front cover painting of someone screaming in agony, and was appropriately promoted with "Brain Drain" surgical caps. Joey considered it the band's best album ever, and *Stereo Review* recognized its new maturity together with the diverging approaches apparent in Joey's poppier songs and Dee Dee's "boot-stomping crypto-metal." Jeffrey Ressner's concert review in *Rolling Stone*, meanwhile, indicated that live, at least, the band still took no prisoners. At the Iguanas Club in Tijuana, the article said, "watching the show became secondary to surviving it," what with raucous Ramones-heads climbing upon each others' shoulders and chicken-fighting in the mosh pit while scores of drunken skinheads flung themselves onto the crowd from the balcony. Of course, the Ramones just kept playing while the fans tore the room apart, including the metal pipes and electrical fixtures.

"People always ask why we're still together," Dee Dee said, as the Ramones celebrated their fifteenth anniversary. "[It's] because we don't have a hit single, and we still gotta work for a living." Then, in July 1989, Dee Dee quit the Ramones.

Chapter Seventeen

The Changing of the Guard

'm not really sure why Dee Dee quit," says Johnny. "I never really knew what went on in his head. He'd left his wife a month before— I suppose that was a bad sign. But I never thought he'd ever quit. It wasn't a good career move, was it?"

"It was a combination of things," says Vera Ramone of the split. "He'd been really straight for a long time, about five years without drinking or taking drugs. There was the pressure of touring and constant songwriting and recording. He was writing most of the songs, mostly to please Johnny and not himself. And he was being sober for me and everybody else, but not for himself. People say he was going through a midlife crisis early. It was total insecurity. Everybody was shocked when we broke up, which happened in one day. I thought he'd snap out of it early and come back to reality. I couldn't believe he could behave like this: 'I don't want to play any more, I don't want to live in Queens, I don't know what I want to do.' He hated everybody, and he stopped taking his medication. Even now when we talk, we'll have a good conversation, then he'll dwell on one little thing and it becomes a big thing. I guess it's called schizophrenia."

No doubt you've surmised that Dee Dee declined to be interviewed for this book, saying through Vera that he intends to author his own account. Of course, Dee Dee had been quite candid about his problems with himself and the band over the years in numerous interviews, often quite graphically. (Vera, who now manages the Federal Government Building in Queens—but still wears short skirts, and has a *pink* office—corroborates the story of years of heavy alcohol and substance abuse, though admitting she was naive about it at first.)

"When we met he was making one hundred dollars a week and had a one hundred-dollar-a-day habit. But I never knew he was a junkie. If he told me it was just Quaaludes, I took his word for it. Time went on and I'd get worried, but he'd always say Valiums or Seconals or Tuinals, and he was really getting high on junk. He OD'd so many times—he couldn't help himself. But it was more mental than anything else. He suffered mood swings, depression. When he was really having a bad day, it was like walking around on eggshells. Sometimes he'd get violent, but we always worked it out. We went to therapy from 1987 to 1989; he'd been going since 1980, and went to A.A., N.A., C.A. I drove him everyday, to his shrink, my shrink, and we went to a third shrink together. Then he stopped the programs, quit his prescribed medication, we broke up, and he quit the band—all within three weeks. At the end he thought he was normal and everybody else was crazy. He wouldn't listen to anybody because they were all enemies and were out to get him.

"He had an obsessive personality. He'd been straight quite a long time and then he started buying watches, wearing five watches on one arm and three on the other. We'd sit over coffee and he'd go, 'Hurry up and get dressed, I want to buy a watch!' Then he had a tattoo phase where he'd get a tattoo, then the next day he'd want another tattoo. 'I want one now!' He'd always get what he wanted, so we drove out to Long Island and he'd look through a tattoo book and pick out another tattoo, then two tattoos at a time. Needless to say, he was covered with tattoos! He had two huge scorpions or crabs on his chest, and his arms were totally full. He had a heart with 'Mama' and 'Vera and Dee Dee,' 'Too Tough to Die' with a little devil and horns. A 'Baby Doll'—a little girl

Dee Dee performing a short bass riff. (Ian Harper)

with blonde hair. I wish he never would have left the band, because he was the heart and soul. But with Dee Dee it was all or nothing—when his solo album didn't happen, he went off the cliff."

With Dee Dee gone, the Ramones survival was at stake. They immediately commenced tryouts for a new bassist. First up was Christopher Joseph Ward, who was born in 1965 on October 8, exactly fourteen years after Johnny's birth.

C.J., as he is now known, had started playing bass when he was thirteen, after his parents bought him one for his eighth-grade graduation. Learning from records, he listened to all kinds of music: from the "classic" rock of the Beatles, Creedence Clearwater Revival, and Neil Young, to the harder, heavier likes of Led Zeppelin, Pink Floyd, and especially Black Sabbath. "I was a mega, mega Sabbath head, and thought [bassist] Geezer Butler was God!" He liked the anger and flash of heavy metal, and with the band Axe Attack, he recorded two albums for the British label Heavy Metal America. But he then grew tired of the metal genre, and its image and attitude. Seeking a less phony, more honest style, he discovered punk rock and hardcore, and three new bass-guitar role models: Sid Vicious of the Sex Pistols, Paul Simenon of the Clash, and Dee Dee Ramone of . . . the Ramones.

He had heard about the Ramones audition through a friend from his hometown of Deer Park, Long Island who was in Joey's brother Mickey's band Tribe 375. He got the call at 3 P.M., with instructions to be there at six. The only problem was that by this time, C.J. was a Marine, and was absent without leave.

"I'd enlisted because I was having a lot of problems, doing a lot of drugs," says C.J. "I was doing them just to do them, and I knew I needed a real strict change in my life. So I tried to enlist in the Navy, but they said I had a heart murmur. But the Marines are bullet-catchers—they take anybody!"

So C.J. joined up, but at boot camp at Paris Island, South Carolina, he contracted Rocky Mountain spotted fever from a tick bite, and was hospitalized with a 106-degree fever; he was so sick, in fact, that his vital signs failed, and his doctors feared he'd suffer brain damage. But he recovered, and never mentioned the severity of the disease when he commenced his infantry training. Meanwhile, there were problems back home. C.J.'s dad, a military aircraft worker, lost his job when the factory closed down, and his mom was stricken with lupus. So he decided to seek a discharge to be with his family. The Marines agreed that C.J. had reason and promised him a discharge, but kept reneging on it. Stationed at Camp Pendleton in California, he was ordered to Japan, but went to stay instead with a sister in Hollywood. He returned to camp two weeks later for his court martial, where the Marines again agreed that he had good cause for discharge, again promised him one, and again reneged.

So C.J. returned to New York, and while he stayed in touch with the Marines, he refused to go back. A year and a half later came the Ramones audition. It was a two-hour drive from his home in Long Island to New York City, so he had essentially one hour to learn a few Ramones songs on a tape player.

"I hadn't played bass in a long time, and never used a pick before. But I auditioned once, and they said I was okay and they wanted me back next week, and then I went back three or four times." Recalls Johnny, "C.J. was the first person who came down. He said, 'Hi. I'm Chris,' and shook hands, and all I could do was hope I didn't have to shake hands with everyone who came down to try out. I didn't want to go home and catch a cold! But he was great—an easy breeze. I expected hundreds of clones who grew up with Dee Dee as their idol. So we tried out one hundred more and they were all horrible—'I don't even play,' 'I can't believe I'm meeting you'—that sort of thing. I kept signaling Monte to get them out!"

The only good thing about the others, according to Marky, was that they came from all walks of life. "Chinese, black, women, white—which was great because it showed that anyone can play all kinds of music. It doesn't have to be one race or sex. But the first guy—C.J.—that was it."

Johnny and Marky also determined that C.J. had a proper musical background, and more important, was neither a junkie nor an alcoholic. Johnny also viewed C.J.'s military experience as a distinct plus, in terms of self-discipline and ability to listen. So C.J. quit his job installing dry-cleaning machines, and after a few more auditions and days and nights of constant practicing (to a point where he knew thirty-five songs), C.J. got the gig . . . but there was still that *slight* problem with the Marines. "I called them to say I thought I'd be leaving the country soon because of the gig, and I needed to get the discharge. They said they weren't familiar with the case, that they'd have to call back in fifteen minutes. Fifteen minutes later the police came in and ran me in jail!"

Since there were no Marines in Long Island, a "bounty hunter" picked C.J. up the next day and brought him to Fort Hamilton in Brooklyn, where he was immediately put to work washing pans before being transferred to a naval brig in Philadelphia. After a two-night stay, he was taken to the Marine Corps brig in Quantico, Virginia, where he was stuck for the next three weeks. The lawyer appointed to handle his case said that if he would waive court-marshall proceedings and admit guilt, they'd grant him a BCD, or "big chicken dinner"—that is, a bad-conduct discharge. But he also felt that C.J. had an unusually just case for *honorable* discharge with full veteran's benefits. "But I hadn't even served a year! I didn't want anything from them *but* a discharge," C.J. recalls.

But what would the Ramones think about this unforeseen mess?

"I thought I'd blown the gig for sure, then two days after I got arrested, I got a call from Monte and Marky telling me not to worry, I got the gig, do the time and don't get into trouble! They understood the whole story! I'm glad they didn't forget about me, and I really thought they would, because with a major organization like the Ramones, it was like holding up a train for a conductor who has to piss! It was unheard of! But I could tell that I really earned their respect because I went back and did what I had to do."

C.J. got his discharge. His debut with the Ramones came on September 4, 1989, at 8 A.M., during Jerry Lewis's annual Labor Day muscular dystrophy telethon. Sammy Davis, Jr. gave the introduction from Atlantic City, though the Ramones were in the local studio in Secaucus, New Jersey. Since C.J.'s head had been completely shaved during his stay in the brig, he wore a bandana over it.

"It was really bad," recalls Johnny. "He forgot everything we rehearsed—stay calm, don't move around, move around as you become comfortable. Pick easy, make it *look* like you're picking hard. But he threw it all out the window! His finger was cut up after one song, he was moving around. But he was fine for the second show."

The second show was in Leicester, England, on September 30, the start of the next tour. "It was a real baptism of fire, swear to God!" continues C.J. "I went on stage totally out of my mind. I knew I had to totally cut loose and just go off, but let me tell you I made a million mistakes! Meanwhile, I was getting pelted with every thing you can imagine, and I was covered in spit. I can't believe that the last time I saw the Ramones at Lamour in Brooklyn, I stood in front of Dee Dee and spat at him the whole time! He held his bass up overhead and the spit was just pouring on him."

C.J. quickly got used to his new role, though not without a little breaking in.

"I don't worry about proper hand position—I just *grind* at my bass. But I had to start taping my fingers, because I play so hard that I'd break strings, and since a set of bass strings is twenty-five dollars, playing four gigs a week, I'd blow one hundred dollars a week on strings! And in the beginning, I'd leave chunks of skin on the bass, and I'd short out the pickup with blood because I'd be bleeding so heavily. One time I broke a fingernail halfway down! It's ridiculous, but that's how I am onstage: I just go for it and pull out all the stops.

"If you mess up, Johnny tells you! 'Don't do it again! I know you know the song, and you fuckin' play it wrong! People pay money to come see you—you got to be good!' and it works. Sometimes you go onstage so tired and you're ready to die but you still got to do it. It's very difficult and I make a mistake and he gives me a sneer, 'Pay attention to what you're doing!' but that's good. It's like being in the Marines: You do a job in the field but you fuck up and somebody lets you know! You find out that being in a band isn't an easy job, but definitely a business with ups and downs, the highs are really high, but the lows are really low. I used to work construction jobs, landscaping, and painting in a military aircraft factory, but this is the toughest job ever."

As for the transition from Dee Dee to C.J. in the hearts and minds of Ramones fans, C.J. is grateful to have been treated well by everyone since the change.

"I try not to look like I'm taking his place, but go up there and do my job and entertain people. I sing a couple of songs of his and feel really good about doing it, because he's someone I totally identify with, you know what I mean? He wrote some songs for the new album, and dropped them off at Arturo's with a note for me: 'C.J.—This is the best I could do, so get to it.' It made me feel good that he was happy for me. He was so wild, unique, original—there will never be anybody like him! I really wish there was a way I could work with him some time."

C.J. was like "the missing piece to a puzzle," says Johnny. Like Dee Dee, C.J. was heavily tattooed, and one writer felt that he looked like a cross between Mel Gibson and Sid Vicious depending on the light, smiling more in a single set than all the Ramones ever have in all of their shows put together! It was also noted in reviews, interviews, and by the Ramones themselves that C.J.'s youth was a swift kick in the pants.

"They have to suck in their stomachs to keep up with him, to be that *intense*," says Monte Melnick. "It was incredible how it worked out. And such a pleasure! My God! You tell the band to be on time, and they're on time!"

"If C.J. didn't work out it would be over, but he pulled it off," says Vera. "He wasn't Dee Dee, but Dee Dee wasn't C.J., either."

And what became of Dee Dee? He continued contributing songs to the Ramones as well as to the Chesterfield Kings, an upstate New York garage band that had impressed Dee Dee after opening for the Ramones at the Ritz (he had cuts on their "Don't Open Til Doomsday" and "The Berlin Wall of Sound" albums). He played guitar and sang in a band called the Spikey Tops, which also included bassist Carla Ola, formerly in the all-girl hardcore group PMS. Various reports had him starting up a psychedelic rock band, the Sprockets, with a new girlfriend, pursuing a career in a biker band, and recording in Paris with the late Stiv Bators.

In autumn of 1990, a shirtless Dee Dee made the papers after getting busted—along with twenty-five others—in a drug raid at Washington Square Park in Greenwich Village, where he was caught buying a small amount of pot. A picture in *The New York Post* showed him covered with tattoos, and he was said to have screamed profanities at the photog-

Dee Dee in his new incarnation after leaving the band. (Sire Records)

raphers at the police station. "He thought he was Dee Dee Ramone and was allowed to do anything he wanted and get away with it—but not that one day," says Vera. "If he'd just kept his mouth shut and didn't tell anyone who he was, there wouldn't have been any picture in the paper!"

Two weeks later another item in the *Post* reported that Dee Dee had been thrown out of a nightspot after allegedly doing up drugs in the bathroom. Then came the article in *Spin* in which Dee Dee aired as much dirty laundry as the clothesline would hold (besides detailing his substance abuse and mental health problems and the hostility among the band members, Dee Dee went so far as to admit that he *hated* playing "Pinhead," since he chipped his teeth when the three-hundred-pound roadie who played the pinhead jumped around on stage, causing his microphone to bang into his mouth!).

"I think it's evident that it's sour grapes," Joey responded in the *Boston Phoenix*, wishing Dee Dee the best. "He quit, but nobody wanted him back. I think he thought we were going to beg him to come back but we didn't, and that's it."

In April 1992, Dee Dee performed in the four-day Kick Out the Jams festival at Detroit's State Theater, helping to raise thirty-four thousand dollars for the education of the children of late MC5 singer Rob Tyner. Dee Dee had moved to Ann Arbor, Michigan, after returning to New York following a six-month stay in England.

"He's doing great now, with a new manager and his own punk rock band, the Chinese Dragons. It symbolizes heroin, but he's straight. He's let his hair grow again [Dee Dee had cropped it short in an effort to redefine his image apart from the Ramones], and he's pulling together," Vera relates.

Concludes Daniel Rey, "Dee Dee is definitely the best person I ever wrote with. He came out with lines and feelings that were so deep and honest and from the heart. He just has a way of putting on paper angst, anger, happy or goofy. 'Chewing out a rhythm on my bubblegum' . . . That's pure genius."

he Ramones fifteenth anniversary
year gave journalists cause to
celebrate, and the Hard Rock Cafe
reason to party.

In New York, the Ramones
presented the Hard Rock with an
autographed leather jacket. Kurt
Loder, now an MTV music news
anchor, was the master of
ceremonies. "Fifteen years ago,
Barry Manilow, Helen Reddy, Olivia
Newton-John, and John Denver all
had Number One hits," said Loder.
"Think how dreary a decade the
seventies might've been had not the
Ramones come along in 1974. For
fifteen years, they've remained true
to their vision of rock 'n' roll as
fast, fun, music, and today they
remain one of the greatest bands

The Ramones

Revisited

(Arturo Vega)

that music has ever produced." At the Los Angeles Hard Rock, the band donated an autographed "Gabba Gabba Hey" concert banner.

Meanwhile, the Ramones were busy on numerous fronts. Joey made a cameo appearance in *Roadkill*, which won an award at the Toronto Film Festival, a movie about a woman named *Ramona* (the director was a Ramones fan) sent to track down a renegade rock band. In another Canadian film production, *Car 54*, the Ramones performed "I Believe in Miracles" in a club scene; the film, based on the classic TV sitcom "Car 54, Where Are You?", starred David Johansen and was directed by Ramones video ace Bill Fishman. "They're the greatest rock and roll band that ever lived and ever will live," Fishman explained.

On television, Joey sat in with Cycle Sluts from Hell, Scott Ian of Anthrax, and Ace Frehley of Danger Danger Bang Tango, and Jethro Tull in a discussion of heavy metal on "The Morton Downey, Jr. Show." He and his mom joined members on a "Heavy Metal, Moms" installment of "Geraldo" (Charlotte Ramone sang a verse each from "Beat on the Brat" and "I Wanna Be Sedated"). Joey and C.J. hosted a segment of MTV's "120 Minutes" alternative music video program.

Joey, actually, was becoming an entrepreneurial tornado. He had always been one to help other bands, be it his brother's new Crown the Good or the Mystics, the Brooklyn doo-wop group (they had the 1959 hit "Hushabye"), for whom he also wrote and recorded.

On a larger scale, Joey had begun staging music *extravaganzas*, putting together a club night offering as many as fifteen up-and-coming bands, regulars including Cycle Sluts from Hell, Manitoba's Wild Kingdom, and Raging Slab. There would also be plenty of celebrities and scene makers about, along with kooky entertainment like beauty pageants, dance productions, and poetry readings. Joey would perform, too, in star-studded jams featuring the likes of Marky Ramone, Richie Stotts, Daniel Rey, Andy Shernoff, Deborah Harry and Lemmy to mention just a few. These events had names as grandiose as their concepts, including: the Holy Inquisition Circus of the Perverse; the Magical Mystery Assault on D.C. and Roadkill Buffet (this one was in the nation's capital); the First Annual Glitter Acid Rock-and-Roll Trash Ball; CBGB; Under Siege—The Spring Offensive; Joey Ramone's Beach Party Bash; and Joey Ramone and His Mom Present A Mother's Day Massacre. Each one, Joey said, created a "whole environmental situation, so that you walked into something that doesn't exist."

On New York station Z-Rock, Joey brought the same eclectic blend to radio, with his monthly "Joey Ramone's Radio Rampage," which featured music, interviews, and politics. On the first show he started out by playing MC5's "Kick Out the Jams" and segued to the Stooges' "TV Eye," later moving to the glam rock of Mott the Hoople and T. Rex before interviewing Lemmy from Motorhead and Richie Stotts, and then bringing on Handsome Dick Manitoba and conducting a panel discussion on the new censorship, a segment also featuring members of the Black Rock Coalition. "I never understood why you can't play the Beatles and Motorhead on the same station," he explained to a reporter. "I hate it when things get so categorized. It's just alienating people from being turned on to good stuff."

Besides music-related activities, Joey was always willing to lend his support to just causes. He participated in benefits on behalf of the rain forest, AIDS, the environment, the homeless, and animals. Because of such high visibility—and the public's awareness of who he was—Joey became a bona fide *star*, sitting on a rock talent show judges' panel at the Ritz with the likes of Marla Maples and Don Kirshner. *Interview* magazine even saw fit to run a picture of his refrigerator! (For the record, its contents were: Crabtree & Evelyn strawberry preserves with orange liqueur; After the Fall apple-raspberry juice; two Diet Cokes; four Dannon light yogurts; bowl of green grapes; Low Sodium Austrian Alps Swiss Cheese; thirteen unmarked American cheese singles; one pint Élan vanilla frozen yogurt; frozen Stouffer's cashew chicken.

But Joey's paramount concern was censorship. Like numerous rock, heavy metal, and rap groups, the Ramones had come under fire by the Parents Music Resource Center (PMRC), an activist watchdog group headed by Tipper Gore and Susan Baker, the respective wives of then Tennessee Senator Al Gore and then Secretary of State James Baker. The PMRC had struck fear throughout the music industry for its crusade against song lyrics that it deemed suggestive or offensive—and songs like "Cretin Hop," "Teenage Lobotomy," and "I Wanna Be Sedated," whatever their real meaning or intention, made easy targets.

In August 1989, Joey and Marky took part in a panel discussion of the PMRC and the issue of censorship at the Ritz, along with other participants including Run-DMC and journalist Dave Marsh. "These right-wing, ultraconservative extremists are trying to go back to the fifties," said Marky. "Soon they'll be telling us what restaurants we can eat in." Said Joey, "It makes you wonder about America. I'm proud to be an American and live in this country, but I just wonder about where we're heading. It seems like we're going back to the fifties and it's really kind of a scary thought . . . everything is so fuckin' conservative, what's happening with the right-wing Moral Majority . . . I mean, they always picked on rock 'n' roll right from the inception of rock 'n' roll, with record-burning, and this and that, saying that 'You listen to rock 'n' roll, it's devil's music, it's this, it's that,' it's nothing new, y'know? The ignorance of it all is just so sickening."

On the career side, though, the Ramones were equally busy. They appeared in two other videos from *Brain Drain*, both with C.J. in the lineup and directed by George Seminara. "Merry Christmas (I Don't Want to Fight Tonight)" starred Skip Lackey (who played Tom Sawyer in the Broadway musical *Big River*) and Jessica Lundy (*Caddyshack II*) as a quarrelsome couple right out of *The War of the Roses*. The politically minded "I Believe in Miracles" had the band performing in front of footage of historic figures and events as a steady stream of names (those of Ramones and rock 'n' roll heroes) and slogans (such as "House the Homeless" and "Vivisection Should Be a Crime") crawled across both the top and bottom of the frame. This clip, which also contained material culled from Marky's personal Ramones world-tour video collection, debuted on CBS News "Nightwatch," with host Charlie Rose commenting that it "looks back on the musical, social, and political history of rock."

This tribute to history was followed by another in June 1990. *All The Stuff (and More)—Vol. I*, which contained all of the tracks from *Ramones* and *Ramones Leave Home* (with "Sheena Is a Punk Rocker" again substituting for the forever banned "Carbona Not Glue") as well as unreleased material, and launched a series of CD reissues of the other early Ramones albums. Among the rarities included on the first disc were the unreleased early demo of "I Don't Wanna Be Learned/I Don't Wanna Be Tamed" and the B-side gem "Babysitter." The CD booklet's cover art was a reproduction of the contact sheet of Roberta Bayley's shoot of a live show at CBGB back in 1976.

Also in 1990 came the home video "Lifestyles of the Ramones," a compilation of the Ramones video clips (including the uncut "Psycho Therapy") with additional interview footage, directed by George Seminara. Seminara's story is by now almost standard. "My mother was big on getting me involved early in youth culture, but I'd given up on music completely because it was so boring. Then one day she went out and came back with albums by Kiss, Bowie, and the Ramones, and told me to pick which one I liked. The Ramones were perfect."

No surprise, then, to learn that Seminara had a high IQ and no friends. "I'd hear the roar of the Ramones and be *liberated*. They didn't ask for a big emotional commitment, but were there just to amuse and be sarcastic and have a good time."

Seminara used to live around the corner from CB's, and would sneak out the window to go there and catch the Ramones ("Once I was gone three days before my parents missed me!"). You see, he was only fourteen at the time, but he looked like all the other Ramones fans—with his long hair, leather jacket, Converse sneakers, blue jeans—that they let him in with a "Nobooze foyouz" underage stamp.

Years later, Seminara directed a video for New York hardcore band Agnostic Front, which Joey liked.

"He got my number and called and asked me to do a Ramones video, and I said, 'I don't think so!' and hung up on him. I thought it was a friend playing a joke!" Seminara said. He went on to re-cut "Merry Christmas (I Don't Want to Fight Tonight)," and then direct "I Believe in Miracles."

"The Ramones never get the kind of production money they deserve," says Seminara. "For 'Pet Sematary,' they only had enough money for three rolls of film! We even shot a video for 'Somebody Put Something in My Drink' which hasn't been edited because the band switched labels after it was shot and we couldn't get any more money from Sire. It's a thirty-seven-thousand-dollar video, and it only cost us fifteen-thousand dollars."

Seminara's way with stretching a dollar and his time-saving efficiency strongly impressed Johnny. "He said his favorite video was 'Sedated,' because all he did was sit there for three hours and then do it and then go home. He said, 'If you can do a video in less than three hours, you're our director.' 'Merry Christmas' took one hour and forty-five minutes, and 'Miracles' was one hour and fifteen minutes! I just shot take after take as fast as possible."

Seminara enjoyed full support when it came time to put together "Lifestyles." The concept called for hiring "Lifestyles of the Rich and Famous" 's Robin Leach as the program's host, but he was too expensive. So instead, a similarly stuffy-sounding off-camera speaker introduces the tape, which also features comments from the likes of Deborah Harry, Chris Frantz, Little Steven, Tina Weymouth, Jerry Harrison, Living Colour's Vernon Reid, Chris Isaak, the members of Anthrax, New York Yankee pitcher Dave Righetti, and various other music-business professionals.

So you aren't misled into thinking that was the height of intelligence found in "Lifestyles," I'll mention that Little Steven said, "Really good rock 'n' roll is very simple, and to maintain that simplicity record after record after record is actually very very difficult"; while Daniel Rey said, "To have been able to work with them is like a younger generation working with the Beatles, because that's how important they were in shaping my musical tastes and directions, and they're still as great as they ever were and ten years from now probably still will be."

There were a couple of noteworthy incidents in 1990. In February, Joey tore some ligaments in his ankle while leaving the stage during a guest spot with Raging Slab at the Wetlands club in New York, causing cancellation of several dates. And in June, C.J.'s tattoos drew the attention of actress Julia Roberts, who was at a Ramones show in Wilmington, North Carolina, with her then-fiancé Keifer Sutherland. C.J. explained them all to her before the hot media couple slam danced the night away.

The Ramones also taped a tribute to the Ventures' thirtieth anniversary along with Springsteen's drummer Max Weinberg, Rick Derringer, and the Doobie Brothers, and Joey spoke before the college radio trade at the annual CMJ Metal Marathon. That summer, the Ramones took part in the "Escape from New York" tour with fellow CBGB alumni Deborah Harry, Jerry Harrison, and Tom Tom Club, which featured ex-Talking Heads Chris Frantz and Tina Weymouth. The package drew between five thousand and ten thousand fans each night wherever it played, topping twenty-five thousand in Austin and seventeen thousand in Milwaukee.

In September, the Ramones authored a piece in *Musician* magazine about the growing censorship debate and the move to sticker albums to warn parents of their potentially offensive contents. Wrote the Ramones, "Teenagers are going to want to listen to music. It's rhythmic, it's part of life, and part of growing up and experiencing things. Music is a sense— you feel it as well as hear it. You can't take that away from them. Kids like rock 'n' roll, baseball, Burger King, and going to concerts. They're smart, and see what's going on in the world around them. They've just seen the wall coming down in Germany and Communism crumbling, and certainly don't want repression to start happening here. Because that's how it starts. Certain freedoms and rights are taken away, and then you have revolt."

In July 1991, *All The Stuff (and More)—Vol. II* was released. The Spector-ish "Slug" was one of its bonus tracks—"a true melodramatic love story," according to Joey, originating from the Bingenheimer/Kessel Brothers sessions. The tune also appeared as a computer program in *K-Power* a children's magazine edited by John Holmstrom after *Punk's* demise. Joey, incidentally, wrote a column for *K-Power*, and later interviewed Pia Zadora for *Spin*.

Motorhead's tribute to the band, *Ramones*, was released in 1991 as well. Major Motorhead-head Joey called it "the ultimate honor," the equivalent of having John Lennon write a song for them. Another tribute came from Perry Farrell, the creative force behind the group Jane's Addiction, which headlined that summer's Lollapalooza Tour (also featuring Siouxsie and the Banshees and Living Colour), who said that the Ramones weren't asked to join the event out of respect, since *they* should be the ones headlining it.

Respect of a different kind came with the use of "Blitzkrieg Bop" in a car race-themed Bud Light commercial. "The Ramones music was picked because the band is representative of today's generation," said Fred Smith, executive producer of the commercial, who also liked the song's beat. "During the shoot we played the song over and over again, and it kept the producers and camera people in a happy mood." But the band turned down another lucrative offer, to star in the sequel to *Rock 'n' Roll High School*. "We already did the original," Joey explained.

Still more respect came late in the year when Joey was asked by Soundgarden to introduce the band during their opening set for Guns N'

**Johnny with Semie Moseley, the late founder of
the Mosrite guitar.
(Johnny Ramone)**

Roses at Madison Square Garden. Turning to the newest Ramone, Joey told the sellout house, "This is C.J. Ramone and I'm Joey Ramone. It was C.J. who turned me on to Soundgarden to begin with. I'm very excited to be here. There's no way we were gonna miss a show like this. No one could keep me away. What a great bill!" Since Guns N' Roses bassist Duff McKagan was regularly photographed wearing a bootleg Ramones T-shirt, Joey and C.J. presented him backstage with an official tee from the Ramones recent tour of Spain, where they recorded a live album ("Loco Live").

The Ramones South American jaunt deserves mention as well. Joey served as a guest deejay on a Sao Paulo station, programming the likes of Motorhead, Stooges, New York Dolls, MC5, Hendrix, the Who, Bowie, Blondie, Mott the Hoople, Jane's Addiction, AC/DC, Alice Cooper, and of course, the Ramones. In Buenos Aires, the band played before a rabid crowd of fifteen thousand. "It was a case of almost literally loving us to death!" said Joey. "We couldn't leave our hotel because we were mobbed by the kids waiting in the street. A crazy thing happened at the airport when we arrived. After the plane landed and we were walking to the terminal, we looked up to find the viewing deck filled with fans. They were waving, and chanting, 'Hey ho, let's go!' "

Joey was also heavily active in politics in 1991. During the annual New Music Seminar held in New York in July, he and Marky took part on the "Rock the Vote" panel, while the whole band filmed a public service announcement on behalf of the "Motor Voter" bill. Directed by Bob Dylan's son Jesse, the ad sat Ramones in front of an oversized American flag while "I Believe in Miracles" played in the background.

Also during the time of the seminar, Joey introduced Birdland at the Marquee and his brother Mickey's new band Crown the Good at the Limelight club. The next night he took part in the ASCAP songwriters night, and later helped end the seminar with a performance at the CBGB Gallery of Sam Cooke's "Bring It on Home to Me," aided partially by bassist Fred Smith (of Television) and guitarist Ivan Julian (Richard Hell and the Voidoids); Joyce Bowden on vocals; Al Maddy on keyboard and Rene Valentine on snare drum; and a cover of the Dave Clark Five's "Glad All Over," with Andy Shernoff helping on guitar.

In September Joey emceed a "Rock the Vote" night at the Cat Club, and for the same cause the next night at CB's gathered together numerous friends, musicians, poets, political activists, and performance artists under the banner "The Resistance Featuring Joey Ramone." Among the assembled: Marky and C.J. Ramone, radio personality Vin Scelsa, Andy Shernoff, The Living Theater founder Judith Molina, and Acid Bones guitarist Garrett (Skinny Bones) Uhlenbrock. Debuting at this gig was Joey's new anticensorship song "Censorshit," and an updated version of John Lennon's classic "Gimme Some Truth," which he especially liked as a comment on governmental deception. "Welcome to the New World Order," he said, introducing it. "Register and vote. Let's get those fuckers out of office. He suggested Frank Zappa and ex-Dead Kennedys (and one-time San Francisco mayoral candidate) Jello Biafra as suitable replacements.

Of "Gimme Some Truth," Joey said, "I always loved that song and thought it was appropriate to do but needed to be more reflective of today's social environment. Otherwise it doesn't make any sense. So I rewrote the song with my neighbor Robin Rothman, who's a poet, and performed it at CB's with a lot of artists and musicians that I wouldn't have the opportunity to work with otherwise. I wanted to create an event, a colorful situation, like Lennon's Toronto Peace Festival, or something. It worked out great—six hundred people came in."

The response to Joey's version of "Gimme Some Truth" was so positive that he decided to record it. But first he needed permission from Yoko

Ono, since he had made changes in the lyrics. Luckily, Joey ran into Sean Lennon at a party for Bob Gruen, the CBGB-era photographer who was also John Lennon's photographer. Luckily again, it turned out that not only was Sean a big Ramones fan, but the first song that he'd ever played on the guitar was "I Wanna Be Sedated"! Sean spoke to his mom that night, and after Yoko heard the song, she gave Joey the okay. It was the first time anyone had changed a John Lennon song.

Joey's goal now is to record the song, with his share of the royalties going to "Rock the Vote," and Yoko's going to the American Civil Liberties Union. "Maybe we'll throw in an acoustic version of 'Censorshit' and another song I wrote, 'Fascists Don't Fuck, They Just Screw,' and maybe 'Bring It on Home,' and put out an EP on Radioactive."

Which brings us to Radioactive Records, Gary Kurfirst's new label, to which the Ramones are now signed.

When he became the Ramones manager, Kurfirst saw his primary function as keeping the record company at bay, "like an offensive line man protecting the quarterback." People loved the Ramones for who they were, Kurfirst knew. His thoughts were, Don't try to change or mold them—just let them have artistic freedom and stay away. The philosophy had worked well enough for twelve years, but there had long been a feeling on the Ramones end that they had been forgotten at Sire/Warner Bros.; Having been there fifteen years without "fantastic" sales, they were hardly regarded as something new and exciting. As Kurfirst had recently launched his Radioactive label, via MCA distribution, with such attention-getting bands as Londonbeat, Live, and Fatima Mansions, it made sense that he bring the Ramones in as well. No longer would they have to worry about budgets, promotions, or getting lost in the shuffle.

"It's a new day in the life of the Ramones," says Kurfirst. "Finally, they'll get the push they deserve, which will translate to the success they deserve."

He wished them the best, but after all they'd been through together, Seymour Stein was sorry to see the Ramones leave. "As long as there was Sire Records, the Ramones had a home," he says. "I look back at my association with them, and it is one of my proudest accomplishments. When people look back on Sire, they'll look back at the Ramones, more than artists who sold fifty times the amount of records that they sold. They are beyond a band—they're an institution."

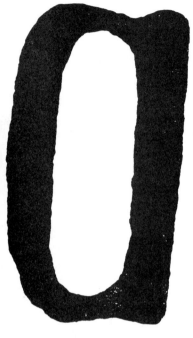

On institution indeed. Now a reputable songwriting expert Joey closed out 1991 by returning to the Bottom Line, the famed Manhattan club the Ramones had blown out back in 1976, for a songwriters' showcase hosted by Vin Scelsa; the discussion also included Grammy winner Don Henry, former DB's Peter Holsapple and Chris Stamey, and John Wesley Harding. Joey was accompanied on electric guitar by Andy Shernoff, and brought the house down with his songwriting secrets (his "most creative moments" are "at 5 A.M. in bed, taking a shit in the toilet, or any time when I'm supposed to be doing something else"), as well as by his revelation that the "Twenty-

The Ramones
Today

GARY KURFIRST PRESENTS

ESCAPE FROM NEW YORK

90

RY HARRISON · DEBORAH HARRY · RAMONES · TOM TOM CLUB

Escape from New York tour program cover '90.

twenty-twenty-four hours to go" chorus on "I Wanna Be Sedated" was patterned after the Ohio Express 1968 bubblegum smash hit, "Chewy Chewy."

Another institution was the Ramones annual New York holiday show, held at the Ritz just before New Year's Eve. The place was typically packed and primed by the time the Ramones opening music (the theme from the film *The Good, the Bad and the Ugly*) came up and the band blasted into "Teenage Lobotomy." It was an all-ages crowd—no generation gap here. Ramones T-shirts and *no* T-shirts, black leather jackets and Princeton sweatshirts, Guns N' Roses denim jackets and Hell's Angels denim jackets, tie dyes and dyed hair, miniskirts and nose rings, jackets-and-ties and tattooed torsos. All these plus the band that never ages, that never changes. The Ramones really are the Grateful Dead of punk rock!

"I hope we don't change too much!" says Johnny. "Basically, we're too old!" Yet their fans keep getting younger and younger—except for the ones that keep getting older and older. And the Ramones have long recognized and appreciated the loyalty and devotion of the legions who have kept the band alive for nearly two decades.

In March 1992, right around the time Donna Weinbrecht won the gold medal in mogul skiing in the Albertville, France Olympics to the tune of "Rock 'n' Roll High School," the Ramones last album for Sire was released. *Loco Live* was also the first live Ramones album released in America (though numerous bootlegs have long been available). It was recorded in April 1991 in Spain. "Yeah! *Que pasa teyos?* It's great to be back in Barcelona tonight! Take it, C. J.!" It could be anywhere in the world: After C. J. shouts, "One-two-three-four!" and the first power chords of "Blitzkrieg Bop" ring out, the masses inevitably chant along, "Hey, ho! Let's Go!," as they did at this show. The Ramones are truly universal.

"Blitzkrieg Bop" was also made into a concert video by George Seminara, using blistering performance footage shot on tour in 1991 at festivals in Belgium (the Ramones headlined the Punkelpopp Festival there before one hundred thousand fans) and what was then East Germany. Seminara hopes eventually to release a documentary of this European tour, since he shot so much background material.

And it seemed that the Ramones momentum was continuing at full throttle. The music paper *Alternative Press* included a track from "Loco Live" in a cassette compilation giveaway, and *Sassy* magazine had a similar promotion that featured Joey introducing the tape's Ramones cut and twelve others by new musical acts. *Creem* included the Ramones in a compilation as well.

Joey's outside interests also continued unabated. Encouraged by Marky's liberalism, he performed his set at two presidential campaign rallies for Jerry Brown before the New York primary elections—along with Marky, Andy Shernoff, and Skinny Bones. He also found time to assist old friend Deborah Harry on her next album: The duet "Standing in My Way" was "classic Blondie meets the Ramones," he said. Producer and ex-Blondie creative force Chris Stein openly predicted that a backlash against "conservative music" was shortly forthcoming, and that the Ramones and Deborah would finally get their due.

The Ramones, Harry, and Stein had renewed their mutual friendship during the "Escape from New York" tour, which Harry referred to in her raunchy liner notes for *Loco Live*. Ed Stasium was also affected by seeing that tour when it came to Los Angeles; according to Kurfirst, "He said he'd give everything to produce the next record."

The Ramones duly waited until Stasium became available in January 1992, then recorded their first album on the Radioactive label at the Magic Shop and Baby Monster studios, with help from Andy Shernoff,

The Turtles met the Ramones during the recording of *Mondo Bizzaro*. The legendary Mark Volman and Howard Kaylan, a.k.a. Flo and Eddie who had recorded with everyone from John Lennon to Bruce Springsteen, added their inimitable backup vocals to two tracks on the album. L–R: Volman, Joey Ramone, Kaylan. (Chuck Pulin/Star File)

Daniel Rey, and guitarist Vernon Reid of Living Colour, whom Stasium had produced. (In "Lifestyles of the Ramones," incidentally, Reid had said that the Ramones sound, which he loved, was "like a locomotive or something.")

Lending their distinguished backup vocals were Mark Volman and Howard Kaylan, a.k.a. Flo & Eddie, a.k.a. the Turtles, who flew in from Los Angeles to harmonize on "Poison Heart," one of three songs by Dee Dee, and on the Beach Boys soundalike song, "Touring."

Besides their classic Turtles hits from the sixties, Flo & Eddie are best known for their work with Frank Zappa. But at one time or another, they've backed up everyone from John Lennon to Bruce Springsteen, T. Rex to Blondie. Joey was a big fan of theirs, and got to know them when they hosted a radio show at New York's K-ROCK. "Neither of us have relied on commercial success to keep our careers going," says Volman. "That's hard to do in a business that does its best to squelch individuality. But you don't really need to sell records to assure your place in history."

Volman also expects that the new Ramones album, entitled *Mondo Bizarro*, will finally put the Ramones over the top. "With *Spin* picking the Ramones as one of the seven greatest rock bands, and with the success of Nirvana and all the other alternative bands, the doors are really open for the Ramones now. A lot of people are really aware of their credibility."

The new album was released in September 1, 1992, with the track listing as follows: "Censorshit," "The Job That Ate My Brain," "Poison Heart," "Anxiety," "Strength to Endure," "It's Gonna Be Alright," "Take It as It Comes," "Main Man," "Tomorrow She Goes Away," "I Won't Let It Happen," "Cabbies on Crack," "Heidi Is a Headcase," and "Touring."

Besides "Poison Heart," Dee Dee penned "Main Man" and "Strength to Endure," which was originally written for Marianne Faithfull. "That's about living life on life's terms," he told *Boston Rock's* Brett Milano, "trying to endure your alter ego, finding your true heart and soul, finding serenity, and reaching your goals. We've got a responsibility to the younger generation. I mean, I like a lot of heavy metal groups like Guns N' Roses and Metallica. But the other day I saw an ad that Metallica put out and it said, 'Alcoholica.' I don't think that's good, for bands to be encouraging people to drink. That's a thing of the sixties, you know, flower power and acid."

Marky wrote a couple songs on the latest album as well, including "Anxiety," with help from Garrett (Skinny Bones) Uhlenbrock. Besides singing originals, the band chose to cover a lesser-known Doors song, "Take It as It Comes," in a harder, heavier, and faster manner, and tried to get Ray Manzarek to reprise his classic keyboard part on it but when he proved unavailable, they brought in Joe McGinty of the Psychedelic Furs.

"The Ramones have a little help now and then," says Rey, who added "a little coloring" with his guitar playing, songwriting, and arranging assistance. "But it's all Ramones. If somebody adds anything, it's just Johnny's pragmatism: 'If he can do it in five minutes and I do it in a half hour, we save this much money.' That's the true spirit of punk!"

Joey penned seven of the songs on *Mondo Bizzaro*. "It's more topical, like 'Censorshit,' which deals with right-wing fascists trying to take away our freedom. 'Cabbies on Crack' came out of a hellride home from the manager's office. He was definitely on *something*. I'm lucky to be alive! Then there's one song that's dedicated to the fans, 'It's Gonna Be Alright.' It shows our appreciation for their loyalty and the fact that they're a breed of their own—total diehard loyalists.

"I think it's the best album we ever made, a real turning point. For one thing, Ed's back, so it's like a reunion, and with C. J. in the band, there's just a real healthier attitude and enthusiasm. And the band's a lot closer and really enjoyable for me."

Also helping immensely is Joey's new attitude toward *himself*. For the last two years, Joey has been completely alcohol- and substance-free, and totally committed to healthful living. "I wasn't that heavy a drinker but I was hanging out and partying all the time, drinking and cocaine. Not like I was this or that, but I got disgusted with the lifestyle and stopped everything cold. Now I'm more focused, more in control and in touch with myself. I'm into holistic medicine and go to a homeopathic chiropractor, and I've never been more happy or creative in my life. It was like after two weeks, I had this intense flow of creative energy and started writing great songs again. And I'm doing all these other things I enjoy, too.

"Mark's been a total inspiration. I always loved him as a drummer—he's up there with Ginger Baker and Keith Moon and John Bonham. But I only got to know him as a person the second time around because he was always so drunk. And John, he's been real supportive. It's like he's there for you. I've learned a lot from him about the business, and I like him more than ever. We enjoy each other's company now. Before, everything seemed like an uphill battle, but now everything's more in unison.

"It's just believing in what we're doing. It's hard to articulate—the fans, the music, the power and energy. There's something very special about the band, that's totally unlike anything else. People always talk about needing a 'Ramones fix.' For me the Ramones are the best therapy in the world. I just want to take them farther!"

So, of course, does management. "Finally, they'll get their just desserts," says Andrea Starr, the Ramones "hands-on" manager in Gary Kurfirst's Overland management firm, who has devoted her energies—

not to mention heart and soul—almost exclusively to the band for nearly a decade. Like many others who share in the Ramones longevity, she feels that *Mondo Bizarro* is the band's best.

"They're getting along better than ever, there's an excitement that didn't exist before. Everyone's become warmer toward each other, and closer together. It's like a marriage—four people married. Two are bad enough! But this is four, and everyone with a distinct personality, particularly Dee Dee, who changed from week to week. C. J.'s really the ultimate hero: He was able to capture the essence of Dee Dee's spirit. He sings like Dee Dee and even looks like Dee Dee!"

What also makes it work, though, is that the Ramones each have their interests outside the band. Joey's have already been detailed extensively, though it should be added that he has a more spiritual side in addition to the political, and has visited the *siddha yoga* teacher Gurumayi.

Marky, as viewers of "Lifestyles of the Ramones" know, is a car freak—and a Bruce Lee fan. So his pride and joy is a 1965 Imperial, the "Black Beauty" of the classic sixties "The Green Hornet" TV series starring Lee.

Less known, though, is C. J.'s interest in Native American causes. "I have a little Huron blood in me, and now and then I play with some friends of mine in a group called Rotten Belly. That's the name of an underground Indian society of *contrary people*, who would talk or smoke when they weren't supposed to. But they were very useful, too, and taught the children. So I'm trying to put a single out and send the money to the Lakota Sioux, because their reservations are in such bad shape."

C. J. always brings tapes of music along with him on the road, and besides artists like the Doors, Hendrix, the Beatles, Sinead O'Connor, and Tanita Tikaram, he listens to Native American flute music. Johnny, the utter baseball maniac, listens only to baseball games, and when he's home, he'll spend much of his morning at the supermarket and the post office, comparing stats with the guys in his rotisserie baseball league. Even on the road, he listens to ballgames on a tiny red Panasonic AM radio, which doesn't even have headphones!

He was listening to it, in fact, backstage at a gig at Columbia University just after completing *Mondo Bizarro*. Then Johnny and the Ramones went onstage, before a packed house of college kids and guests (including photographer Bob Gruen and Sean Lennon). They played "Beat on the Brat," "Gimme Gimme Shock Treatment," "Psycho Therapy," "I Wanna Be Sedated," "Rockaway Beach," and "Pet Sematary." Like they say, it's the soundtrack of your life—even if it's a decidedly *different* life!

"We believe in freedom, and we believe in human rights!" Joey announced. "Register and vote!" The next song, appropriately, was "I Wanna Live." Outside, Arturo Vega was selling six different T-shirts, not to mention an autographed bass drum head, a Ramones baseball hat, and a set of pins. The clothing and accessory designs all were derived from the same T-shirt that Arturo had created from stick-on block letters eighteen years earlier.

C.J., the newest Ramone, doing what he does best. (Rena Cohen)

e play all the outlands and ports from Des Moines to Pocatello," says Joey. "Every little place is just as important as everywhere else, and nothing is more exciting than hitting new territories and turning them on to something new and exciting."

Johnny adds to the sentiment. "We're just middle-class kids from Queens—same as middle-class kids from Nebraska. Ain't no different."

Except that for nearly twenty years, Johnny and Joey—with Dee Dee, Tommy, Marky, Richie, and C.J.—have been making records that have assured them all their place in history.

It seems hard to imagine now that when it all started, Johnny had

From Des Moines

To Pocatello

RAMONES

in JAPAN 1990

just been laid off from a construction job, and figured on recording one album at most before his dad got him another job. In fact, back then he was too embarrassed even to tell his parents about the *existence* of the Ramones, or even that he was in a band, until the first album was not only recorded but already *released*. "They'd have said, 'Stop this! You can't even play a song!' " he says.

After *Ramones* was released, a lot of people agreed. A lot more didn't. "They were a prototype, like Elvis, the Beatles, the Rolling Stones, the Velvet Underground, the New York Dolls," says former Dolls manager Marty Thau. "You can't begin to guess how many thousands of bands came after them." Howie Klein, the journalist/deejay who moved on to work for Sire Records, saw the Ramones as "the Johnny Appleseeds" of the punk/new wave movement, leaving the seeds wherever they went for new bands to sprout up. "People saw that you don't have to study guitar for twenty years and copy Jeff Beck, that you play rock 'n' roll for fun, because that's what it's all about."

Likewise, journalist and Ramones first manager Danny Fields recalls that the most gratifying thing about the early days was that they'd play a small out-of-town venue, "then six months later we'd return and these adorable little kids in black leather would come up and say, 'We saw you guys and started a band. If you could, we could.' It sounds like an insult, but it was a great compliment—it's what the Ramones said when they saw the Dolls and what the Clash said when they saw the Ramones: 'Let's get out of rehearsal and onto the stage, because we're never gonna be Eric Clapton and it doesn't matter.' They just lit fires all over world. Every hardcore band I interview says they were a defining moment."

In early 1992, a consensus of *Spin* critics, on the occasion of the magazine's seventh anniversary, placed the Ramones among the top seven rock bands of all time. "My feeling is that it was justified because they really did create punk," says publisher Bob Guccione, Jr. "Although the Sex Pistols did more with the image, the Ramones were as original as Led Zeppelin causing heavy metal out of the blues. The *Spin* readership still goes to their shows—in a sense, they're to punk what the Grateful Dead is to the sixties. There's a new generation that was in diapers when the Ramones were discovered at CBGB's, and what's great about them is that they still *matter*."

Hard to believe that a few years ago, Joey told an interviewer that he'd kill himself if the Ramones didn't start selling records. He's still alive, of course, and if *Mondo Bizarro* really is the commercial breakthrough we've all waited for since 1974 (and, as with every Ramones album since then, it *should* be), he must be more alive now than ever.

Because now, more than ever, *everyone* loves the Ramones. Kids of all ages, aging kids who were at that first CB's gig, kids who back then weren't even born yet. And why not? I mean, what's not to like? The

Ramones really are *The* American Band, wart(hog)s and all. Their symbol is the American Eagle. They even contractually stipulate that Yoohoo chocolate drink is to be provided in their dressing room at gigs, because, as Joey says, "It's the quintessential American drink." And who more than the Ramones stands for freedom, democracy, and The American Way? And in true American Dream fashion, haven't they pulled themselves up by their sneaker laces through hard work and dedication, and, when they got stepped on or held back, didn't they just get up and push forward even harder?

True, it wasn't easy, but nothing ever is in real life, and the Ramones, even with their heads buried in comic books and horror films and dementia, were nothing if not *real*. I mean, look at yourself: Do you look more like David Bowie or Bon Jovi, say, than Joey or Johnny Ramone? Is your life closer to Dee Dee's or Marky Ramone's, say, than Mick Jagger's or Michael Bolton's? And with all the hard times and problems and weirdness that the Ramones have experienced, I mean, really—in "End of the Century" U.S.A., is it really that much different from what all of us have had to deal with—to at least some degree—in our own lives?

I would guess, *of course not!* Which, in a nutshell, is why the Ramones have survived. For when it comes right down to it, the Ramones "R" Us, basically. Most of us aren't beautiful by a long shot. Most of us never got the dream car, the dream girl, the dream family, the dream house, the dream job, The American Dream. But we're glad to see someone that's like us at least appear to do it for all of us. And they've worked so hard at it.

"They *live* to work," says manager Gary Kurfirst. "I often tell them, 'Take time off, you'll burn yourself out,' but they love to work. And when they're not working, they're rehearsing. They never take a vacation. They don't go to the Caribbean or Hawaii like other bands. They don't even take taxis—they take the subway!"

Yes, the Ramones have always stayed true to who and what they are. "Some bands are *chameleonic*," continues Kurfirst. "They change their spots or colors with the times, the climate, or season. But the Ramones never changed their 'spots.' If it's one hundred degrees in July, they'll still wear black leather jackets! They'll never change."

Indeed, the Grateful Dead comparison is accurate. "They've been around forever," Joey told *Island-Ear*, "and they've always been a sort of 'cult' band in their own way, maybe in some way a larger scale version of the Ramones, if you follow what I mean. . . . The great part is that the Dead still sound the way they always did. They didn't go changing their sound in order to have a hit. They sound now just like they did ten years ago and that's the same idea behind us."

Amazingly, although as mentioned, the Ramones today both sound and *look* exactly the same as they ever did, they really *aren't* the same.

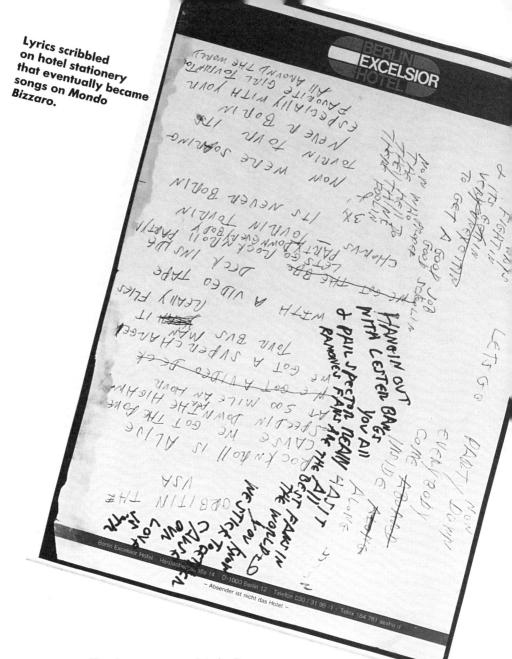

Lyrics scribbled on hotel stationery that eventually became songs on Mondo Bizzaro.

They've grown up (kind of),
or at least grown into who they are. I don't
mean to saddle them with *maturity*, but they're comfortable. They've
made it. They may not know it, but they've made it. Their albums each
have sold in the neighborhood of a quarter-million copies, though "Ramones Mania" is slowly approaching the gold half-million sales mark.
Meanwhile, "Lifestyles of the Ramones," at twenty-five thousand copies
sold, was about to earn a gold video award—then the officials doubled
the required sales total!

But the numbers game never really applied to the Ramones, anyway. In fact, the only number that really matters is 1,800—they've now played more than 1,800 shows!

"People think they're cartoon characters, but they're not," says Kevin Patrick, now the president of Medicine Records, and formerly the a&r executive responsible for signing bands including X, the Georgia Satellites, the Pogues, and Marianne Faithfull—besides being a member of the Ramones privileged inner circle. "They created an entire genre, gave license to a look, a sound. And they offered one hundred percent *escapism*—the ultimate test of any act. They have their own *layer* in the universe, and they'll get their justice, but even if they don't, at the end of the day, *they're* the ones in the history books, not the self-fulfilling, tone-deaf, playlist-paranoid, creatively handcuffed, musically frustrated nobodies that control the radio stations—and I'm being polite!"

So the Ramones didn't get radio airplay. But they made us remember rock 'n' roll radio, taking us back to where we were when music didn't just mean something, it meant *everything*. As superfan Roger Risko says, "This was the stuff that rock was made of." Yet in harking back to the best of the old, it presented a clean breaking point from which to begin anew, with complete freedom, in one last burst of adolescent energy, one last wave of something new like the Beatles, though this time reflecting adult reality instead of teen dreams. And if you were too young to appreciate any of this, no matter! You could still relate on your own terms, because the Ramones never grew up so far that their songs couldn't stay in touch with the kids of today.

By all rights, perhaps, Joey *should* have killed himself. The Ramones *wouldn't* have made it. They would have made that one album and gone back to construction or hairdressing or peddling artificial flowers, like the rest of us. But someone has to make it, if the rest of us are to have any hope, or at the very least, *satisfaction* that people like us *can* make it. As I said, the Ramones "R" Us. So is the creative and personal tension between the hardcore punk of Johnny, the romanticism of Joey, and the uniquely troubled sensitivity of Dee Dee which fell somewhere in between. "If I wasn't in the band, I'd be their number one fan!" says Marky. "We all feel that way, and that's why we've been together eighteen years."

"Everybody thought it was a joke that wouldn't last," says publicist Janis Schacht. "Here it is almost twenty years later and Monte's still behind the wheel!"

In this ever-changing world the Ramones stay the same, as Johnny told *Rolling Stone*. Or as Monte Melnick likes to say, "The song *Ramones* the same."

"Wanchewtreefawww!"

Tour Schedule

1974

Mar 30—Performance Studio
(as a trio)
Aug 16–17—CBGB
Aug 24–25—CBGB
Aug 29, 30, 31, Sep. 1—CBGB
Sept 2—party in Soho
Sept 7, 8—CBGB
Sept 15—CBGB

Sept 17—CBGB
Sept 22—CBGB
Sept 24—CBGB
Oct 1—CBGB
Oct 6—CBGB
Oct 8—CBGB
Oct 12, 13—CBGB
Oct 20—CBGB

Oct 31,—CBGB
Nov 1, 2, 3—CBGB
Nov 16—Perf Studio
Nov 17—CBGB
Dec 7—Performance Studio
Dec 20—Perf Studio

1975

Feb 14—Brandy's II, NY
Feb 28—Perf Studio
Mar 1—Perf Studio
Mar 6, 7, 8—CBGB
Apr 11—Perf Studio
Apr 14, 15—CBGB
Apr 25—Perf Studio, with Blondie
May 12, 13—CBGB
May 30—Conventry, Queens,
with Heartbreakers

June 5, 6, 7, 8—CBGB, Talking
Heads
June 20, 21, 22—CBGB, T Heads
July 4, 5, 6—CBGB, with Blondie
July 11—Waterbury, Conn, with
Johnny Winter
July 16, 17, 18—CBGB, Rock
Festival (Blondie, Tuff Darts,
T Heads, etc)
July 31, Aug 1—CBGB, T Heads

Aug 22, 23, 24—CBGB
Sept 12, 13—Perf Studio, Blondie
Oct 3, 4, 5—Mothers in NY with
Blondie
Oct 24, 25, 26—CBGB, Blondie
Nov 21, 22, 23—CBGB
Dec 18, 19—CBGB
Dec 31—Sea of Clouds in NY
with Heartbreakers

1976

Jan 30, 31, Feb 1—CBGB with
Heartbreakers
Feb 25—Nashua NH
Feb 26—Boston
Feb 27—Brockton MA
Mar 22—My Fathers Place, Roslyn,
L.I. with Heartbreakers
Apr 1, 2, 3—CBGB
Apr 9, 10,—NJ, Phase V, with
Blondie
Apr 18—Max's KC with Blondie
May 10, 11—Bottom Line with
Dr Feelgood
May 13, 14, 15—CBGB
May 20, 21, 22—Boston
May 28—New Cannan CT
(Caanan)
May 29—Fairfield CT
June 10—Dover NJ
June 11, 12—Max's Kansas City

June 19—Cleveland (rainout)
June 20—Youngstown, Ohio
(when Monthe got hired)
(Danny said: If he can get the
money, because we flopped,
you can be the road manager)
July 4—Roundhouse, London,
Flamin' Groovies
July 5—Dingwalls, London, Flaming
Groovies
July 13—My Fathers Place, L.I.
July 16, 17—Islip LI
July 18—Ashbury Park NJ
July 22—New Haven CT
Aug 11, 12—Los Angeles, Roxy
with Flaming Groovies
Aug 16, 17—L.A., Starwood
Aug 19, 20, 21, 22—S.F.
Aug 23, 24—Huntington Beach
CA

Aug 25—Huntington Beach,
diff place
Aug 27, 28—Redondo Beach CA
Sept 2—Hempstead L.I with
Good Rats
Sept 3, 4—Friar Tuck's CT
Sept 9, 10, 11—CBGB
Sept 12—White Plains NY
Sept 17, 18—Westport CT
Sept 19—Dover NJ
Sept 24, 25—Toronto
Sept 27, 28—My Fathers Place, LI,
with T Heads
Oct 8, 9—Max's with T Heads
Oct 16—Detroit
Oct 22, 23, 24—Wash DC
Nov 12, 13—Newport RI
Nov 24, 25, 26, 27—Atlanta GA

1977

Jan 28, 29, 30—Boston
Feb 2—My Fathers Place, LI
Feb 3, 4, 5—CBGB; with Suicide, but also Feb 4 at Nassau Coliseum in LI with Blue Oyster Cult
Feb 8—Dover NJ
Feb 10—Poughkeepsie NY with Blue Oyster Cut
Feb 16–20, L.A., the Whiskey, with Blondie
Feb 22, 23—SF
Feb 24—San Jose CA
Feb 25, 26—Berkeley
Feb 28—Palo Alto
Mar 2—Sacramento
Mar 4—Bremerton, Wash
Mar 5—Aberdeen, Wash
Mar 6—Seattle
Mar 8—visited Phil Spector's house
Mar 10—Encinitas CA
Mar 11—San Bernardino CA
Mar 12—San Diego
Mar 13—Norwalk CA
Mar 15, 16—Denver
Mar 25—Buffalo NY, Buffalo U with the Dictators
Mar 26—Countryside IL
Mar 27—Detroit
Mar 28—Ann Arbor MI, with Sonics Rendevous band (Fred Sonic Smith)
Mar 31, Apr 1, 2, 3—CBGB
Apr 8—Westport CN
Apr 9—Philadelphia
Apr 10—West Islip LI
Apr 13, 14—My Fathers Place, Roslyn, LI with Cramps
Apr 15, 16—Salisbury, Mass
Apr 17—Boston
Apr 20—CBGB with Cramps
Apr 24—Zurich, Switz with T Heads
Apr 26—travelled 18 hours to Marseilles but cancelled for lack of power to run the amps
Apr 27—Geneva, Switz
Apr 28—Lyon, France
Apr 30—La Havre, France
May 2—Paris
May 3—Orleans, France
May 4—Lille, France

May 5—Brussels, Belgium
May 6—Amsterdam, Netherlands
May 7—Eindhoven, Neth
May 8—Groningen, Neth
May 10—Rotterdam, Neth
May 11—Utrecht, Neth
May 12—Copenhagen
May 15—Stockholm, Sweden
May 16—Helsinki, Finland
May 17—Tampere, Finland
May 19—Liverpool
May 20—Leeds
May 20, 21—Glasgow, Scotland
May 22—Manchester
May 23—Doncaster
May 24—Birmingham
May 25—went to see Clash on day off in Brighton
May 26—Aylesbury, England
May 28—Slough, England
May 29—Croyden
May 30—Bristol
May 31—Swindon
June 1—Plymouth
June 2—Penzance
June 4—Canterbury
June 5—London
June 6, London, with Saints and T Heads
June 9, 10, 11—CBGB with Cramps
June 17, 18—Toronto
June 21—Chicago
June 23—Madison, El Tejon
June 24—Waukesha
June 26—Ann Arbor
June 28—Cincinnati
June 29—Waukegan
June 30—Rockford
July 1—Minneapolis
July 2—Minneapolis
July 4—Milwaukee
July 6—Chicago
July 8—Lebanon, IL
July 14—Austin
July 15, 16—Houston
July 18—San Antonio
July 20—Killeen TX
July 24—Dallas TX
July 28—Huntington Beach CA
July 30—SF with Dictators at Winterland

Aug 4—Seattle with Tom Petty & Heartbreakers
Aug 5—Portland, Ore with Petty
Aug 6—Vancouver, Canada
Aug 9—filmed Don Kirshner's Rock Concert
Aug 10—LA at Whiskey
Oct 1—Dover NJ
Oct 4—Waterbury CT, the Palace Theater with Iggy Pop
Oct 6—NY Palladium with Iggy
Oct 8—Montreal with Iggy
Oct 9—Toronto with Iggy
Oct 11—Wash DC
Oct 12—Philadelphia with Iggy
Oct 15—Baltimore with Iggy
Oct 19—Cleveland with Iggy
Oct 20—Detroit with Iggy, Cobo Hall
Oct 21—LA, the Whiskey, with Martin Mull
Oct 22—Chicago with Iggy and Leslie West
Oct 27—through 30—CBGB
Nov 5—Brown U in Providence RI
Nov 7—Poughkeepsie NY
Nov 8—Philadelphia
Nov 11, 12—Pittsburgh
Nov 14—Utica NY
Nov 15—Providence
Nov 16—Amherst MA
Nov 18—Boston (Orpheum with T Heads and Eddie and the Hot Rods)
Nov 19—Passaic, Capitol Theatre, T Heads and Eddie & Rods)
Dec 16—saw Sex Pistols in England
Dec 17—Carlisle, England
Dec 18—Edinborough, Scot
Dec 19—Glasgow, Scot
Dec 20—Newcastle, England
Dec 21—Manchester
Dec 23—Cambridge
Dec 28—Birmingham
Dec 29—Stoke on Trent
Dec 30—Aylesbury
Dec 31—Jan 1 1978—Rainbow Theatre, (the live album recorded) with Rezilloes and Generation X

1978

Jan 5—New Haven CT
Jan 6—Hartford CT
Jan 7—NY, the Palladium with Runaways and Suicide
Jan 9—Dover NJ
Jan 13—Buffalo NY
Jan 14—Detroit with Runaways
Jan 15—Youngstown, Ohio with Runaways

Jan 16—Cleveland with Runaways
Jan 18—Madison
Jan 19—Milwaukee with Runaways
Jan 20—Chicago with Runaways
Jan 21—Minneapolis with Runaways
Jan 23—Kansas City, Kansas
Jan 27—Santa Monica CA Civic Center with Runaways

Jan 30, 31—SF
Feb 2—Eugene, Oregon
Feb 3—Seattle
Feb 4—Portland
Feb 7—San Diego with Runaways
Feb 8—Phoenix with Runaways
Feb 10—Albuquerque NM
Feb 12—Tulsa
Feb 14—San Antonio TX with Runaways

Feb 17—Austin TX with Runaways
Feb 18—Ft Worth with Runaways
Feb 19—Houston with Runaways
Feb 21—New Orleans with Runaways
Feb 22—Baton Rouge with Runaways
Feb 25—Atlanta with Runaways
Feb 27—Charlotte NC with Runaways
Mar 2—Orlando FL with Runaways
Mar 3—Miami with Runaways
Mar 6—Belville IL with Runaways
Mar 8—Ann Arbor
Mar 9—Columbus, Ohio
Mar 10—Cincinnati
Mar 12—Champagne IL
Mar 13—Akron, Ohio with Runaways
Mar 15—Norfolk VA with Runaways
Mar 17—Baltimore MD with Runaways
Mar 18—Philadelphia with Runaways and the Jam
Mar 19—Wash DC with Runaways
Mar 21 and 22—Boston
Mar 24—Hempstead LI with Runaways
Mar 25—Passaic NJ, Capital Theater with Runaways
Mar 31—Syracuse NY
Apr 1—Yatesboro, Penn, with Runaways
Apr 2—Jamestown NY with Runaways
Apr 4, 5—Toronto
Apr 16—Trenton NJ with Dead Boys
Apr 20—Rochester NY
Apr 21—Wilkes-Barre, Penn, with Patti Smith
Apr 23—Toledo OH
Apr 24—Lansing MI
Apr 25—Indianapolis
Apr 27—Sunderland, Mass
Apr 29—Willimantic CT

May 4—CBGB, Johnny Blitz benefit
June 29—Poughkeepsie NY, first job with Mark
July 1—New Cruz Brunswick NJ
July 2—Greenwood Lake NY
July 5—Roslyn LI with Richard Hell
July 7–8, 9—Boston
July 10—Providence RI
July 12—Portland, Maine
July 16—Youngstown OH with David Johansen
July 17—Lansing MI
July 19—Flint MI
July 21—Columbus OH
July 23—Cincinnati
July 25—Palantine IL
July 26—Madison WI
July 27—Dekalb IL
July 29—Kansas City KS
July 30—Springfield, Missouri
July 31—St Louis
Aug 1—Champaign IL
Aug 2—Highwood IL
Aug 5—Ashbury Park NJ with Patti Smith
Aug 11, 12, 13—Hurrah's NY (audition for R&R High School)
Aug 18—Dover NH with Cramps
Aug 19—Willimantic CT
Aug 21—New Haven CT with Shrapnel
Aug 26—New Brunswick NJ
Sept 5—Helsinki, Finland
Sept 7—Stockholm, Sweden (Keith Moon died)
Sept 8—Malmow, Sweden
Sept 9—Ronneby, Sweden
Sept 11—Hamburg, Germany
Sept 12—Berlin
Sept 14—Brussels
Sept 15—Amsterdam
Sept 16—Arnhem, Holland
Sept 18—Paris
Sept 23—Belfast
Sept 24—Dublin
Sept 26—Bristol, England

Sept 28—Newcastle
Sept 29—Manchester
Sept 30—Birmingham
Oct 2—London
Oct 3—Cardiff, Wales
Oct 4—Leeds, England
Oct 5—Coventry, England
Oct 6—Edinburgh, Scotland
Oct 7—Glasgow, Scot
Oct 19—New Haven CT
Oct 21—Queens College NY
Oct 22—Providence RI with Patti Smith
Oct 23—Philadelphia
Oct 25—Albany NY
Oct 26—Amherst, Mass
Oct 27—Wash DC
Oct 28—Richmond VA
Nov 12—Raleigh NC
Nov 13—Atlanta with Black Sabbath and Van Halen
Nov 15—Highwood IL
Nov 17—Omaha, Neb
Nov 18—St Paul MN open for Foreigner (their fans too lame to boo)
Dec 1—San Bernardino, open for Black Sabbath (famous San Bernardino show)
Dec 2—Stockton CA
Dec 4—Long Beach, open for Black Sabbath
Dec 5—Phoenix open for Black Sabbath
Dec 14—filmed concert scene for R&R High School at Roxy
Dec 15—San Diego
Dec 18—Costa Mesa CA
Dec 24, 25, 27, LA the Whiskey
Dec 28—SF with the Tubes
Dec 29—Reno open for Eddie Money
Dec 30—Santa Cruz with Rick Derringer
Dec 31—San Jose with the Tubes

1979

Jan 3—Portland
Jan 4—Seattle
Jan 5—Seattle
Jan 6—Vancouver
Jan 9—Boise, Idaho
Jan 10—Idaho Falls, Idaho
Jan 11—Salt Lake City, Utah
Jan 13, 14—Boulder CO
Jan 18—Dallas
Jan 19—Austin
Jan 20—San Antonio
Jan 21—Houston
Jan 23—Lafayette
Jan 24—New Orleans
Jan 25—Baton Rouge

Jan 26—Lake Charles with Toto
Jan 28—Nashville
Jan 29—Birmingham AL
Jan 30—Atlanta
Jan 31—Raleigh NC
Feb 2—College Park MD
Feb 4—Baltimore
Feb 6, 7—Toronto
Feb 8—Buffalo
Feb 10—Passaic NJ, Capitol Theater with David Johansen and Shrapnel
Feb 14—Shelton CN
Feb 15—Sunderland MA
Feb 16—New Brunswick NJ

Feb 17—Providence RI
Feb 23—Toledo OH
Feb 24—Chicago
Feb 25—Detroit with the Romantics
Feb 26—Ann Arbor
Feb 27—Cleveland with Romantics
Feb 28—Cincinnati
Mar 1—Columbus
Mar 3—Boston with Johansen
Mar 4—Hartford CT
Mar 6, 7—Pittsburgh
Mar 9—NY Palladium with Lester Bangs (Birdland)
Mar 22—West Orange NJ

Mar 23—Princeton NJ
Mar 24—Brown's Mill NJ
Mar 25—Ashbury Park NJ
Mar 29—Dover NJ
Mar 30—NY Columbia U
Mar 31—Jamesburg NJ
Apr 6—Roslyn LI
Apr 7—Roslyn J LI
Apr 8—New Brunswick NJ
Apr 10—CBGB (last time) (benefit
  for police bulletproof vest)
Apr 12—film Uncle Floyd tv show,
  which did numerous times
Apr 18—attended preview of
  R&R High School
Apr 19—Dallas to attend another
  preview
May 1—start LP with Spector
June 8—SF, outdoor show
June 16—Dover NJ
June 17—New Haven
June 19—Amityville LI
June 21—West Orange NJ
June 22—Ashbury Park NJ
June 23—Browns Mill NJ
June 24—Allentown PA
June 26, 27—Staten Island
June 29 and 30—Boston
July 2—Toronto, big show,
  Canadian World Music Festival,
  Exhibition Stadium with
  Aerosmith, Ted Nugent,
  Johnny Winter, ACDC
July 5—Poughkeepsie
July 6—Syracuse
July 7—Rochester
July 8—Albany
July 11, 12—Toronto
July 13, 14—Montreal

July 19, 20, 21—Roslyn LI
July 22—Taunton MA
July 26—Wash DC
July 27—Baltimore
July 29—Ocean City MD
July 30—Virginia Beach VA
July 31—Raleigh NC
Aug 3—Hartford CT
Aug 4—Brooklyn
Aug 6—NY, Central Park
Aug 8—Ashbury Park NJ
Aug 9—Dover NJ
Aug 11, 12—Amityville LI
Aug 13—Port Chester NY
Sept 11—Albany
Sept 14—Port Chester
Sept 15—Port Chester
Sept 18—Wayne NJ
Sept 22—Cookstown NJ
Sept 27—C.W. Post College LI
Sept 28, 29—Brooklyn
Sept 30—New Haven
Oct 2—Bergenfield NJ
Oct 3—Wayne NJ
Oct 4—West Orange NJ
Oct 6—Boston
Oct 7—NYC Hotel Diplomat,
  the Rock n Roll Convention
Oct 8—Queens College NY
Oct 9—Philadelphia
Oct 11—Dayton, Ohio
Oct 12—Galesburg IL
Oct 13—Evanston IL
Oct 14—Grand Rapids MI
Oct 15—Chicago
Oct 17—Marietta OH, with Police
Oct 18—Detroit with Joe Jackson
Oct 19—Chicago
Oct 20—Milwaukee

Oct 23—Denver
Oct 26—Davis, U. of California
Oct 27—Oakland
Oct 28—LA, UCLA
Oct 29—UCLA
Oct 31—San Diego
Nov 2—Costa Mesa
Nov 4—Irvine CA
Nov 5—Claremont CA
Nov 6—Garden Grove CA
Nov 8—Tucson
Nov 9—El Paso
Nov 11—Lubbock
Nov 13—Austin
Nov 14—Dallas
Nov 16—Houston
Nov 18—New Orleans
Nov 20—Birmingham
Nov 22—Atlanta
Nov 23—Nashville
Nov 24—Memphis
Nov 26—St Louis
Nov 27—Madison, Headliners
Nov 28—Minneapolis
Nov 30—Milwaukee
Dec 1—Cincinnati
Dec 4—Ann Arbor
Dec 5—Bloomington IN
Dec 6—Indianapolis
Dec 8—Carlisle Penns.
Dec 10—Lowell MA
Dec 11—New Haven CT
Dec 13—West Islip LI
Dec 21—Hartford CT with
  Johansen
Dec 28—Dover NJ
Dec 29—Freeport LI
Dec 31—NY, the Palladium

1980

Jan 6—Port Chester NY
Jan 16—Brighton, England
Jan 17—Leicester, England
Jan 18—Cambridge, England
Jan 19—Norwich, England
Jan 21—Exeter
Jan 22—Cardiff, Wales
Jan 23—Aylesbury, England
Jan 24—Portsmouth, England
Jan 26—Leeds
Jan 27—Edinburgh, Scot
Jan 28—Glasgow, Scot
Jan 29—Newcastle, Eng
Feb 1—Manchester
Feb 2—Lancaster
Feb 3—Sheffield
Feb 4—Birmingham
Feb 6—Bournemouth
Feb 7—Bristol
Feb 8—Colchester
Feb 9—London
Feb 11—Amsterdam with UK Subs
Feb 12—Brussells with UK Subs

Feb 14—Reggio Emillia, Italy with
  UK Subs
Feb 15—Udine, Italy with Subs
Feb 16—Milan with Subs
Feb 18—Turin with Subs
Feb 20—Paris with Subs
Feb 22—London with The Boys
Feb 23—London with The Boys
Mar 6—Asbury Park NJ
Mar 7—Cherry Hill
Mar 8—Cherry Hill
Mar 21, 22—Toronto
Mar 23—Detroit
Mar 24—Cleveland
Mar 26—Columbus
Mar 28—Atlanta
Mar 29—Atlanta
Mar 30—Gainesville FL
Mar 31—Birmingham
Apr 1—New Orleans
Apr 3—Austin
Apr 4—Houston
Apr 5—Dallas

Apr 7—Phoenix
Apr 8—San Diego
Apr 10—LA
Apr 11—Santa Cruz
Apr 12—SF
Apr 13—Palo Alto with Flaming
  Groovies
Apr 15—Berkeley
Apr 21—Vancouver
Apr 22—Vancouver
Apr 24—Pocatello, Idaho
Apr 26—Boulder
Apr 27—Denver
Apr 29—Omaha
May 1—Dekalb IL
May 2—Champagne
May 3—Lansing MI
May 4—Chicago
May 6—Carbondale IL
May 8—Milwaukee
May 9—Chicago
May 10—Grinell Iowa
May 11—Minneapolis

May 13, 14, 15, 16, 17—Chicago
May 19—filmed Sha Na Na tv show
May 20—London
May 21—Burlington, Canada
May 23—Montreal
May 25—Toronto
May 26—Guelph, Can
May 27—Ottawa
May 29—Albany
May 30—Hartford CT
May 31—Lynn MA
June 2, 3, 4—Boston
June 5—Staten Island
June 6—Great Adventure, New Jersey, Amusement park (second show best I ever played)
June 8—College Park MD
June 10—Tampa
June 11, 12—Allend Hallendale FL
June 15—NY, Club 57
June 27, 28, 29—Tokyo (played with Jap band Sheena and the Rockets)
July 1—Nagoya, Japan
July 2—Kyoto, Jap
July 3—Osaka
July 4—Fukuoka
July 8—Sydney, Aust

July 9—Sydney
July 10—Melbourne
July 11—Adelaide
July 13—Woollongong, Aust
July 14, 15—Sydney
July 16—Canberra
July 18—Brisbane
July 19—Gold Coast
July 21—Auckland, NZ
July 22—Wellington, NZ
July 24—Christchurch, NZ
Aug 7—Long Beach LI
Aug 8—Asbury Park
Aug 9—Hull MA
Aug 10—Cherry Hill NJ
Aug 11—NY, Central Park
Aug 28—Stockholm
Aug 30—Oslo
Aug 31—Lund, Sweden
Sept 1—Copenhagen
Sept 3—Berlin
Sept 4—Hanover, Germany
Sept 6—Alvelgem, Belgium
Sept 7—Rotterdam, Holland
Sept 8—Munich
Sept 9—Zurich, Switz
Sept 11—San Remo, Italy
Sept 12—Genoa
Sept 13—Milan

Sept 14—Rome
Sept 15—Casalmoggiore, Italy
Sept 17—Montpellier, France
Sept 19—Barcelona with Mike Oldfield
Sept 22—Oporto, Portugal
Sept 23—Lisbon
Sept 24—Lisbon
Sept 26—Madrid (in bull ring)
Sept 27—San Sebastian
Sept 29—Lyon, France
Sept 30—Paris
Oct 2—London (UK tour the Spectres, with ex-Sex Pistol Glenn Matlock)
Oct 3—Derby
Oct 4—Manchester
Oct 5—Edinburgh, Scot
Oct 6—Liverpool
Oct 8—Dublin
Oct 9—Belfast
Oct 11—Birmingham
Oct 12—Canterbury
Dec 26—Cherry Hill NJ
Dec 27—Staten Island
Dec 29—Dover NJ
Dec 31—Lido Beach LI

1981

Jan 3—Brooklyn
Jan 4—Rockaway NY
Jan 6—Boston
Jan 7—Providence
Jan 8—Hartford
Feb 13—Philadelphia
Feb 14—Stoney Brook U. LI
Feb 16—New Paultz NY
Feb 19, 20—NY, Bond's
Feb 21—New Brunswick
Feb 27—South Orange NJ, Sexton Hall U
Feb 28—Ithaca NY, Cornell
July 3—Hampton Beach NH
July 4—Hampton Beach
July 5—Hull MA
July 7—Passaic
July 9—Lido Beach LI
July 10—NY Palladium with Stiv Bator
July 12—Staten Island
July 13—Wildwood NJ
July 14—College Park MD
July 15—Long Island NY
July 17—Palladium NY
July 18—Roselle Park NJ
July 25—Tampa
July 26—Miami
July 27, 28—Miami
July 29—Orlando
Jul 31, Aug 1—Atlanta
Aug 4—Dallas

Aug 5—Houston
Aug 6—San Antonio
Aug 7—Austin
Aug 9—Denver
Aug 12—Phoenix with the Kinks
Aug 13—San Diego
Aug 14—LA, Palladium
Aug 15—Pasadena
Aug 18—SF
Aug 19—Petaluma CA
Aug 20—Santa Cruz
Aug 21—SF
Aug 27—Islip LI
Aug 29—NY, the Pier
Sept 3—Albany
Sept 4—Binghamton NY
Sept 5—Saratoga Springs with Peter Frampton
Sept 9—Mt Vernon NY
Sept 11—Hartford
Sept 12—Cherry Hill NJ
Sept 13—New Haven
Sept 14—Providence
Sept 15—Boston
Sept 17—Rochester
Sept 18—Toronto
Sept 19, 20—Detroit
Sept 22—Cleveland
Sept 24—Bloomington IN
Sept 25—Chicago
Sept 26—Twin Lakes WI
Sept 28—Minneapolis

Sept 29—Madison WI
Oct 1—Champagne IL
Oct 2—Chicago
Oct 3—Chicago
Oct 4—Youngstown OH
Oct 5—Ann Arbor
Oct 7—Dayton
Oct 8—Columbus
Oct 10—Virginia Beach show that Mark missed (cancelled)
Oct 11—Wash DC (Mark made it)
Oct 22—London
Oct 24—Amsterdam
Oct 27—Stockholm
Oct 28—Lund, Sweden
Oct 29—Copenhagen
Nov 1—Aachen, Germany
Nov 2—Hanover, Germany
Nov 4—Munich
Nov 6—Milan
Nov 7—Bordeaux, France
Nov 9—Barcelona
Nov 10—Valencia, Spain
Nov 11—Madrid
Nov 12—Madrid
Nov 13—La Coruna, Spain
Nov 15—San Sebastian, Spain
Nov 17—Paris
Nov 18—Brussels
Nov 19—London
Nov 26—Trenton NJ
Nov-Dec 31—Lido Beach LI

1982

Jan 2—Hull MA
Jan 3—New Haven CT
Jan 7—Passaic
Jan 8—Pawcatuk CT
Jan 9—Staten Island
Jan 22—Glen Cove LI
Feb 11—Boston
Feb 12—Delhi NY
Feb 13—Manchester NH
Feb 18—Newark Delaware
Feb 19—Fairfield CT
Feb 20—Providence
Feb 21—Oswego NY
Mar 1—Baltimore
Mar 6—West Islip LI
Mar 13—Buffalo
Mar 16—Cleveland
Mar 17—Detroit
Mar 25—Albany
Mar 26—Beer Mountain NY
Mar 27—Mansfield PA
Apr 3—Madison NJ
Apr 4—Framingham MA
Apr 14—NY Columbia U.
Apr 16—Millersville PA
Apr 17—Mattawah, NJ with Johansen
Apr 18—Saratoga Springs

Apr 21—Montclair NJ with Johansen
Apr 22—Salem MA
Apr 23—Boston, MIT
Apr 24—Waltham MA Brandeis U
Apr 25—Glassboro NJ
Apr 27—Virginia Beach VA (makeup job, free, for Mark missed)
Apr 28—Columbia SC
Apr 29—Morgantown WV
Apr 30—New Rochelle NY
May 1—Hempstead LI, Hofstra
May 2—Newark with Johansen
May 6—Fitchburg MA
May 7—Hull MA
May 8—Farmingham ME
May 9—Hampton Beach NH
May 14—Trenton with Blue Angel (Cindy Lauper)
May 16—Burlington VT
May 18—Jersey City with Rbert Gordon
May 20—Poughkeepsie
May 21—Poughkeepsie
May 22—Brooklyn
May 29—Schenectady with Johansen

May 30—Tyngsboro MA with Johansen and Jim Carroll
July 2—Dover NJ
July 20—Roslyn LI
Aug 24—Brooklyn
Aug 25—Poughkeepsie
Aug 27—Asbury Park
Aug 28—Hampton Beach NH
Aug 29—Easthampton LI
Sep 3—San Bernardino CA, the US Festival with Plice, Talking Heads, B-52s
Oct 1—Providence RI
Oct 3—Washington DC
Oct 4—Virginia Beach VA
Oct 6—New Haven CT
Oct 7—Hartford
Nov 15—Bangor Maine with Cheap Trick promoted by Steven King and went to his house
Nov 16—Boston
Nov 20—Mt Vernon NY
Nov 21—Hempstead NY (Hofstra) with B52s
Nov 26—Islip LI
Nov 27—Islip LI

1983

Feb 13—Utica
Feb 17—Philadelphia
Feb 18—Poughkeepsie
Feb 19—Wellesley MA
Feb 20—Boston
Feb 24—Middlebury VT
Mar 12—Southampton LI
Mar 13—Danbury CT
Mar 14—Burlington VT
Mar 16—Philadelphia
Mar 17—Philadelphia
Mar 18, 19—Brooklyn
Mar 23—24—Wash DC
Mar 25—New Haven
Mar 26—Hartford
Mar 30—Boston
Mar 31—Amherst MA
Apr 8—Atlanta
Apr 9—New Orleans
Apr 11—Beaumont TX
Apr 13—Dallas
Apr 14—Houston
Apr 15—Austin
Apr 16—San Antonio
Apr 19—Las Cruces NM
Apr 20—Phoenix
Apr 22—LA Palladium with the Dickies
Apr 23—San Diego, Jack Murphy Stadium with T Petty, Stray Cats, Bow Wow Wow
Apr 24—Pasadena
Apr 26—Goleta CA

Apr 27—Santa Cruz
Apr 28—Palo Alto
Apr 29—SF
Apr 30—Sacramento
May 2—Eugene OR
May 3—Portland
May 4—Seattle
May 5—Seattle
May 6—Vancouver
May 9—Denver
May 11—St Louis
May 12—Kansas City
May 13—Wichita
May 15—Minneapolis
May 16—Madison
May 17—Milwaukee
May 19, 20—Chicago
May 21—Cleveland
May 22—Detroit
May 24—Indianapolis
May 26—Columbus
May 27—Wheeling IL
May 28—Chicago, North-western U
May 29—Chicago, U of Chicago
May 31—Omaha
June 1—Des Moines
June 2—Rockford IL
June 3—Wausau WI
June 5—Winnipeg
June 7—Calgary
June 8—Edmonton
June 10—Toronto

June 12—Ann Arbor
June 13—Ottawa
June 14—Montreal
June 20—Virginia Beach VA
June 22—Raleigh NC
June 23—Columbia SC
June 24, 25—Hallandale FL
June 26—St Petersberg
June 29—Wash DC
June 30—Wash DC
July 9—Bridgeport CT
July 11—Margate NJ
July 13—Wilkes Barre PA
July 14—Pittsburgh
July 16—NY, the Pier, the Divinyls open
July 22—Hicksville OH
July 24—Richmond VA
July 27—Buffalo
July 28—Roslyn LI
July 29—Philadelphia with B52s
July 30—Cape Cod with B52s
Aug 5—Hampton Bay LI
Aug 6—Poughkeepsie
Aug 12—Brooklyn
Aug 13—Queens
Dec 20—Cedar Grove NJ
Dec 22—Poughkeepsie
Dec 23—Hartford
Dec 27—Levitown LI
Dec 29—NY, Ritz
Dec 30—Providence

1984

Jan 5—New Haven
Jan 6—Boston
Jan 7—Queens
Jan 12—Philadelphia
Jan 14—Roslyn
Mar 9—Portland ME with Joe Perry and David Johansen
Mar 10—Providence
Mar 16—Waterbury CT
Mar 17—Brooklyn
Mar 20—Wash DC
Mar 22—Manchester NH
Mar 23—Albany
Mar 29—Hartford
Mar 30—Brockton MA
Apr 6—Salisbury MA
Apr 26—Charlottesville VA
Apr 27—Bronx, Forhdam U
Apr 28—Rochester
Apr 29—Storrs CT
May 4—Ithaca
May 5—Cortland with Cheap Trick and Johansen
May 17—Garden City LI
May 18—New Haven
May 19—Mt Ivy NY
May 31—Richmond VA
June 1—Norfolk
June 8—Ellington CT

June 9—Keene NH
June 16—Queens
June 28—Providence
June 29—Taunton MA
June 30—Syracuse
July 1—Wash DC
Aug 1—Rochester with Billy Idol
Aug 17—Hacketstown NJ
Aug 28—New Haven
Aug 30—Seldon LI
Aug 31—Hartford
Sept 2—Lido Beach LI
Sept 15—Stony Brook LI
Oct 5—Spring Valley NY
Oct 6—Queens
Oct 9—Wash DC
Oct 11—North Dartsmouth MA
Oct 12—Providence
Oct 13—Manchester NH
Oct 19—Bethany WV
Oct 20—Norfolk
Oct 26—rainout at Tampa Fl
Oct 28—Hallandale FL
Oct 29—West Palm Beach FL
Oct 30—Hallandale FL
Oct 31—Gainesville FL with Beaver Brown
Nov 2, 3—Atlanta
Nov 5—Destin FL

Nov 7—New Orleans
Nov 10—Houston
Nov 11—Austin
Nov 12—Dallas
Nov 14—Albuquerque
Nov 15—Phoenix with Black Flag
Nov 17—LA with Black Flag
Nov 18—San Diego
Nov 20—LA
Nov 21—Pomona CA
Nov 23—SF
Nov 24—Palo Alto
Nov 27—Portland
Nov 29—Vancouver
Nov 30—Seattle
Dec 1—Eugene OR
Dec 3—Sacramento
Dec 4—San Jose
Dec 5—Berkeley
Dec 7—Las Vegas
Dec 9—LA
Dec 12—St Louis
Dec 13—Milwaukee
Dec 14—Chicago
Dec 15, 16—Detroit
Dec 26—West Islip LI
Dec 27—28—Ritz NY
Dec 29—Providence

1985

Jan 3—Boston
Jan 4—Hartford
Jan 9—Mt Vernon NY
Jan 12—Asbury Park
Jan 25—Lexington VA
Jan 30, 31—Wash DC
Feb 8—Brooklyn
Feb 12—Bronx
Feb 14—Lowell MA
Feb 15—Worcester MA
Feb 16—Manchester NH
Feb 17—Philadelphia with Joan Jett
Feb 18—Baltimore
Feb 24—London
Feb 25, 26, 27—London
Mar 7—Garden City LI
Mar 8—Providence
Mar 9—Brooklyn
Mar 14—Athens OH
Mar 15, 16—Detroit
Mar 18—Columbus
Mar 19—Cincinnati
Mar 20—Pittsburgh
Mar 29—Buffalo
Mar 30—Syracuse
Mar 31—Hamden CT
Apr 4—Baltimore
Apr 5—Norfolk VA
Apr 6—Newark, Delaware

Apr 12—Durham NH
Apr 13—Trenton
Apr 27—Worcester MA
May 3—New Haven
May 4—Jamesburg NJ
May 5—Trenton
May 7—Garden City LI
May 9—Rochester
May 10—Buffalo
May 12—Hartford
May 20—Providence
May 25—Hartford
May 27—Blacksburg VA
May 28—Richmond
May 30—New York, Ritz with Murphys Law
May 31—Ritz
June 7—Oyster Bay LI
June 8—Hampton Beach NH
June 14—Scotia NY
June 15—Brooklyn
June 22—Milton Keynes, England with U2 and REM
June 24—Dublin
June 25—Dublin
June 26—Belfast
June 28—Glasgow
June 30—Roskilde, Denmark
July 2—Berlin

July 3—Hamburg
July 4—Bochum, Germany
July 6—Tourhout, Belgium
July 7—Werchter, Belgium with U2, Depeche Mode and REM
Aug 9—Worcester MA
Aug 10—Middletown NY
Aug 11—Hampton Bay LI
Aug 12—New Haven
Aug 21—Boston
Aug 22—Branford CT
Aug 24—Norfolk VA
Aug 25, 26—Wash DC
Aug 27—Ocean City MD
Sept 1—Lido Beach LI
Sept 20—Hartford
Sept 21—Albany
Oct 5—Asbury Park
Oct 11—Spring Valley
Oct 12—Providence
Oct 13—East Meadow LI
Oct 26—College Park MD
Nov 1—Amherst MA
Nov 22—Commack LI
Nov 23—Lewiston, Pennsylvania
Nov 27—Trenton
Nov 29—Brooklyn
Dec 7—Plattsburg NY
Dec 31—NY, The World

1986

Apr 11—Fredonia NY
Apr 12—Rochester
Apr 14—Philadelphia
Apr 19—Burlington VT
Apr 20—Durham NH
Apr 25—Randolph NJ
Apr 26—New Brunswick NJ
May 4, 5, 6—London
May 7—Brighton, England
May 8—Poole
May 9—St Austell
May 11—Bristol
May 12—Birmingham
May 13—Preston
May 14—Edinburgh, Scot
May 15—Newcastle, England
May 17—Leeds
May 18—Manchester
May 19—Rottingham
June 20—Albany NY
June 21—Hartford
June 22—Hampton Beach NH
June 24—New Haven
June 25—Providence
June 27—Brooklyn
June 28—Philadelphia
June 29—Baltimore

June 30—Norfolk with
   Smithereens
July 1, 2—Wash DC with
   Smithereens
July 8—Oyster Bay LI
July 11—Trenton NJ
July 12—Asbury Park
July 17—Pittsburgh
July 19, 20—Detroit
July 21—Cleveland
July 22—Columbus
July 24—Newport KY
July 25, 26—Chicago
July 27—Minneapolis
Aug 2—Veurne Belgium with PIL
Aug 3—Sneek Holland
Aug 4, 5—Amsterdam
Aug 31—Lido Beach LI
Sept 11—San Diego
Sept 13—LA with Social
   Distortion
Sept 14—Sacramento
Sept 15—SF
Sept 16—SF
Sept 17—Santa Clara
Sept 19—Long Beach
Sept 21—LA

Sept 22—Riverside
Sept 23—San Diego
Sept 24—LA the Whiskey
Oct 10—Trenton NJ
Oct 11—Brooklyn
Oct 16—Northampton MA
Oct 17—Hartford
Oct 18—Providence
Oct 24—Wash DC
Oct 25—Philadelphia
Oct 31—Roslyn LI
Nov 1—Bridgeport CT
Nov 3—Boston
Nov 6, 7—NY, Ritz
Nov 15—Kent OH
Nov 16—Buffalo
Nov 18—Montclair NJ
Nov 21—Sayreville NJ
Nov 22—Medford MA
Dec 4—Waltham MA
Dec 5—Rochester
Dec 6—Alfred NY
Dec 19—Queens
Dec 20—Bayshore NY
Dec 31—Roslyn LI

1987

Jan 3—Trenton
Jan 4—Wash DC
Jan 23—Providence
Jan 24—Poughkeepsie
Jan 31—Sao Paolo, Brazil
Jan 31, Feb 1—Sao Paolo
Feb 4—Buenos Aires, Argentina
Feb 20—Pittsburgh
Feb 21—Allentown PA
Feb 26—Wayne NJ
Feb 27—Asbury Park
Feb 28—Philadelphia
Mar 20—Dallas
Mar 21—Austin
Mar 22—Houston
Mar 23—New Orleans
Mar 25—Atlanta
Mar 26—Tallahassee
Mar 27—Tampa
Mar 28—Coco Beach
Mar 29—Miami Beach
Apr 22—Garden City LI
Apr 23—Staten Island
Apr 25—Hartford
Apr 26—New Haven
Apr 30—Williamstown MA
May 1—Brunswick ME
May 2—Albany NY with Joan Jett
May 3—Hadley MA
May 8—Randolph NJ
May 9—Brooklyn
May 15—Providence
May 16—Bayshore LI
May 29—Darien Lake NY
May 30—Poughkeepsie

June 18—Harrisburg PA
June 19—Ocean City MD
June 20—Philadelphia
June 26—Oyster Bay LI
June 27—Flushing NY, Flushing
   Meadow Park
June 28, 29, 30—Wash DC
July 1—Norfolk
July 21, 22, 23—Toronto
July 24—Ottawa
Aug 12—Easthampton NY, Richie
   quits, next three nights can-
   celled including Commack, NY,
   and two nights at Ritz
Aug 28—Providence with Clem
   Burke on drums
Aug 29—Trenton with Clem
Sept 4—Oyster Bay LI with
   Mark back
Sept 5—Wash DC
Sept 6—Comack NY
Sept 10, 11—NY Ritz
Sept 16—San Diego
Sept 18—LA
Sept 19—Fresno
Sept 21—SF
Sept 22—SF
Sept 23—Santa Clara
Sept 25—Long Beach
Sept 26—Northridge CA with
   Dickies
Sept 27—LA
Oct 5—Copenhagen
Oct 6—Hamburg
Oct 7—Amsterdam

Oct 8—Dusseldorf, Germany
Oct 9—Munich
Oct 11—Milan
Oct 12—Zurich, Switzerland
Oct 13—Paris
Oct 15—Sheffield, England
Oct 16—Newcastle
Oct 17—Leeds
Oct 18—Glasgow
Oct 20—Nottingham, England
Oct 21—Norwich, England
Oct 22—Manchester
Oct 23—Liverpool
Oct 24—Cardiff
Oct 25—Birmingham
Oct 26—London
Oct 31—Alexandria VA
Nov 12—Wilmington NC
Nov 13—Greenville NC
Nov 14—Charlotte NC
Nov 15—Charlottesville VA
Nov 18—Boston
Nov 19—Providence
Nov 20—Allentown PA
Nov 21—Brooklyn
Nov 22—Glassboro NJ
Nov 27—Bayshore LI
Dec 3—New Haven
Dec 4—Randolph NJ
Dec 5—Poughkeepsie
Dec 9—Baltimore
Dec 10, 11—Wash DC
Dec 12—Oyster Bay LI
Dec 13—Philadelphia
Dec 31—Bayshore LI

R
a
m
o
n
e
s

1988

Jan 1—Trenton
Jan 2—NY, Ritz
Jan 28—Dallas
Jan 29—Austin
Jan 30—Austin
Jan 31—Houston
Feb 1—New Orleans
Feb 3—Atlanta
Feb 4—Tallahassee
Feb 5—Jacksonville
Feb 6—St Petersburg
Feb 7—Miami
Feb 19—Aguadilla, Puerto Rico
Feb 20—Aguadilla
Mar 11—Sayreville NJ
Mar 12—Queens Village NY
Mar 13—Hempstead NY
Mar 18—Oswego NY
Mar 19—Rochester
Mar 24—Staten Island
Mar 26—Allentown PA
Apr 22—Trenton
Apr 23—Philadelphia
Apr 27—Providence
Apr 29—Comack NY
Apr 30—Oswego NY
May 3–4, 5—Toronto
May 6—Buffalo with
  Grandmaster Flash
May 7—Rochester
May 19—Brewster NY
May 20—New Rochelle NY
May 21—Philadelphia
June 2—Stockholm
June 3—Lund, Sweden
June 4—Seinajoki, Finland
June 6—Paris

June 7—Tilburg, Holland
June 8, 9—Amsterdam
June 10—Groningen, Holland
June 11—Guttingen, Germany
  with Stranglers and Godfathers
June 12—Berlin with Stranglers
  and Godfathers
June 13—Dusseldorf with above
June 15—London
July 1—Brooklyn
July 2—Poughkeepsie
July 7—San Diego
July 8—LA's Dickies
July 10, 11—SF, Fillmore
July 12, 13—Santa Clara
July 15—Anaheim
July 16—LA
July 17—Santa Barbara
July 18—LA, Roxy
Aug 2—New Haven
Aug 3—Easthampton
Aug 4—Brewster NY
Aug 5—Trenton
Aug 12—Comack NY
Aug 13—Philadelphia
Aug 14—Baltimore
Aug 15–16—Wash DC
Aug 19, 20—NY Ritz with Dickies
Aug 26—The Reading Festival,
  Reading, England with Iggy and
  Smithereens
Aug 27—Hechtel, Belgium
Sept 13—Sayreville NJ
Sept 14—Boston
Sept 15—Providence
Sept 21—Pittsburgh

Sept 22—Kent OH
Sept 23—Chicago with Iggy
  and Dickies
Sept 24—Detroit
Sept 26—Cincinnati
Sept 27—Columbus
Sept 28—Indianapolis
Sept 29—St Louis
Oct 1—Cleveland
Oct 6—Staten Island
Oct 7—Poughkeepsie
Oct 8—Rochester
Oct 9—Albany
Oct 13—Island Park NY
Oct 14, 15—Trenton
Oct 24, 25—Tokyo
Oct 26—Kobe, Japan, the Fish
  Dancehall
Oct 27—Osaka
Oct 28—Tokyo
Nov 11—Dallas
Nov 12—Austin
Nov 13—Austin
Nov 14—College Station TX
Nov 15—Houston
Nov 16—New Orleans
Nov 18—St Petersburg FL
Nov 19—Miami Beach
Nov 20—Orlando
Nov 22—Atlanta
Dec 1—Bronx
Dec 2—Baltimore
Dec 10—Durham NH
Dec 11—New Haven
Dec 30—Providence
Dec 31—NY, Irving Plaza

1989

Jan 16, 17—Wash DC
Jan 19—Nashville
Jan 20—Lexington KY
Jan 21—Louisville
Jan 23—Columbia SC
Jan 24—Charlotte NC
Jan 25—Norfolk VA
Jan 27, 28—NYC, Ritz
Feb 7—Madrid
Feb 8—Barcelona
Feb 9—Valencia, Spain
Feb 10—Valencia
Feb 11, 12—San Sebastian, Spain
Feb 24—Poughkeepsie
Feb 25—Philadelphia
Mar 24—Canton NY
Mar 25—Albany
Mar 31—Queens Village NY
Apr 1—Baltimore
Apr 6—New Haven
Apr 7—Lancaster PA
Apr 15—Stoney Brook NY
May 2—Monfalcone, Italy

May 3—Milan
May 4—Florence
May 6—Bicenza, Italy
May 7—Rimini, Italy
May 8—Modena, Italy
May 9—Rome
May 10—Perugia Ellera, Italy
May 12, 13, 14—Athens
May 15—Athens
May 26—Boston
May 27—Providence
June 2—LA
June 3—Long Beach
June 4—Reseda CA
June 17—SF
June 18—Petaluma CA
June 19—Santa Clara
June 20—Santa Barbara
June 22—San Diego
June 23—Tijuana, Mex
June 24—San Pedro CA
June 25—Reseda
June 27—Portland OR

June 28—Vancouver
June 29—Seattle
July 1, 2—SF Fillmore
July 3—Santa Cruz
July 4, 5—Santa Clara, DD's
  last show
Sept 30—Leicester, England
  with CJ
Oct 1—Liverpool
Oct 2—Glasgow
Oct 3—Newcastle, England
Oct 4—Manchester
Oct 6—Leeds
Oct 7—Birmingham
Oct 8—Bristol
Oct 9, 10, 11—London
Oct 31—Auckland, New Zealand
Nov 1—Auckland
Nov 3—Melbourne
Nov 4, 5—Melbourne, Aust
Nov 6—Perth
Nov 7—Adelaide
Nov 9, 10, 11—Sydney

Nov 12—Brisbane
Nov 22—Offenbach, Germany
Nov 23—Bonn
Nov 24—Oberhausen, Germany
Nov 25—Hamburg
Nov 27—Berlin

Nov 28—Bielefeld, Germany
Nov 29—Neumarkt, Germany
Nov 30—Boblingen, Germany
Dec 1—Deinze, Belgium
Dec 2—Utrecht, Holland
Dec 3—Rotterdam, Holland

Dec 4—Amsterdam
Dec 12—New Haven
Dec 13—Poughkeepsie
Dec 14—Philadelphia
Dec 15, 16—NYC, Ritz

1990

Feb 23—Trenton
Feb 24—Sag Harbor LI
Feb 25—Albany
Mar 1—Charlottesville VA
Mar 2—Fredericksburg VA
Mar 3—St Mary's MD
Mar 4—Reading PA
Mar 8, 9—Boston
Mar 10—Providence
Mar 22—Copenhagen
Mar 23—Tampere, Finland
Mar 24—Turku, Finland
Mar 25—Helsinki
Mar 27—Stockholm
Mar 28—Gothenburg, Sweden
Mar 29—Lund, Sweden
Mar 30—Karlskoga, Sweden
Mar 31—Hultsfred, Sweden
Apr 1—Oslo, Norway
Apr 18—Norman OK
Apr 19—Dallas
Apr 20—Austin
Apr 21—Austin
Apr 23—New Orleans
Apr 24—Birmingham AL
Apr 26—Miami Beach
Apr 27—Melbourne FL
Apr 28—Tampa
Apr 29—Orlando
May 1—Atlanta
May 2—Nashville
May 4—Winston-Salem NC
May 5—Wilmington NC
May 6—Raleigh NC
May 8—Columbia SC
May 9—Charlotte NC
May 11—Baltimore MD
May 12—Norfolk VA
May 13—Richmond VA
May 14, 15—Wash DC

June 23—Loreley, Germany, The Bizarre Festival
June 28—Seven week tour with Tom Tom Club and Debby Harry (Escape NY) Columbia MD
June 29—Bristol CT
July 1—Milwaukee
July 2—Detroit
July 3—Toronto
July 4—Montreal
July 6—Boston
July 7—Portland ME
July 8—Burlington VT
July 9—Philadelphia
July 11—Jones Beach LI
July 12—Holmdel NJ, Garden Arts
July 13—Darien NY
July 14—Cleveland
July 16—Columbus
July 17—Chicago
July 18—Cincinnati
July 19—Atlanta
July 22—St Louis
July 23—Memphis
July 24—Kansas City
July 25—Tulsa
July 26—Dallas
July 27—Houston
July 28—Austin
July 30—Sante Fe
July 31—Denver
Aug 1—Salt Lake City
Aug 2—Irvine CA
Aug 4—San Diego
Aug 5—Las Vegas
Aug 6—Mesa AZ
Aug 8, 9—LA
Aug 10—Ventura
Aug 11—Berkeley

Aug 12—SF
Aug 14—Portland
Aug 15—Seattle
Aug 16—Victoria, Can
Aug 17—Vancouver
Sep 3—Osaka
Sep 4—Nagoya
Sep 5, 6—Kawasaki
Sep 8, 9—Nagoya
Sep 10, 11—Osaka
Sep 13, 14, 15, 16—Kawasaki
Oct 4—Philadelphia
Oct 5—Baltimore
Oct 6—NYC, Ritz
Oct 7—Trenton
Nov 13—Paris
Nov 14—Munich
Nov 15—Volkingen, Germany
Nov 16—Bremen, Germany
Nov 17—Gent, Belgium
Nov 19—Lyon, France
Nov 20—Zurich, Switzerland
Nov 21—Vienna, Aus
Nov 22—Graz, Austria
Nov 24—Zagreb, Yugoslavia
Nov 25—Ljubljana, Yugoslavia
Nov 26—Milan
Nov 27—Rimini, Italy
Nov 29—Zaragosa, Spain
Nov 30—Madrid
Dec 1—Barcelona
Dec 2—San Sebastian
Dec 4—Valencia
Dec 5—Murcia
Dec 7—Manchester, England
Dec 8—London
Dec 27—Providence
Dec 28—Boston
Dec 29—NYC, Ritz
Dec 30—New Haven

1991

Jan 22—Gold Coast, Australia
Jan 23—Byron Bay
Jan 25—Brisbane
Jan 26—Sydney
Jan 27—Wollongong
Jan 29—Sydney
Jan 31—Adelaide
Feb 1—Melbourne
Feb 2—Perth
Feb 5, 6, 7—Tokyo
Mar 6—Madrid
Mar 7—Madrid
Mar 8—Valladolid, Spain

Mar 9—Vigo
Mar 11—Barcelona
Mar 12—Barcelona
Mar 13—Valencia
Mar 15—Pamplona
Mar 16—Mondragon
Mar 17—Bilbao
Mar 18—Melgar
Apr 4—New Haven
Apr 5—Philadelphia
Apr 6—Baltimore
Apr 12—Allentown PA
Apr 13—Columbus OH

Apr 14—Detroit
Apr 15—Cincinnati
Apr 16—Pittsburg
Apr 26, 27, 28—Buenos Aires
Apr 30, May 1, 2—Sao Paulo, Brazil
May 4—Porto Alegre, Brazil
May 28—New Haven
May 29—Trenton
May 30—New Britain CT
May 31—Spring Valley NY
June 1—Asbury Park
June 7—Tampa

Tour Schedule

June 8—Miami
June 9—Orlando
June 11—Atlanta
June 12—Charlotte NC
June 14—Raleigh NC
June 15—Winston-Salem NC
June 16—Greeneville NC
June 18—Athens
June 19—Knoxville TN
June 21—Norfolk VA
June 22—Richmond VA
June 23—Wash DC
July 6—Las Pezia, Italy
July 8—Torino, Italy
July 10—Leysin, Switzerland, Leysin Rock Festival with INXS and Jethro Tull
Aug 6—Toronto
Aug 8—Kitchener, Canada
Aug 9—Toronto

Aug 10—Bala, Canada
Aug 11—Canada
Aug 13—Montreal
Aug 14—Ottawa
Aug 15—St Catherine's, Canada
Aug 16—Hamilton, Canada
Aug 24—Berlin with Iggy Pop
Aug 25—Hasselt, Belgium
Aug 27—Helsinki, Finland with Iggy
Aug 28—Stockholm, festival with Iggy
Oct 4—Trenton
Oct 5—Philadelphia
Oct 6—Middletown NY
Oct 7—Northampton MA
Oct 11—Warwick RI
Oct 14—Cleveland
Oct 15—Columbus OH
Oct 16—Pittsburgh

Oct 18—Baltimore
Oct 19—Wash DC
Oct 24—Boston
Oct 25—New Britain CT
Oct 26—Sea Bright NJ
Nov 25—Utrecht, Holland
Nov 27—Hamburg
Nov 28—Dusseldorf, Germany
Nov 29—Deinze, Belgium
Nov 30—Rennes, France
Dec 2—Birmingham, England
Dec 3—Newcastle
Dec 4—Glasgow, Scotland
Dec 5—Manchester, England
Dec 7, 8—London
Dec 27—New Haven
Dec 28—Baltimore
Dec 29—NYC, Ritz

1992

Mar 14—Fontanafredda, Italy
Mar 15—Florence
Mar 16—Milan
Mar 17—Correggio, Italy
Mar 19, 20, 21—Athens
Apr 9—New Haven
Apr 10—New York, Columbia U.
Apr 11—Sea Bright NJ
Apr 12—Trenton
Apr 23—Baltimore
Apr 24—Norfolk VA
Apr 25—Wash DC
Apr 26—Allentown PA
May 3—Bourges, France
May 4—Lyon
May 5, 6—Paris
May 7—Mulhouse, France
May 9—Pau, France
May 10—Niort, France
June 4—Kitchener, Canada
June 5—Oshawa, Canada
June 6—Hamilton
June 7—London
June 9, 10—Toronto
June 12—Quebec City
June 13—Ottawa
June 14—Montreal

June 19—Hummijkrvi, Finland
June 27—Alsdorf, Germany, the Bizarre Festival

TENTATIVE

Sept 13—Santiago, Chile
Sept 16, 17, 18, 19—Buenos Aries
Sept 22, 23—Rio de Janeiro
Sept 26, 27—Mexico City
Oct 7—Seattle
Oct 8—Portland
Oct 10—Berkeley
Oct 11—Reno
Oct 13, 14, 15—LA
Oct 17—San Diego
Oct 18—Phoenix
Oct 19—Albuquerque
Oct 21—Dallas
Oct 22—Austin
Oct 23—Houston
Oct 24—New Orleans
Oct 26—Atlanta
Oct 28—Detroit
Oct 29—Chicago
Oct 30—Milwaukee
Nov 2—Cleveland

Nov 3—Cincinnati
Nov 5—Buffalo
Nov 6—Pittsburgh
Nov 7—Philadelphia
Nov 8—New Haven
Nov 11—Wash DC
Nov 13—Boston
Nov 14, 15, 16—NYC, Ritz
Nov 26—Munich
Nov 27—Stuttgart
Nov 29—Leipzig
Dec 1—Erlangen, Germany
Dec 2—Offenbach
Dec 3—Freiburg
Dec 5—Cologne, Germany
Dec 6—Hanover
Dec 7—Berlin
Dec 8—Hamburg
Dec 10, 11—Amsterdam
Dec 13—Bristol, England
Dec 14—Birmingham
Dec 15—Cambridge
Dec 17—Glasgow, Scotland
Dec 18—Manchester
Dec 20—London

1993

Jan 9, 10, 11, 12—Tokyo
Jan 14–15—Nagoya
Jan 17, 18, 19—Osaka

R a m o n e s
U . S .
D i s c o g r a p h y

label	record #	title	year
SINGLES			
Sire	SAA-725	Blitzkrieg Bop/Havana Affair	1976
	SAA-734	I Wanna Be Your Boyfriend/California Sun (live)/I Don't Wanna Walk Around With You (live)	1976
	SA-738	Swallow My Pride/Pinhead	1977
	SA-746	Sheena Is A Punk Rocker/I Don't Care (dist. by ABC)	1977
	SRE-1006	Sheena Is A Punk Rocker/I Don't Care (dist. by Warner Bros.)	1977
	SRE-1008	Rockaway Beach/Locket Love	1977
	SRE-1017	Do You Wanna Dance?/Baby Sitter	1978
	SRE-1025	Don't Come Close/I Don't Want You	1978
	SRE-1045	Needles And Pins/I Wanted Everything	1978
	SRE-1051	Rock 'N' Roll High School/Do You Wanna Dance/(live)	1979
	SRE-49182	Baby I Love You/High Risk Insurance	1980
	SRE-49261	Rock 'N' Roll Radio/Let's Go	1980
	RSO-1055	I Wanna Be Sedated/Return Of Jackie And Judy	1980
	SRE-49812	We Want The Airwaves/You Sound Like You're Sick	1981
	7 28599	Something To Believe In/Animal Boy	1986
	7 27663	I Wanna Be Sedated/Sedated Mega-Mix	1988
	7 22911	Pet Sematary/Sheena Is A Punk Rocker	1989
ALBUMS			
Sire	SASD-7520	Ramones (dist. by ABC)	1976
	SR-6020	Ramones (dist. by Warner)	1977
	SASD-7528	Ramones Leave Home (with "Carbona"; dist. by ABC)	1977
	SASD-7528	Ramones Leave Home (with "Sheena"; dist. by ABC)	1977
	SR-6031	Ramones Leave Home (with "Sheena"; dist. by Warner Bros.)	1977
	SRK-6042	Rocket To Russia	1977
	SRK-6063	Road To Ruin	1978
	SRK-6070	Rock 'N' Roll High School	1979
	SRK-6077	End Of The Century	1980
	SRK-3571	Pleasant Dreams	1981
	7 23800	Subterranean Jungle	1983
	7 25817	Too Tough To Die	1984
	7 25433	Animal Boy	1986
	7 25641	Halfway To Sanity	1987
	7 25709	RamonesMania	1988
	7 25905	Brain Drain	1989
	7 26220	All The Stuff And More Vol. 1	1990
	7 26618	All The Stuff And More Vol. 2	1991
Chrysalis	1901-3219012	Loco Live	1991
Radioactive	RARD-10615	Mondo Bizzaro	1992

R a m o n e s
U . K .
D i s c o g r a p h y

label	record #	title	year
SINGLES			
Sire	6078 601	Blitzkrieg Bop/Havana Affair	1976
Sire	6078 603	I Remember You/California Sun (live)/I Don't Wanna Walk Around With You (live)	1977
Sire	RAM 001	Sheena Is A Punk Rocker/Commando/I Don't Care	1977
Sire	6078 607	Swallow My Pride/Pinhead/Let's Dance (live)	1977
Sire	6078 611	Rockaway Beach/Teenage Lobotomy/Beat On The Brat	1977
Sire	6078 615	Do You Wanna Dance?/It's A Long Way Back To Germany/Cretin Hop	1978
Sire	SRE-1031	Don't Come Close/I Don't Want You	1978
Sire	SRE-1031	Don't Come Close/I Don't Want You	1978
Sire	SIR-4009	She's The One/I Wanna Be Sedated	1979
Sire	SIR-4021	Rock 'N' Roll High School/Rockaway Beach (live)/Sheena Is A Punk Rocker (live)	1979
Sire	SIR-4031	Baby I Love You/High Risk Insurance	1980
Sire	SIR-4037	Do You Remember Rock 'N' Roll Radio?/I Want You Around	1980
RSO	-70	I Wanna Be Sedated/Return Of Jackie And Judy	1980
Sire	SREP 1	Meltdown With The Ramones EP (Includes I Just Wanna Have Something To Do/Here Today, Gone Tomorrow/I Wanna Be Your Boyfriend/Questioningly)	1980
Sire	SIR-4051	We Want The Airwaves/You Sound Like You're Sick	1981
Sire	SIR-4052	She's A Sensation/All Quiet On The Eastern Front	1981
Sire	W-9606	Time Has Come Today/Psycho Therapy	1983
Beggar's	BEG-128	Howling At the Moon/Smash You	1985
Banquet	BEG-128D	Howling At The Moon/Smash You/Chasing The Night/Street Fighting Man (gatefold double pack)	1985
	BEG-140	Bonzo Goes To Bitburg/Daytime Dilemma	1985
	BEG-157	Somebody Put Something In My Drink/Something To Believe In	1986
	BEG-167	Crummy Stuff/She Belongs To Me	1986
	BEG-198	Real Cool Time/Life Goes On	1987
	BEG-201	I Wanna Live/Merry Christmas	1987
Chrysalis	CHS-3423	Pet Sematary/All Screwed Up	1989
12-INCH SINGLES			
Sire	Ram 001	Sheena Is A Punk Rocker/Commando/I Don't Care	1977
Sire	6078 611	Rockaway Beach/Teenage Lobotomy/Beat On The Brat	1977
Sire	SRE-1031	Don't Come Close/I Don't Want You (red or yellow vinyl)	1978

Sire	W9606T	Time Has Come Today/Psycho Therapy/Baby I Love You/Don't Come Close	1983
Beggar's Banquet	BEG-128T	Howling At The Moon/Smash You/Street Fighting Man	1985
	BEG-128TP	Chasing The Night/Howling At The Moon/Smash You/Street Fighting Man	1985
	BEG-140T	Bonzo Goes To Bitburg/Daytime Dilemma/Go Home Ann	1985
	BEG-157T	Somebody Put Something In My Drink/Something To Believe In/Can't Say Anything Nice	1986
	BEG-167T	Crummy Stuff/She Belongs To Me/I Don't Want To Live This Life	1986
	BEG-198T	Real Cool Time/Life Goes On/Indian Giver	1986
	BEG-201T	I Wanna Live/Merry Christmas	1987
Chrysalis	CHS12 3423	Pet Sematary/All Screwed Up/Zero Zero/UFO	1989

ALBUMS

Sire	9103 253	Ramones	1976
Sire	9103 254	Ramones Leave Home (with "Carbona")	1977
Sire	9103 254	Ramones Leave Home (with "Baby Sitter")	1977
Sire	9103 255	Rocket To Russia	1977
Sire	SRK-6063	Road To Ruin	1978
Sire	SRK-603	Road To Ruin (yellow vinyl)	1978
Sire	SRK 2-6074	It's Alive	1979
Sire	SRK-6077	End Of The Century	1980
Sire	SR-6020	Ramones (reissue)	1980
Sire	SR-6031	Ramones Leave Home (reissue)	1980
Sire	SR-6042	Rocket To Russia (reissue)	1980
Sire	SRK-3571	Pleasant Dreams	1981
Sire	923 800	Subterranean Jungle	1983
Sire	925 709	RamonesMania	1988
Beggar's Banquet	BEGA 59	Too Tough To Die	1984
	BEGA 70	Animal Boy	1985
	BEGA 89	Halfway To Sanity	1987
Chrysalis	CHR 1725	Brain Drain	1989
	CCD 1901 3219012	Loco Live	1991
Radioactive	RARD 10615	Mondo Bizzaro	1992

Index